# A Study of
# Pueblo Architecture
# in Tusayan and Cibola

## Victor Mindeleff

Introduction by Peter Nabokov

SMITHSONIAN INSTITUTION PRESS
WASHINGTON AND LONDON

© 1989 Smithsonian Institution
Introduction

Originally published 1891
Reprinted 1989
New material for reprint edition edited by Debra Bertram

**Library of Congress Cataloging-in-Publication Data**
Mindeleff, Victor, 1860–1948.
   A study of Pueblo architecture in Tusayan and Cibola.
   (Classics of Smithsonian anthropology)
   Reprint, with new introd. Originally published:
Washington, D.C.: U.S. G.P.O., 1891 in 8th Annual
report of the Bureau of Ethnology for the
years 1886–1887.
   Bibliography: p.
   Includes index.
   1. Pueblo Indians—Architecture.  2. Pueblo Indians—
Antiquities.  3. Indians of North America—Southwest,
New—Architecture.  4. Indians of North America—
Southwest, New—Antiquities.  I. Nabokov, Peter.
II. Title.  III. Series.
E99.P9M65 1989    722'.91'09789    88–43115
ISBN 0–87474–619–1

Manufactured in the United States of America

93 92 91 90 89    5 4 3 2 1

⊗ The paper used in this publication meets the minimum requirements of the
American National Standard for Permanence of Paper for Printed Library
Materials Z39.48–1984.

# CONTENTS

# PUBLISHER'S NOTE

Victor Mindeleff's monograph appearing in this volume is a photographic reprint of the first edition, published as pages 3–228 in the *Eighth Annual Report of the Bureau of Ethnology to the Secretary of the Smithsonian Institution 1886–87* by J. W. Powell (Washington: U.S. Government Printing Office, 1981). Cosmos Mindeleff's monograph, reprinted here as Appendix 1, was also reproduced photomechanically from the first edition, published as pages 635–53 in the *Nineteenth Annual Report of the Bureau of American Ethnology to the Secretary of the Smithsonian Institution 1897–98*, Part 2, by J. W. Powell (Washington: U.S. Government Printing Office, 1900). The original text pagination, punctuation, and spelling have been retained for both. All illustrations have been reproduced, in clusters throughout the text; in order to accommodate the two-page plans and foldout maps for the Victor Mindeleff work on facing pages, Plates VII, XIX, XXXV, L, LIII, LVI, LXI, and LXX have been transposed with their immediately preceding plates.

*Victor Mindeleff, date unknown,*
*Smithsonian Institution National*
*Anthropological Archives, Portrait 54–C.*

*Cosmos Mindeleff in 1897.*
*From "Authorities on the Southwest,"*
Out West, *vol. 6, no. 5 (April 1897),*
*186. The Bancroft Library, University*
*of California, Berkeley.*

# INTRODUCTION

*Peter Nabokov*

When Victor Mindeleff and his younger brother Cosmos began their fieldtrips to the Southwest late in the summer of 1881, Victor was barely twenty-one years old, Cosmos only nineteen. The incomplete documentation on their careers tells us little of that first journey, probably by rail from Washington, D.C., to Fort Wingate in western New Mexico, then by wagon through the Zuni Mountains to arrive at the Pueblo of Zuni around the beginning of August. Nor is it clear how these untrained brothers were recruited for this ethnographic assignment: measuring the Pueblo of Zuni in western New Mexico in order to construct a scale model of the community for exhibition in the new U.S. National Museum, part of the Smithsonian Institution. They appear to have been the sort of talented, curious minds with entrée to Washington's scientific circles who were able to find a niche in American anthropology and archeology at this adventuresome time.

The Mindeleffs were joining the second major southwestern expedition conducted by the Smithsonian's fledgling Bureau of Ethnology, later renamed the Bureau of American Ethnology, and led by Col. James Stevenson, a close associate of the Bureau's energetic director, Maj. John Wesley Powell. At Zuni Pueblo their party was greeted by a young man who was fast becoming a legend in southwestern anthropology, twenty-four-year-old Frank Hamilton Cushing. Two years before, Cushing had stayed behind after Colonel Stevenson's earlier sojourn at Zuni. He became so absorbed in Zuni culture that he was on the verge of undergoing the initiatory rites to make him a member of their Bow Priesthood.

Thus from the outset these young Russians were thrust into the heroic heyday of southwestern Indian studies. Over the following nine field seasons (1881–89) they would work with and learn from the pioneers of southwestern ethnography: Cushing; Colonel Stevenson and his wife, Mathilda Coxe; Frederic Webb Hodge; Alexander M. Stephen; John G. Bourke; Washington Matthews; and others. The Mindeleffs were clearly "tenderfeet," as Washington Matthews once tagged Victor (Hinsley 1981:197), and they picked up their fieldwork techniques on the job. In the process the region's Indian peoples and their architectural heritage cast a lifelong spell on both men.

Victor's active involvement would climax with the publication of this ground-breaking study of Western Pueblo house-building traditions. Cosmos would continue to explore and preserve southwestern ruins, build architectural models for the Smithsonian to send to national and international expositions, and write popular articles drawing upon the years covered in this study long after its publication. The brothers' collaboration, summarized in this goldmine of information and description, would constitute the major data base for the study of Pueblo architecture and town planning up to the present day. As Bainbridge Bunting, the late scholar of Pueblo building history, wrote in 1976, "In many ways the most illuminating treatment of early Indian architecture of the Southwest is the first one written" (1976:115). Neill M. Judd likewise praised the work in his history of the Bureau of American Ethnology: "Never has there been an equal to Mindeleff's 'Pueblo Architecture'. It describes the pueblos of the 1880's [sic] inside and out, pictures their external irregularities, illustrates interior features that give individuality to individual rooms, and introduces their occupants" (1967:63–64).

Three hundred and forty-one years before the Mindeleffs entered Zuni Pueblo, the first Europeans in the Southwest visited an earlier village of the same tribal group. This was probably Hawikuh, whose ruins the Mindeleffs photographed about fifteen miles southwest of modern Zuni Pueblo. In 1539 the Spanish priest, Fray Marcos de Niza, possibly had glimpsed the modest village from afar. But his enthusiastic report to Spain was written as if from the inside, and he claimed that the village was a storehouse of precious stones and metals.

After Francisco Vásquez de Coronado saw Zuni architecture at first hand in the summer of 1540, he realized that "everything is the opposite of what he [de Niza] related." Coronado lamented, "They [the buildings] are not decorated with turquoise, nor made of lime or good bricks, nevertheless, they are very good homes and good rooms" (Hammond and Rey 1940:170). Coronado noted the "estufas," chambers for religious and social usage, now known by the Hopi term kivas; the narrow corridors between buildings; and the removable house ladders for entering and exiting from the living units through roof openings. However, this initial impression of architectural intricacy caused the early Spanish some confusion. They were disposed to evaluate American Indian buildings for what they suggested about the level of culture and material wealth attained by their inhabitants. Yet Coronado turned up no gold, silver, or precious jewels, and as for their inhabitants, he commented, "I do not think they have the judgement and intelligence needed to be able to build those houses in the way in which they are built, for most of them are entirely naked" (Hammond and Rey 1940:171).

Following Coronado's conquest of Zuni, the Spanish made few impositions upon Western Pueblo lifeways—with such exceptions as the brutal conquest of Acoma Pueblo—until 1629. At that time Franciscan missions were established among the Zuni and the Hopi, and the most pronounced architectural expressions of a colonial presence were the bell towers of adobe Catholic churches that interrupted the horizontal Pueblo rooflines like jutting watchtowers. Spanish influence would also become evident in the beehive-shaped baking ovens, or *hornos*, which were built outdoors, and the chimney pots sprouting from rooftops. Inside, it would be evidenced by the built-in corner fireplaces, or *fogons*, which gradually replaced the old open-fire hearths that used to be located directly below the roof opening that served as both ladder well and smokehole.

After fifty years of intensifying Spanish oppression, the combined Pueblo peoples of east and west rebelled. The rare example of inter-Pueblo solidarity saw many of those bell towers toppled, and it reshaped the map of Pueblo locations as well. Fearing eventual Spanish reprisal, many villages resettled in more defensible sites. This was particularly the case in the western lands visited by the Mindeleffs, where the Zuni consolidated into one community—present-day Zuni—and a number of Hopi towns reestablished themselves on the remoter summits of First and Second Mesas.

Even after their military reconquest of the region in 1692–96, the Spanish never regained dominion over the Western Pueblos. When one Hopi community, Awatovi, returned to Christianity, it was attacked in 1700–1701 by other Hopis. The Zuni mission was temporarily reactivated, only to be abandoned in 1820. Until the end of Spanish and later Mexican control, with the Treaty of Guadalupe Hidalgo in 1848, these people and their architecture remained fairly resistant to outside change. Word of mouth from trappers, traders, and other travelers described these conservative communities, their rituals and distinctive housing, but the American military expeditions that explored road and railroad routes around the mid-nineteenth century produced the fullest descriptions of their self-sustaining and highly religious worlds. The Pueblo of Acoma to the east of Zuni was described by the topographical engineer Lt. James W. Albert in 1846; the first account of the prehistoric remains within Chaco Canyon north of Zuni were provided by Lt. J. H. Simpson in 1849; the mesatops inhabited by the Hopi Indians—known to the Spanish as the kingdom of Tusayan—were visited by U.S. Army personnel such as P. G. S. Ten Broeck and J. C. Ives in the 1850s.

Their eyewitness accounts of living American Indian villages and abandoned ruins helped to inspire the scientific expeditions run by the U.S. Department of the Interior little more than a decade later. Professor F. V. Hayden's Geological and Geographical Survey of the Territories began dispatching men like Colonel Stevenson into the field. Maj. John Wesley Powell's surveys commenced in 1867, producing somewhat rivalrous government explorations. Inaugurating work in the private sector was Dr. Edward Palmer, who began digging for Harvard's Peabody Museum in southern Utah in 1876. The period also saw visits to the region's ruins and inhabited villages by major cultural scholars of the time, Lewis Henry Morgan (in 1878) and Adolph F. A. Bandelier (in 1880).

Visual documentation played an important part in these survey expeditions (see Goetzmann 1966 for a historical review of the military and scientific explorations). As photographer for the Hayden surveys from 1874 to 1877, William Henry Jackson measured various southwestern pueblos. Then he crafted plaster models of the communities for exhibition at the 1876 Philadelphia Centennial (a few remain in Harvard University's Peabody Museum). William Henry Holmes—"perhaps the greatest artist-topographer and man of many talents the West has ever produced," according to historian William Goetzmann (1966:512–13)—was Jackson's colleague in these inaugural efforts of the Hayden crew to document Pueblo town architecture. Finally, photographer John "Jack" C. Hillers had been working on most of the Bureau expeditions to the southwest—from 1879 through 1885, with the exception of the 1884 field season. Powell's favorite photographer, he was compiling a virtual album on Western Pueblo buildings in the decade just before milled lumber, glass, sashes, stovepipes, and changing settlement patterns began modifying rapidly the pre-Hispanic look of Zuni and Hopi architecture.

Such were the waves of scientific activity on which the Mindeleffs were riding. While these fieldworkers were accumulating information about Pueblo life and architecture, the "father of American anthropology," Lewis Henry Morgan, was trying to relate this data to theories about American Indian cultural development that he had been developing since the 1840s. Morgan's final work, published the year the Mindeleffs traveled to the Southwest, was *Houses and House-Life of the American Aborigines* (Morgan [1881] 1965). The study was an ingenious appropriation of data on every form of American Indian architecture to buttress his thesis that human sociocultural evolution had advanced by stages. Pueblo architecture was especially pertinent because its compact room clusters were evidence to Morgan of "communism in living." In his grand social scheme, this feature and the customs of Pueblo land tenure placed these "sedentary Village Indians" a cut above the "middle status of barbarism" ([1881] 1965:82). Morgan also noted the influence of "the defensive principle" ([1881] 1965:140) in this architecture and included lengthy quotes from available ethnographic and archeological reports. For his Zuni material Morgan had relied upon the report of the Sitgreaves expedition in 1851 (he handcopied the Zuni Pueblo backdrop sketched by the expedition's artist, Richard Kern) and descriptions by Colonel Stevenson's wife, Mathilda Coxe, which originated from her 1879 trip. For his Hopi data he drew upon Lieutenant Ives's report of Second Mesa; Ives's phraseology must have been particularly gratifying, since it echoed Morgan's own emphases: Ives observed that the stepped house-tiers of the Hopi enclosed a "court [that] is common, and the landings are separated by no partitions, it involves a certain community residence" (Ives [1861] 1969:122).

These forerunners set the stage for the job that lay before the Mindeleff brothers and enhanced their final work. Thanks to the early documentation undertaken by Holmes and Hayden of southwestern Indian architecture in 1874–77 for the Hayden surveys, the topic was already credible. Thanks to the personal encouragement provided by Holmes, they probably won the assignment in the first place. Thanks to the rich photographic coverage provided by Hillers and the fortuitous availability of a fine Smithsonian staff artist, their book would be enriched by ample illustrations. And probably thanks to the interest of Morgan in the relationship between American Indian houses and social life, and Morgan's profound influence on Major Powell, they were encouraged to pursue the fuller role that architecture played in the Pueblo world.

We do not know what the Mindeleffs thought about Morgan's theoretical use of architectural data, nor whether Powell even assigned his manuscript as reading material before they left for Zuni. It earns only a few passing references in their study, although Cosmos pays fuller homage in a later 1898 overview of southwestern Indian buildings (Mindeleff 1898a). While clearly they did not feel obligated to second Morgan's theory with their own material, they did seek to satisfy Major Powell's concern that the study of houses should be more than the recording of built forms. In a letter to Spencer F. Baird, Secretary of the Smithsonian, Powell made a point to place "technology— especially with reference to domestic life" (BAE File 4677, p. 5) high on the list of eight major subject areas that his new Bureau of Ethnology should address. Powell believed strongly that "the collection of the arts is but the collection of curiosities unless the relation between arts, institutions, languages and opinions are discovered" (Powell

1883:iii). Almost certainly Morgan had helped to convince Powell of this tie between architecture as an art to social life as an institution. Perhaps Powell also communicated to the Mindeleffs some concern for deriving information about intangible aspects of culture such as social organization (and possibly aspects of religion and worldview) from the buildings and spaces that people have built for themselves.

The Mindeleff brothers brought sharp eyes into mesa country and probably were encouraged from childhood onward to observe and render reality with care. They were the children of émigré parents whose scientific and artistic leanings were apparently inherited by their sons. Victor was born 2 June 1860, of two Russians then living in London. That same year his mother, Julia Feodorovna (who apparently was a portraitist), and his father, Dimitri Victorovitch (who seems to have been a chemist), emigrated to the United States, settling in Washington, D.C. Cosmos was born in 1863, and a third son, Charles, in 1867. Victor attended public schools and advanced to the Emerson Institute College Preparatory School, where he won their Pinkney Medal for scholarship. What he studied, whether it entailed draftsmanship, and if he became an architectural intern before his southwestern period, we still do not know.

Possibly it was the fondness they shared for art and watercolor in particular, or merely the fact that they were neighbors, that brought Victor into contact with the cultivated scientific explorer and artist William Henry Holmes. Holmes's passion for the Southwest had been fired at age twenty-six, when, in 1872, he joined the Hayden Survey. Trained as a landscape artist, he was soon turning out exquisitely subtle, geologically precise watercolors of southwestern canyonlands. In 1875 Holmes first laid eyes on cliff dwellings along the San Juan drainage, a powerful experience to which he attributed his lifelong devotion to archeology (see Mark 1980:131–71 for profile of Holmes).

Holmes apparently introduced Victor into the Bureau of Ethnology, and the tone of the letters he would receive from the young amateur in the field ring of those to a patron. Holmes also drew Mindeleff into the lively circle of explorers, architects, and natural scientists who collected around Washington's prestigious Cosmos Club and the city's Anthropological Society. Throughout Victor Mindeleff's Bureau years his official letters, reports, and budgetary requests were addressed to Major Powell or his assistants, but his unofficial correspondence with Holmes often allowed him to express more personal reflections. As he confided toward the close of that first stay in Zuni:

> No matter what I may have to take to in the future I shall never regret my trip in the West—I think it has been rather exceptional in the

peculiar experiences I've met with—The fact of my being located so long a time among this one people, instead of wandering around more and having more hasty glimpses of a greater variety of people will afford me all the more satisfaction from knowing them so much more thoroughly—I shall always be greatly indebted to you for having kindly taken an interest in the undertaking as you did—and you have been the one to give me this chance. My present work in helping the Col [James Stevenson] may not be of much good to me, but I feel confident that my own special task on Zuni has been done with satisfactory completeness—I hope to have your criticism however when I reach home to tone down this boyish over-confidence (Mindeleff to Holmes, 3 December 1881).

Even after Victor left the Bureau he could count on Holmes's support. In 1918, when Holmes recommended Mindeleff's nomination for Cosmos Club membership, he characterized him as "my old friend and near neighbor of many years past . . . a man of ability, an architect of excellent standing and of superior taste in all matters of art" (Holmes to Cosmos Club, 18 May 1918).

The nine field seasons spent in the Southwest by Victor and Cosmos were times of high adventure, hard work, rough travel, diminishing budgets, and hospitable, hostile, or indifferent Indians. Despite interruptions to satisfy Bureau directives to collect museum specimens—pottery in particular—the brothers always returned to their central passion: native buildings, how they were made and arranged together, and, to some degree, how they were conceived and used.

Yet the prospect of a monograph on Pueblo architecture appears to have been less on their minds during the last five months of 1881 than the pressing assignment to produce the scale model of Zuni Pueblo. Cushing had introduced the brothers to the receptive Pueblo governor, and on 9 August they began measuring his house, recording their data in U.S. Geological and Geographic Survey sketchbooks. It could not have taken them long to realize that recording the odd-angled, irregularly lined, and ad hoc Pueblo constructions made of water, mud, and sandstone would call for improvised surveying techniques.

This architecture was premised on unfamiliar and unwritten rules. Its apparent durability was a mask, for these buildings were in a constant state of flux. Not only were they vulnerable to the rains of July and August and required much upkeep, but the Zuni and the Hopi seemed continuously to be sealing up or adding on new units, freely recycling stone, wood, and mortar from any unused quarters nearby. The Mindeleffs dutifully applied their instruments to "record the minute variations from geometric forms which are so characteristic of the pueblo work," but they never quite appreciated the improvisational nature of its engineering. To the Indians, what was important were the specific uses of their rooms and the meanings associated with them. The Mindeleffs, however, concluded that the Pueblo builders betrayed "an absence of high architectural skill," and they sought in their descriptions to correct any impression left by previous visitors that just because these constructions were big they were also well made.

It was surely at Zuni that they first worked out procedures for documenting building irregularities on paper. With compass and tape they ran the straight lines of every house or houseblock and then carefully recorded on their graph paper all deviations from these outlines—the jogs and odd angles that had developed from years of washed-out walls and rooms eroding from disrepair, from units intentionally closed up or hastily added on. This tedious process was then applied to the second and higher stories, recording each with a different color tone while noting vertical measurements. Numerous external features were also jotted down, such as coping stones, chimney locations, trapdoors, ladders, and vents.

Since these measurements were initially directed toward model building, the Mindeleffs also surveyed the topography on which the villages stood. They first sighted through their levels all around Zuni in order to establish accurate heights for each building and wall. Later on, when they measured abandoned ruins, they established fixed positions that they connected with cross sights rather than wall lines for their control grid, since it was often impossible to ascertain whether disintegrated walls merely turned corners or actually terminated.

As the Mindeleffs lugged their equipment between buildings and up ladders, the guidance of Cushing allowed them to circulate among Zuni families in the midst of their daily lives. But the Indians drew the line at their sacred *kivas* and also refused to let the Mindeleffs measure interiors in the core houseblocks—numbers one and four on their town plan. On the verge of their departure, however, the outsiders were privileged to witness a performance by the sacred clowns, or *newe.kwe* society. It occurred on 17 November in the house of the governor, whose earthen floor had been specially swept and sprinkled for the occasion. These clowns were sanctioned to break rules, present dramatic parodies, and expunge the sense of shame commonly associated with certain acts. In front of Mindeleff, John G. Bourke, and others (as described by Bourke 1886:400–403), the performers conducted a mock Catholic mass that climaxed in the gleeful consumption of cupfuls of human urine.

Back in Washington, Cosmos took charge of the first of many models he would mold in the Bureau's workshops. On his worktable he reduced the measurements of Zuni—roughly 1,200 by 600 feet—by a sixtieth. His model village also acquired miniature sheep corrals and gardens along with the five-storied houseblocks, and a miniature of Nuestra Señora de Guadalupe Church was added alongside the Pueblo's largest plaza. Finally, the model was mounted on an 11 by 20 foot wood base for immediate exhibition in the U.S. National Museum.

The youthful Mindeleffs had apparently shown sufficient mettle to be attached to the following summer's mission to northcentral Arizona. This 1882 season would prove the richest specimen-collecting expedition the Smithsonian would ever enjoy in the Southwest (it is reviewed in Parezo 1985). Before they ever reached their destination in Hopi country, however, the Mindeleffs underwent the usual impediments to travel at this time. As a government agency, the Bureau of Ethnology aspired to militarylike precision in its timetables and communiqués, but rugged country and unreliable transportation made punctuality difficult. The leg from Kansas City to Fort Wingate was completed—presumably by train—in the normal three days, but then they were held up nearly a week until the group's leader, Colonel Stevenson, could coax the post commandant to loan them a six-mule-team wagon for the five-day haul to Keams Canyon. There they were delayed for another five days as they packed burros and sought permission to bivouac in the old government schoolhouse up on First Mesa (based upon V. Mindeleff to Powell, 30 September 1882).

The same good fortune that had given them the services of the knowledgeable Cushing at Zuni was also awaiting them in Hopi country. Recently in residence at the trading post—established by Thomas V. Keams seven years earlier—near the Hopi mesas was a remarkable Scotsman named Alexander M. Stephen. He was an ex-Army officer who was studying Navajo language and culture. The Mindeleffs' visit coincided with Stephen's new curiosity about Hopi lifeways, which had been helped by the experience of another resident Anglo scholar, Dr. Jeremiah Sullivan (who would provide the Mindeleffs with folklore about the Hopi-associated ruin of Payupki). In fact, Stephen was moving up to First Mesa at the time, and the appearance of the Mindeleffs lent direction to his new inquiries. While Stephen helped the Mindeleffs to survey, he also began recording the Hopi clan migration legends that would make the Hopi's own version of their architectural history an unexpectedly vital aspect of the Mindeleffs' final study.

Through Stephen's assistance, the Mindeleffs were also able to document (1) the native architectural glossary; (2) the rituals for blessing houses and *kivas* during and after construction; (3) the lore concerning the meanings and use of *kivas*; (4) the location of clan groupings within the village plans; and (5) the critical role of women in Hopi house customs. Stephen's apparent rapport with the Hopi enabled the Mindeleffs to imbue their book with a native point-of-view despite their reservations about the craftsmanship and character of the Hopi themselves. (As edited by Elsie Clews Parsons, Stephen's intimate account of daily Hopi life offers a complement to the Mindeleff study: Stephen 1936, 2 vols.) Stephen was roundly considered an exceptional fieldworker and human being; as Victor later wrote the Bureau endorsing fieldwork support for him, "Mr. Stephen not only has the advantage of ready access to the sources of such legendary information—an access that can be secured only by gaining the confidence of the Indians through long contact with them, and by exercise of much tact—but he is also a gentleman of exceptional culture and scholarship" (V. Mindeleff to Powell, 26 July 1886).

Then as now, the Hopi towns were situated on three picturesque mesas that extend south from Black Mesa into the Painted Desert. During the latter half of September 1882, the Mindeleffs measured, sketched, and photographed the houseblocks of the three villages on First Mesa: Hano, Sichomovi, and Walpi. With Stephen smoothing the way, their efforts progressed well enough to allow a side trip to the Awatovi ruins, or "Tallah Hogan" (Singing House) as it was called by the Navajo. This older Hopi site lay about ten miles southeast of First Mesa and promised evidence for a thesis that would permeate the Mindeleffs' study: the close link between contemporary Pueblo settlements and their direct archeological antecedents. Awatovi was also a symbol of the tragic extremes of tribal factionalism; the village was brutally destroyed by Hopis themselves when its inhabitants seemed to be returning to Catholic control after the 1680 all-Pueblo rebellion (see Montgomery, Smith, and Brew 1949 for a full description of Awatovi based upon Peabody Museum archeological work in 1935–39).

With First Mesa documented, Victor also took a six-week break for side trips with Colonel Stevenson to the ruins of Canyon de Chelly and with Major Powell into the Grand Canyon. Upon his return in early December 1882, Victor was ordered by Washington to oversee the collecting of "ethnologic specimens" among the Hopi. He decided to start with Oraibi Pueblo on Third Mesa, leaving the three villages on the Middle or Second Mesa for last because they were closer to supplies. Cushing was assigned as Mindeleff's advance man. But when Cushing departed in the third week of December for Oraibi Pueblo to make preliminary arrangements, he would also set the stage for Victor's first field disappointment and confront a reality that, at one time or another, has been part of the experience of many American ethnographers: the Indians' negative response to being studied and to having their artifacts collected and exhibited.

The years 1881–83 would bring the Bureau of Ethnology and the U.S. National Museum more specimens, primarily painted pots, from the Western Pueblos than it would ever collect again. Most of the 3,429 artifacts from Zuni and the 2,952 items from Hopi would originate from expeditions in which Victor participated. "Collecting" at this time was basically trading. Word was put out for Indians to bring in their old ceramics, baskets, stone implements, and other cultural materials—the older the better. Displayed atop packing crates would be trade goods hauled in by burro or wagon: red calico, lead bars, sleigh bells, flour, clothing, and the like. Business was usually brisk, and the native items piled up rapidly to be packed in sheep pelts, stuffed into hastily built wooden crates, and carried by wagon to the railhead for transport to Washington.

By the time the Mindeleff party appeared in northern Arizona, relations between the Oraibi villagers and European-Americans had declined from poor to worse. The earliest Anglo visits in the 1850s had coincided with fearful smallpox epidemics among the Hopi. Raiding by both Navajos and white settlers, plus waves of drought and consequent famine, caused population loss and an atmosphere of anxiety and resentment. In the same period, aggressive proselytizing by competing missionaries heightened tensions within a number of Hopi villages. The previous season had gone well for the Mindeleffs at the First and Second Mesa communities, but the membership of Oraibi Pueblo was riven with debate over political relations with whites (see Whiteley 1987 and Dockstader 1979).

Cushing had been effective at establishing rapport with the Zuni because he was studying only a single community, of which he had been accepted as a resident for over a year. The Hopi occupied a number of different communities, however, each displaying their own attitude toward outsiders. Stephen's contacts had paved the way for efficient work at First Mesa, but when Cushing maneuvered through his friendly contacts from there—especially Tom Polacca—to set up shop in one of the Oraibi *kiva*s, opposing elements in the village were infuriated.

On 23 December a courier brought Victor alarming word from Cushing. During a confrontation in one of their *kiva*s, the Oraibi "hostiles" ordered Cushing out of the village; his Indian friends were powerless. As Cushing quoted from their eviction speech, "When the Caciques of the Americans sit on our decapitated heads then they can dress our bodies in their clothes, feed our bodies with their victuals. Then, too, they can have our things to take with them to the houses of their fathers" (Cushing to Mindeleff, 23 December 1882). Although

Cushing defiantly stood his ground, collecting at Oraibi was clearly out of the question. Mindeleff must rush wagons to Oraibi so they could cart their goods to safety. "I have passed through no small personal risk this night," Cushing added in his letter to Mindeleff. "They like me, they say. My mission they do not like. They will have nothing to do with it, or with the Americans. No, not even though they come with all their power."

Mindeleff immediately telegraphed Powell about this turn of events, copied Cushing's letter and forwarded it to Washington, and hastened to rescue Cushing and the trade goods. He pushed to Oraibi through the snow, whereupon the expedition shifted to a safer base camp just below Mashongnavi village on Second Mesa. Here they conducted a brisk trade with Hopi from the First and Second Mesa villages. The wares were displayed on wooden crates, and the expedition amassed pottery, basketry, stone implements, and dance paraphernalia—1,200 specimens all told, including 150 prehistoric pots. At the same time Victor drew and photographed the pottery collection of trader Keams, and, quite likely, both brothers used their free moments to doublecheck their Hopi village measurements in anticipation of more model building.

Cosmos was already in his Smithsonian work studio by February 1883, molding the clay replica of Second Mesa. Victor wrote Holmes that he wished to "personally attend to the first mesa model." He wanted to "make a damn big thing of it, modeling the entire mesa with the three towns on top. It would be a fine thing if executed to the same scale as the Zuni model." Work on these models preoccupied the brothers until June. First they were molded in clay after the field measurements, then tissue paper and glue produced a papier-mâché cast. Finally emerged the plaster miniature, which was painted, detailed, and carefully mounted for safe transport. These models, and the earlier Zuni example, met uncertain fates. Cosmos was constantly turning out duplicates as old models became chipped or mishandled and upcoming exhibitions demanded fresh material. Eventually the Zuni Pueblo model disappeared, and perhaps never returned from the St. Louis Exposition of 1904 (possibly it met the same wrecking ball that is believed to have pulverized the Frederic Remington sculptures also displayed at St. Louis).

One model of Walpi, perhaps the initial cast, was destroyed in early winter 1890, while it was en route to the New Orleans Exposition. Another copy from the Walpi mold, however, apparently found safe harbor at the Panhandle-Plains Museum in Canyon, Texas. Cosmos himself was worried about the fate of his creations, and possibly about his own professional security as well. He warned the Bureau that the models his workroom was turning out—including subjects other than

Pueblo architecture—would be lost unless a curator of models was appointed (he was turned down).

The forthcoming Louisville Exposition called for models not only of inhabited Indian villages but also of abandoned prehistoric cliff ruins. Cosmos hurried to provide them and then departed for the Southwest again. As if the Mindeleffs had had enough of studying architecture whose inhabitants could talk back, this coming 1883 season was slated for the recording of uninhabited, pre-Hispanic ruins. They were to begin with Canyon de Chelly before shifting to the sites of Kin-Tiel and Kimma-Zinde not far away. However, the de Chelly sites lay in the heart of Navajo country, on the reservation the tribe had been given in 1868. When the expedition received reports of troublesome Indians north of Fort Defiance, a last-minute shift in plans saw them detour to Kin-Tiel, an extensive ruin situated between Zuni and Hopi country.

Shaped like a butterfly with extended wings, the village of Kin-Tiel (Wide Ruins) measured roughly 600 by 350 feet and was bisected by an arroyo. Here Victor discovered well-preserved walls, a grave recently exposed in a wash containing pottery offerings, and a curious doorway stone, a large piece of sandstone with a manhole cut through it. To Victor, numerous architectural details made the site especially interesting: stone-paved floors, fireplaces with ancient ashes still in them, stone griddles "similar to those used at present by the Zunis and Mokis," as well as paint-grinding stones, needles and awls.

By November the expedition felt comfortable about turning to Canyon de Chelly, but with the season so far advanced only a superficial survey was possible. Guided by Navajos and following local tips, they wended their way up unexplored branches of the canyon containing more ruins. Concerned about obtaining more measurements for new models, the last days of December 1883 were devoted to a quick visit to Acoma Pueblo. Victor collected specimens and measured the old parallel-street village that was situated in a highly defensible and dramatic location, 375 feet atop a sandstone mesa.

Back in Washington the brothers cooperated on their map of the Chaco Canyon sites, put finishing touches on the Hopi models, and produced working drawings for models to be displayed at the government's upcoming New Orleans exposition. During the 1884 fieldtrip, Victor returned to Chaco Canyon for another look in August and then traveled to Etowah mound in Georgia, which was under study by Dr. Cyrus Thomas of the Smithsonian. Sketches from these visits were turned over to Cosmos's shop, which kept late hours until December, when Cosmos personally installed the completed exhibits in New Orleans.

Now Victor seemed to feel compelled to turn from collecting back to architecture, to plug up holes in research, and to consolidate his findings. In June 1885 he sent Powell an ambitious proposal for the 1885–86 field season: he wanted to return to Hopi country for a closer look at their houses and especially their room interiors. Then he would record the cell-like shelters found in the San Francisco Peaks area before moving to the Walnut Creek ruins. More work was needed in Canyon de Chelly, with special focus on its round *kivas*. Victor suggested an itinerary for documenting the eastern Rio Grande pueblos, first sketching and measuring the Jemez Pueblo *kiva* before continuing to Cochiti Pueblo and taking a look at the nearby caves carved into the tufa cliffs of Rito de los Frijoles Canyon, which Bandelier had studied. After noting down the remaining modern Eastern Pueblo villages, "comparing some details of construction with those used in the houses of lower class Mexicans," he would record Laguna and Acoma. His final stop would be Zuni, for further work on both the modern town and its ancestral villages. Weather permitting, Victor wanted to explore Round Valley near the headwaters of the little Colorado, especially the "remains of archaic Circular stone houses." The seven-month itinerary would cost $5,525.90, including salaries for himself and Cosmos, a cook, and two packers.

While it did cover a lot of ground, the 1885 season did not fulfill that grand design. Late June found Victor again encamped below Second Mesa, where Cosmos joined him in July. Presumably with Stephen at their side, they again meandered through the Hopi villages—Oraibi excepted. *Kivas* were intensively studied, construction details were analyzed, and more house-building processes and traditions were recorded. On August 18 they also witnessed the Snake Dance at Walpi village—their camera was one of five at the ceremony, but most of their eighteen plates turned out thin because of poor light.

In August they were confronted by a party of Navajos who were worried about white strangers using measuring instruments in their territory. They were reassured, however, that the Mindeleffs presented no threat to their hard-won reservation, and in fact the expedition obtained valuable information on Navajo mythology, their methods for building hogans (the traditional Navajo house), and the cosmological meanings associated with parts of the frame and covering. The Navajo shared their songs associated with hogan construction and blessing. This was probably the material that went into the first published account of a Navajo house dedication ritual (Stephen 1893) and Cosmos's lengthier treatment of Navajo architecture (Mindeleff 1898b).

Next the expedition explored such Hopi-related ruins as Payupki, Tenkibi, and Old Walpi before heading for the Keams Canyon trading post to overhaul equipment and shoe horses. In September they visited Mummy Cave in Cañón del Muerte and White House ruin. Lack of water deterred them from Chaco Canyon, and they returned to the Zuni territory, collecting surface pottery and measuring the old farming pueblos believed to be the rest of the fabled "seven cities" of Cibola—early Zuni-related sites such as Ojo Caliente, Hawikuh, Keteupaui, and Chalowe.

But funds were running out. Victor mailed a plea for $600 to collect more material around St. Johns, Arizona, and from several Rio Grande Pueblos—"both localities rich in material that would prove very useful for comparison in the study of the Moki [Hopi] and Zuni architectural groups." When this was not forthcoming, he returned to Washington for his first stab at assimilating the data the brothers had been collecting for four years now. Cosmos reentered the modeling work-room, duplicating exhibits for new expositions and producing a new Chaco Canyon series.

It seems to have been here that the present report was born. Cosmos was handed the job of editing the Hopi "traditional history" material collected by Stephen into an introductory chapter. Indeed, at this early stage the work was apparently envisioned as having joint authorship, and Cosmos prepared a number of chapters that were cut from the final publication: a 10-page description of the region, a 17-page review of Spanish expeditions, and a 137-page "review of the descriptive literature" (see Acknowledgments and Archival References for citations on the excised Cosmos Mindeleff materials).

After Victor drafted separate chapters on the Hopi and Zuni materials, he launched into the comparative section, highlighting whenever possible those details that might also illuminate the ruins they had visited. He reluctantly found himself turning into a bureaucrat, for another function of his desk-bound role as a Bureau "assistant ethnologist" forced him to interrupt his writing to answer queries about the whereabouts of ruins for other fieldworkers to visit. Not until September 1887 were the brothers able to return for their last full-scale working sojourn in the Southwest. First they sketched ruins in the San Francisco Mountains, Walnut Canyon, and near Keams Canyon that were traditionally associated with Hopi culture history. It seems the antiwhite atmosphere at Oraibi had momentarily subsided, for next they were able to examine house construction there as well as at the outlying farming community of Moen-Kopi—rarely described by early anthropologists—and inspect nearby ruins before pressing on to Chaco Canyon.

There they spent six weeks surveying the architecture in order to discern its structural principles. Some similarities between the living and abandoned pueblos seemed obvious, such as the practice of hasty mortaring up of temporarily unused rooms, the occasional use of interior air vents between stories within, the size of the multistoried houseblocks, and the forms of inside doorways. Some of their observations today's archeologists still find useful, and theirs were the first photographs of Chaco's ruins (see Lekson [1984] 1986 for an excellent summary of Chaco Canyon architecture). All the while they collected material on the "more primitive Navajo architecture" they observed from horseback. The season closed with only a dent into the envisioned Rio Grande survey: a side trip to Jemez Pueblo where they drafted a plat of the village.

From now on Victor undertook shorter Bureau assignments to the field. In fall 1888 he visited Arizona to paint the pottery collection of the Navajo trader, Lorenzo Hubbell, and managed an excursion to Zuni for last-minute building details. Shortly afterward he visited Casa Grande ruin, outside present-day Phoenix, Arizona. But his primary burden now was pulling together the architecture manuscript. This was probably not easy, since he was still adding and revising in December 1889. A few months later Holmes wrote Powell advising the dropping of most of Cosmos's contributions, since Victor's work was monographic, while Cosmos was "but a fragment of a great field which is not separable into parts" (Holmes to Powell 24 February 1890). However, Holmes urged their expansion in a separate publication later on. We do not know Cosmos's feelings about being demoted from author to contributor, but his attention was quickly absorbed with meeting new demands for models both at home and abroad.

By "Pueblo" architecture, the Mindeleffs actually meant what has become classified as Western Pueblo, the Hopi and Zuni villages in Arizona that lay west of the Eastern Pueblos along the Rio Grande River in New Mexico. Often lacking the luxury of water within easy reach, the houses here had a rawer, stonier, and more modest look than those to the east. But their history was no less ancient, and the Mindeleffs sought to investigate it using one of the more controversial approaches of architectural reconstruction, the application of American Indian mythology. Although Victor did write Holmes that he considered the Hopi oral narratives of "secondary importance" (V. Mindeleff to Holmes, 26 July 1886), his brother's synthesis of Hopi migration stories was located prominently—it was the study's opening section. These narratives were interlaced with accounts of ancient settlements, house-buildings, and village abandonments. They established a basis for Mindeleff's interest in comparing uninhabited ruins with their occupied descendants among the Zuni and the Hopi. This arrangement also implied that the white scholar's reconstruction of Pueblo culture history could possibly be compatible with the native cultural memory, an implication that would be a matter of some debate between nineteenth-century and Boasian anthropologists a generation later.

When it was finally finished, this work proposed no grand interpretative scheme, as Lewis Henry Morgan's study of Indian houses had accomplished a decade earlier. It was a fairly straightforward description, moving from those intermingled accounts of clan migrations that led to the ultimate consolidation of the Hopi on their mesas, to two chapters that studied, respectively, the living villages of the Hopi and the Zuni. (This was perhaps the last time, however, that the antiquated Spanish names for these legendary Indian "provinces" were employed—Tusayan and Cibola). For Victor the final, fourth chapter was perhaps the most satisfying: the close-grained comparison of architectural details at Zuni and Hopi.

While not driven by any guiding theory, the work was underlain with numerous suppositions and concerns. Implicit comparison played an important role, as Victor juxtaposed contemporary pueblos with their (presumed direct) pre-Hispanic antecedents, and Zuni buildings with Hopi constructions. Although he tried to evaluate Pueblo architecture on its own terms, Victor often found the contemporary Pueblo construction wanting. Like most first-time visitors, initially Victor was impressed by the tidy, uniform stonework of the ruined Chaco Canyon walling techniques. But he appears unaware that these chunks of shaped sandstone were actually plastered over. On later visits he became less enchanted when he realized that pueblo walls were generally not bonded, and he detected a decline between the fine work of old Anasazi sites and the "careless and chaotic," "shiftless" craftsmanship of contemporary Hopi buildings with their "absence of a definite plan."

What is remarkable about the book is that despite Victor's lack of appreciation for why Hopis did not employ sounder building principles, he provided abundant detail from the native persepctive. No doubt this is in large measure due to the contributions of Cushing at Zuni and Stephen at Hopi. It was Cushing, for instance, who directed Victor to the Zuni myth of the "stone close," which helped to decipher the function of a large stone with a round hole that had probably served as a prehistoric doorway. And it was Stephen who enabled Victor to interpret the *kiva* as a model of Hopi cosmology. In the area of ceremonial usages and practices, the Mindeleff data offers a rare window onto an American Indian belief system and worldview.

While Victor grasped the idea that *kivas* might encode cosmological principles, it was still too early in the development of southwestern archeology for him to realize that they could reflect architectural history as well. Early in the study he promised to demonstrate how "an important type of primitive architecture . . . had developed from the rude lodge into the many-storied house of rectangular rooms." He was also aware "of the well known tendency of the survival of the ancient practice in matters pertaining to the religious observances of primitive people." Despite these insights, it would be another thirty years before southwestern archeologists would propose that those earliest "rude lodges" were in fact pit-houses, a building form converted into religious use as the surface "unit house" developed above ground to multiply into the early multiroom pueblos. But the pit-house was retained, later emerging as the *kiva;* by the time of the Mindeleffs' arrival *kiva*s were found in rectangular form at Hopi and Zuni and, predominantly in circular form, among the Eastern Rio Grande Pueblos.

Mindeleff made breakthroughs in other aspects of architectural history. His sequence of drawings plotting the growth of the Hopi village of Mashongnavi is the first serious attempt to illustrate the morphological growth of one Pueblo village. He also sensed the abiding tension in Pueblo architecture between change and conservatism. While he documented such Spanish-borrowed modifications as the use of straw in adobe, the application of hot gypsum whitewash with the aid of sheepskin gloves, and the addition of the interior and outdoor fireplaces, he also described the rejection of other imported ideas.

For instance, he learned that the Hopi refused to roof with oven-fired tiles because in their belief system the notion of kiln treatment was associated with forced loss of precious moisture, a belief that did not pertain to adobe, as it was allowed to slowly harden beneath a baking sun. Mindeleff seemed to appreciate the arena of architecture as a place where historical and cultural ideas were in dynamic competition. His descriptions are thick with the minutiae of historical change—the effect of axes, oxen, dynamite, window sashes, and the railroad on Pueblo construction, and also on features of Pueblo tradition that seemed impervious to those innovations.

As far as the relationship of domestic space to social organization and history was concerned, the Mindeleffs were not grand theorists like Morgan, but they were pioneers. Down-to-earth ethnographers, they linked society and buildings. Their access to the inner world of Hopi social organization enabled them to chart clan locations for most Hopi villages. While the completed study only illustrated one town plan indicating clan affiliation and residence pattern, Cosmos published the rest in his valuable addition on Hopi clan localization (Mindeleff 1900), which we have added to this new edition. In this paper Cosmos hypothesized that the process of pueblo growth and fission followed two courses: outlying or "summer" villages that every pueblo used during the peak of the farming season gradually became occupied permanently, and migrating clans attached themselves to developing villages, grouping their living units into new village "wards," or separate house clusters. Mindeleff suggested that this process had continued from prehistoric times through to the present, and his work underscored the conservatism of Pueblo architecture. The allocation of rooms and buildings for specific social, domestic, or ceremonial purposes, and specific details such as door shape, ladder usage, roofing techniques, and arrangement of corn-grinding basins were shown to be remarkably consistent since pre-Hispanic times.

To the Mindeleffs' credit, they also paid attention to what were probably unfamiliar customs regarding the social order of architecture and the care for the spiritual welfare of a house and its occupants. They noted the custom of the female rights over the house both as property and as architecture: a man generally moved into the clan cluster of his wife's family, and a woman usually took charge of all but the heaviest part of house construction. Religious customs included house offerings held before construction to "root" the new quarters, prayers during the actual work, and the placement of prayer feathers, or *paahos* in the rafters to bless and protect the completed room (see Saile 1977 for a summary of Hopi, Zuni, and other Pueblo material on construction rituals). Mindeleff detailed such practices as the fact that some plastering was purposefully left incomplete, so that a supernatural spirit—a Kachina—might complete the job, and he observed that a house was blessed before a chimney (of postcontact origin) was added, as if to exclude the foreign element from sanctification. When it came to Hopi *kivas*, Mindeleff's collection of building lore was especially rich, including an architectural glossary and beliefs associated with these special-use buildings.

Unlike later scholars of vernacular built forms, Mindeleff dignified his subject matter with the term "architecture," despite the fact that the Hopi disregard for solid, permanent construction went against his architect's grain. What he found among those inhabited pueblos, and on closer inspection among many of their prehistoric antecedents, were honeycombs of individual huts of sandstone and sticks shakily stuck together by dried mud and plastered over each year. To block the doorway of an unused room, the Hopi or the Zuni filled it quickly with unfinished rubble and adobe. They added rooms with equal expediency, unworried about structurally bonding new walls to old. Mindeleff often found it difficult to tell whether he was watching walls going up or falling apart.

As for design principles, Mindeleff believed that defense was an overriding motivation for perpetuating the enclosing, clustered character of Pueblo architecture, in both their valley and their mesatop locations. This was demonstrated by the fact that while communities in the open valleys were organized around enclosed courtyards, or plazas, he did not find such clustering on the mesatops, which were natural barriers to surprise attack. Interestingly, he made little of the role of thermal comfort in the evolution of these pueblos. And while environment constrained town plans on cramped mesa sites where the Hopis located their villages, he maintained that Indians did not consciously enhance conformities between landscape and architecture for purposes of concealment, for visual appeal, or for any religious reasons.

By 1887 Victor became concerned about the quality of illustrations for his prospective publication. His mentor, Holmes, was anxious to have both brothers on hand when the actual drawings were being prepared. To visually document the study Victor had not only the photographs he and Cosmos had taken, but also the extensive collection shot by Hillers between 1879 and 1885 (see Fowler 1972 on Hillers's career). In the finished work some were retouched and cropped, and for production purposes they were often inserted in the published work (unfortunately, far from their textual references). What lent the work even greater graphic appeal, perhaps, was the enhancement afforded those photographs that were not reproduced but were instead converted into engravings. This transformation was devoted to negatives that were too thin, such as a number of Victor's rather uninteresting pictures of prehistoric remains, and to sections of Hillers's photos in order to highlight their architectural details. Another benefit of engravings was that, unlike photographic plates, they could be inserted directly on the printed page to illustrate the immediate discussion.

Here the book's artwork profited from an unsung contributor. H. Hobart Nichols (1869–1972) was the resident Smithsonian artist who produced 114 renderings that were included in the published study. An employee of the Bureau of Ethnology from 1889 to 1895, Nichols had been trained at Washington's Art Students League and the Académie Julien in Paris. He was about twenty years old when he began these drawings, and his contribution cannot be minimized. Nichols's careful depictions of fireplaces, roof drains, chimneys, ladders, room interiors, and crumbling facades help the reader focus on Mindeleff's crucial comparison between prehistoric and historic architectural details. They parade before us a delightful variety of cooking spaces, they show us myriad ways that rainwater was deflected from vulnerable adobe walls and floors, and they review the imaginative diversity of doorway and ladder forms that Pueblo builders devised for moving in and out and through their buildings.

Hillers's photos and the drawings by Mindeleff and Nichols help complement Victor's efforts to describe how Hopis and Zunis used this architecture. We get a better sense from the illustrations than from the text that these house clusters were actually food-processing plants. Inside were entire rooms devoted to food storage and preparation; outside we see the spaces where much of workaday life was spent—the terraces strewn with drying peaches, strings of cut pumpkin and squash being prepared for winter use, and raw sheepskins pegged to adobe walls drying in the sun. The pictures also allow us to compare the skylines of Zuni, splintered with the angled poles of entry ladders and punctuated with chimney pots, with the lower rooftops of the Hopi, where the coping walls are less refined, unplastered walls are more evident, and the shorter ladders—wood is at a premium in this Western Pueblo territory—do not break up the horizontal terrace planes.

Although Victor was a talented graphic artist in his own right, his work was nonetheless redrawn, except for a watercolor of a Hopi room interior. Apparently he was too busy reworking the text, which he was still revising in autumn 1888, to prepare the finished visuals. His last task was executing maps with locations of known Pueblo ruins identified on them, which were also redrawn by a Bureau illustrator. At this point Victor's association with the Bureau apparently came to a close, and he entered the design career that this sidetrack had delayed for almost nine years.

Critical response to the work—even notice of publication—was slow in coming. The 200-page study was underplayed as an "accompanying paper" to the Bureau's eighth annual report. It represented work finalized during the 1886–87 period, its publication date was officially 1891, and it was not available until 1893. That year the *American Anthropologist* cursorily listed its availability, but apparently never reviewed it. As an official document of specialized distribution, it received little notice in architectural circles.

Only the *American Antiquarian and Oriental Journal* appears to have reviewed the study, calling it "a very important monograph" that is "splendidly illustrated and convey[s] a vast amount of information." The *Antiquarian*'s interest was probably aroused because aboriginal architecture held special interest for its founder-editor, Rev. Stephen D. Peet. The writer added that "those who secure this volume will form a pretty clear idea of the Pueblos and of the changes which have occurred in their location during the past three hundred years." His only reservation was that "the description is confined to one particular locality," but he advised readers that they would thus "have the opportunity of comparing the structures here and elsewhere by taking the different reports which have been published" (1893:389).

Reviewers might have overlooked the importance of the Mindeleff contribution, but scholars began mining it almost immediately. Over the years it acquired a distinguished reputation: as an unheralded classic, as a model for the study of vernacular architecture, as the principal sourcebook on traditional Western Pueblo buildings and their ancient prototypes, and as a major data base for studies of Pueblo culture change.

In an overview of southwestern ethnology, anthropologist Keith Basso points out that "the history of research in the Southwest has been—and still is—a mirror of American anthropology" (Basso 1979:14). The study of southwestern architecture, in turn, is a microcosm of the regional research; the research directions implied in the Mindeleff work render it a crystal ball for the field. Hardly a decade has passed that the Mindeleff study has not been appropriated for one or another theoretical approach to the interpretation of Pueblo culture.

Even before the study appeared, Mindeleff was being cited for his ideas on how this architecture had evolved. In a provocative essay Mindeleff's guide, Frank Cushing, suggested that the precontact development of Zuni housing might be reconstructed through a careful gloss of key architectural terms in the Zuni language. Cushing became the first to cite Mindeleff, "whose wide experience among the southwestern ruins entitles his judgement to high consideration" (Cushing 1886:476). Mindeleff suggested to Cushing that some archaic Zuni terminology perhaps referred to the time when the early Zuni had tried to cluster their old, round stone houses and discovered that it was more convenient to straighten and combine adjoining curved walls, thereby producing the first apartment complexes.

While French sociologists Emile Durkheim and Marcel Mauss made much of Cushing's work and cited Mindeleff as early as 1903, full appreciation at home took longer. Victor and Cosmos had mentioned the thermal and defensive determinants of Pueblo architecture but had never spelled out the environmental argument. Cosmos addressed the subject later (1897a), but it was not until 1906 that Jesse Walter Fewkes hit upon the study's most glaring omission. In "The Sun's Influence on the Form of Hopi Pueblos," Fewkes paid homage to Mindeleff's "valuable memoir" and acknowledged Mindeleff as the first to note that Hopi houses were generally arranged in parallel rows separated by courts. Fewkes added, however, that Mindeleff might also have mentioned the uniform directional orientation to these house rows that did not always conform to the mesa shape. While he felt Mindeleff was right in suggesting that the need for defense had initially led to "the grouping of clans into composite villages with united rooms" (Fewkes 1906:99), another principle was at work. This was the "desire to obtain a maximum amount of heat through heliotropic exposure" (1906:99), which had necessitated the extension of these houseblocks so that living units would customarily face south to southeast. Their stone-and-adobe walls could thus soak up the sun's heat during daylight and radiate it inside at night, as well as minimize exposure from cold winds to the rooftop terraces where people worked and socialized. Fewkes's insight also explained why new construction usually occurred along the northwestern or southeastern walls of standing buildings.

Fewkes was still studying the Hopi when Alfred L. Kroeber arrived at Zuni Pueblo in 1915 with a different agenda. During these years American anthropology was following exciting new directions under the guidance of Franz Boas. Among his favored students, Kroeber epitomized the empirical, systematic philosophy of his mentor. The Boasian era was also intent on making anthropology a respectable member of the academic sciences; the day of gifted amateurs like the Mindeleffs was in decline. Kroeber was at Zuni to apply ideas on kinship and social organization inspired by the British anthropologist W. H. Pitt-Rivers. He produced what anthropologist Elsie Clews Parsons would later praise as "the first study of the relations between housing and kinship" (Parsons 1936:229), while his colleague, Leslie Spier, conducted archeological exploration at the pueblo.

For both investigators Mindeleff's work must have served as a field guide. Spier's excavations verified Victor's contention that the northwestern houseblocks were the oldest structures. Kroeber began using the book's map to plot current family and clan distribution. But he soon realized that while Mindeleff's plan looked "tantalyzingly" [sic] like the Zuni he was discovering, hardly a dozen walls were standing where they had been noted thirty-five years before, and most of the buildings had lost upper stories. After witnessing the almost daily dismantling and reconstruction of room units that occurred over their summer field season, Kroeber realized that his map of Zuni would look quite different than Mindeleff's "excellent plot" (1919:180). But he produced his own map at the same scale to measure change at Zuni over the previous thirty-five years.

The discrepancy, of course, was not to Mindeleff's discredit. But Mindeleff's and Fewkes's use of native migration narratives to help reconstruct historical migrations and phases of town settlement was, in Kroeber's opinion. He saw in this pre-Boasian tendency "a remarkable exemplification of the fatal check to knowledge invariably dealt to studies in the field of civilization when the temptation of seeking specific origins is yielded to and the path of merely but deeply understanding phenomena is abandoned" (1919:135). Thus Kroeber was not surprised that Mindeleff's own list of Hopi clans mentioned in native texts bore little resemblance to the clan names Stephen had collected for him. "In other words," Kroeber dryly observed, "how a society is organized today is of little interest or moment compared with what its organization may have been a thousand years ago; and the facts at hand were neglected in favor of speculation on those beyond reach" (1919:135).

Some of this Boasian superiority regarding the work of nonacademic fieldworkers had lessened by the time Mischa Titiev from the University of Chicago began studying the Hopi Pueblo of Old Oraibi in the 1930s. Working under Leslie White, Titiev and his colleagues reflected a new synthesis of functionalism with an abiding respect for culture history. Titiev found the Mindeleff data quite useful as he drew up a fresh survey of Oraibi's streets, houses, and clan locations. He learned that "out of 136 houses that were capable of exact comparison, 88 or 65% had been given identical clan names, a satisfactory degree of correspondence when it is considered that fifty years had elapsed between the two investigations" (Titiev 1944:53). As far as phratry affiliation—the grouping of clans into larger social aggregates—was concerned, Titiev estimated that 86 percent of the houses were assigned to the same one as in Mindeleff's day, which led him to conclude that phratry cohesion was more stable than clanship.

By the time Titiev's colleague, Fred Eggan, produced his synoptic study of Western Pueblo social organization (1950), he too had grown more charitable toward the Mindeleffs' approach to clans than had Kroeber. While he believed they had been overly confident in identifying specific ruins as the work of specific migratory clans, he felt they had been on the right track in assuming that farming villages, evidenced by small ruins, had played a significant prehistoric role, and that small bands, which coalesced into larger groups, had settled Hopi territory over a long time period. When Eggan compared Fewkes's work with the later paper by Cosmos Mindeleff on the evolution of clan house-complexes among the Hopi, he concluded, "It is Mindeleff's reconstruction rather than Fewkes' which modern archeological and ethnological studies support" (Eggan 1950:80).

While Titiev used a portion of Mindeleff material, linguist Benjamin Whorf used none at all. But Whorf's interest in Hopi architecture deserves brief citation here, since it harkens back to Cushing's hunch that native vocabulary might contain clues to the meanings of built forms. Mindeleff had taken pains to incorporate the glossary collected by Stephen: sixty-six terms associated with house elements, eight with roof construction, and twenty-nine with *kiva* parts. As analyzed by Whorf, such terms revealed concepts of space more systematic and sophisticated than those that could be expressed in English (Whorf 1953).

The most predictable use of the Mindeleff survey was as a baseline against which to measure architectural change. Yet by the 1950s, southwestern fieldworkers were more interested in problems of acculturation, assimilation, and revitalization, and to a large measure they turned from the conservative Pueblos to the more accessible Athapaskan and Piman speaking groups. When the Western Pueblos did return to anthropological scrutiny in the 1960s, it was less to discover changes occurring since Mindeleff's work than to use that material to reconstruct the relationship between prehistoric social organzation and built forms.

It remained for scholars from other disciplines to make better use of the Mindeleff data. In 1968 geographer Elliot G. McIntire depended upon Mindeleff in order to substantiate his thesis that "houses [of the Hopi] have changed gradually from the 'Southwestern pueblo' type to styles common in poorer parts of rural America. The densely nucleated villages with a clearly defined internal organization have given way to sprawling settlements with no noticeable pattern" (McIntire 1971:510). Architectural historian Bainbridge Bunting was heavily indebted to the Mindeleff contribution for his 1976 profile of spatial change at Zuni Pueblo. The wealth of detail provided by Mindeleff's measurements, visuals, and descriptions allowed him to plot the curve of Zuni's decline from a classic Pueblo VI period village to a discouraging example of suburban sprawl.

Bunting noted that just about the year the Mindeleffs were measuring Zuni the railroad reached the community. Within a few years milled lumber doors began replacing ladders; glazing opened up facades that had been only penetrated before by tiny, irregular selenite-covered holes in the wall; stovepipe was erected whenever an old chimney made of mortared pots crumbled down. Bunting chronicled the effect upon the town plan of new foci of human activity, such as the school, the railroad, paved roads, and nearby commercial centers. New building materials and social and economic conditions eroded the integrity of the enclosing pueblo shape and the integrated massing of its houseblocks. Bunting's case study provided an example to other scholars, such as the member of Santa Clara Pueblo, Dr. Rina Swentzel, who made a similar analysis of changing spatial patterns in her home community.

More recently, the Mindeleff documentation helped revive interest in pairing ethnology and archeology. Between 1975 and 1977 the Pueblo of Walpi offered an interesting opportunity for archeologists who study the correlation between room size and function. A contract between the Museum of Northern Arizona and the Hopi tribe admitted scholars into unused rooms slated for rehabilitation through a Housing and Urban Development program. The project was directed by E. Charles Adams, who credited Mindeleff's work as "a monumental study of Pueblo architecture . . . [that] forms a considerable portion of groundwork for the present study" (1983:47). As Adams estimated the work in personal correspondence, "Its broad score would seldom be dared today and much could not be gathered today due to change or Pueblo reticence toward photography and sketches. It still provides information on Pueblo architecture that is essential reading for any modern student of Pueblo or even non-Pueblo architecture" (Adams to Nabokov, 9 September 1983).

Like Bunting, Adams used the Mindeleff material as his baseline. From examination of over ninety years of changing residence patterns at Walpi, Adams agreed with Titiev that while clan localization was variable, features such as room size, tier location, and number of doors seemed consistently related to room purpose. They were also good indicators of boundary lines between the matrilineal residences. Adams concluded that this continuity of room dimension over a period of nearly eleven hundred years suggests that architecture could yield predictive data for reevaluation of old archeological work.

The Mindeleff book has also been a helpful source for recent scholars examining Zuni spaces. However, T. J. Ferguson and Barbara J. Mills, attached to the Pueblo's archeological program, reached a somewhat less pessimistic interpretation of spatial continuity at Zuni than had Bunting. They conceded that "changes in activities have resulted in the almost complete structural transformation of the built environment since 1881" (Ferguson and Mills 1978:12), but they focused instead on surviving concepts and ceremonies associated with Zuni spaces. The viability of the annual Shalako (a major house-blessing ritual that, for some reason, the Mindeleffs did not discuss), plus the "conceptual bounding of different areas of the pueblo with traditional place names" (1978:12), indicated that a cognitive dimension to classic Zuni architecture had survived.

The Mindeleffs had envisioned their study as the first of a trilogy on their southwestern investigations, but they never finished the projected volumes on Canyon de Chelly and Chaco Canyon. Perhaps the Smithsonian was changing its qualifications for field personnel; perhaps Victor felt the call of family and a neglected architectural career. Cosmos, on the other hand, would remain in the Smithsonian's model-building shop for a while. He would also conduct important explorations of the Verde Valley and complete restoration at Casa Grande ruins for the Bureau well into the 1890s. Until 1898 he combined this work with writing for architectural and popular journals about his southwestern adventures. Then he either exhausted his experiences or the outlets for such articles became restricted to the academic community; whatever the case, Cosmos faded into obscurity. The paucity of information about the working relationship between the brothers is unfortunate, for it has left underappreciated Cosmos's deep personal investment in the work and writings about it.

In the years after the project, Victor conducted an architectural practice out of his Washington home. Among his clients was the U.S.

Zoological Park, and during 1890–92 he designed its Carnivora House, Buffalo House, bear dens, and prairie dog fences. Thereafter he began a twenty-year association with the U.S. Life Savings Service, apparently working on seacoast facilities. Other architectural assignments included a young women's seminary near Washington, D.C., which would later be converted into the Glen Echo Amusement Park, and the Public Roads Group at Gravelly Point. According to his colleague and Cosmos Club companion, architect Delos H. Smith, Victor's work expressed his special combination of designing, decorating, and gardening talents. He became a familiar figure in Washington artistic circles, joining the Society of Washington artists and the Washington Water Color Club, and he painted the murals for the local Army-Navy Club.

In 1917 he became an associate of the American Institute of Architects, assuming full membership in 1920; six years later he became a lifetime fellow and chaired the AIA's fifty-ninth convention committee. In 1924 he had been named president of the AIA's Washington chapter, and in 1926 he was one of nine Washington architects selected by the *Evening Star* to build a model house—the Dutch colonial that, somewhat remodeled, still stands on the southwest corner of Alaska Avenue and Hemlock Street. During the 1926 AIA convention Victor's touch was evident in the sightseeing map of the Potomac he had handdrawn for visiting architects.

We have few personal glimpses of the man. In the AIA Washington chapter's history, Edwin Morris recalls him as "always companionable and unpredictable, was a good painter and a good architect, though he was apt to shrug off credit" (Morris 1951:3). Mindeleff left no memoir of his own about his southwestern adventures, but he talked of them fondly with Cosmos Club mates. Before the ethnographer and editor Frederick Webb Hodge left for the Southwest he visited Mindeleff for advice on equipment. He recalled that Mindeleff "put his hand in a jar on the mantle and pulled out a handful of piñon nuts. I'd never seen piñon nuts before, so I cracked two or three and ate them. I said, 'I can't say that I like them very much; they taste like coal oil.' " Mindeleff explained that he had once leaked coal oil on his food at Hopi, and everything tasted of it. When his three months were up, "darned if I didn't like it. Now I never sit down to a meal without a coal oil can beside me" (Hodge n.d.:39–40). He also entertained Hodge with sidelights about his trips, especially concerning the overbearing Mathilda Coxe Stevenson.

In the late 1930s Victor and his wife Jessie Louise left the city for retirement in Wayside, a town in Charles County, Maryland. He visited Washington periodically, and in 1941 lunched with Neil M. Judd of the Smithsonian. He followed up with a donation to Judd of three albums of photographic prints, largely of prehistoric sites such as Chaco Canyon and Canyon de Chelly.

On 26 March 1948, Victor Mindeleff died. For his AIA obituary, Delos H. Smith praised the painter and landscaper who "made gardens to dream about." Smith also harkened back to Mindeleff's glory days in the Southwest: "The character of his work was no doubt influenced by his early years with Dr. J. W. Powell's expeditions to the prehistoric ruins of the Southwest. The sketches he drew and brought home of aboriginal Indian dwellings made a valuable contribution to American ethnology and doubtless inspired his innate talent. And a certain common sense in viewpoint may well have been gained on the prairie" (Smith 1948:219).

Mindeleff's study seemed to intuit the spectrum of interpretations to which Pueblo architecture would be subject. It also accepted as given the rather progressive proposition that one level of culture might be decoded from another. It touched upon the mythic origins of built forms, the contribution of archeology to architectural morphology, the role of women and ritual in house-making, the possible significance of language in interpreting architecture, the linkages between the past and the present in the evolution of Pueblo material culture, the ties between social organization and spatial arrangement.

But one of the work's enduring virtues was derived from what one might expect from a gifted observer: precise description in picture and word. Victor looked well, and he made the most of a time when inexperience was no barrier to an interdisciplinary adventure. Beneath its prophetic, theoretical shadows and accurate observation, the work's hidden strength lay in the appreciative light it shed on an architectural heritage and the human beings who maintained it. Mindeleff kept his personal opinions about the poor quality of the architecture in proportion to what Cushing and Stephen taught him about its deeper role in Zuni and Hopi culture.

He insisted that we consider the prehistoric builders part of a cultural continuum with their contemporary descendants. Given the nature of his material, he could not help but see architecture as a window onto culture. If Mindeleff did not meet modern anthropology's call for an "anthropology of architecture," he provided marvelous data for it. Perhaps the freshness of his study's ideas stemmed from the learning process its innocent authors underwent during this frontier period of southwestern anthropology, and the unusual assistance that good fortune placed in their path. Because of such insightful and enthusiastic guides as Cushing and Stephen, and such gifted collaborators as Hillers, Nichols, and his brother Cosmos, Victor Mindeleff authored an enduring landmark in the study of vernacular architecture.

# ACKNOWLEDGMENTS AND ARCHIVAL REFERENCES

My unfinished pursuit of the elusive careers of Victor and Cosmos Mindeleff has been aided by a number of generous archivists and researchers.

In the National Anthropological Archives I am especially indebted to Paula Fleming and James Glenn. They provided me with such primary documents as the Mindeleff sketchbook from their first season at Zuni (NAA #2138), the two boxes of fieldplans and descriptions of inhabited pueblos and pueblo ruins in Arizona and New Mexico (NAA #2621), and the three albums of photographs of archeological work that were sent to Neil M. Judd by Victor Mindeleff in February 1942 and which Judd turned over to Matthew Stirling of the Bureau of Ethnology (NAA #4362). In addition, the archives provided me with "Letters Received" files for the Mindeleffs and Holmes, and the separate files associated with preparation of the various BAE reports themselves, especially the *Eighth Annual Report.*

I am extremely grateful to the anonymous reviewers of this introduction, especially the individual who alerted me to the manuscript (file #428) in the Hodge-Cushing Collection at the Southwest Museum, Los Angeles. Apparently deposited at the Southwest Museum by Frederick Webb Hodge, this material contains Holmes's letter to Powell (25 February 1890) transmitting the original manuscript of this study by the two brothers, and another letter the day before suggesting that some of Cosmos's contributions be withheld from this publication. This file also contains the expunged chapters.

Tony R. Wrenn, archivist for the American Institute of Architects, copied files on Victor's activities with the Washington-Metropolitan Chapter of the AIA, an association obviously dear to Mindeleff. Mr. Wrenn also provided me with salient facts from such District of Columbia sources as the Morris (1951) history of the AIA and Virgil E. McMahan's *Washington, D.C., Artists Born Before 1900: A Biographical Directory* (1976), with citations on Victor, his wife and mother, and H. Hobart Nichols.

For the more elusive and in some ways more interesting career of his brother Cosmos, I am indebted to William A. Longacre, who has been tracking Cosmos for some time—losing him around 1905, at which time he was a freelance writer in New York City. It was Dr. Longacre who turned up, for instance, the sketch in *Out West* (vol. 6, no. 5, April 1897, 186–87) characterizing Cosmos as an authority on the Southwest.

Susan W. Glenn, assistant archivist of the Smithsonian Institution Archives, provided pertinent Record Units: #201, letters received by departments and bureaus of the government; and #112, letters file, U.S. National Museum, which contains much Mindeleff correspondence.

Mary C. Ternes of Washington's Martin Luther King Memorial Library was imaginative in using such references as *Who's Who in the Nation's Capital* (1920–30 edition, edited by Stanley H. Williamson, Washington, D.C.: Ransdell, Inc.); Washington, D.C., street directories; and U.S. Census documents.

I am also grateful to Paula Roberts-Pipes, formerly of the Smithsonian Institution Press, who first encountered this reissue, and to Daniel Goodwin, the Press's editorial director, who saw it into print; to Lucy A. Young, librarian of the Cosmos Club; to Dr. E. Charles Adams for his contributions; to John Aubrey of Chicago's Newberry Library; to Peter Whiteley, who wrote me at the last moment with extremely helpful corrections and queries; and to the late Bainbridge Bunting, aficionado of Pueblo architecture, who first introduced me to the Mindeleff work.

# REFERENCES

Adams, E. Charles
    1983    "The Architectural Analogue to Hopi Social Organization and Room Use, and Implications for Prehistoric Northern Southwestern Culture." *American Antiquity* 48(1):44–61.

Amer. Ant. J.
    1893    Review of *A Study of Pueblo Architecture in Tusayan and Cibola*, by Victor Mindeleff. *American Antiquarian and Oriental Journal* 15(6):389.

Basso, Keith H.
    1979    "History of Ethnological Research." In *Handbook of North American Indians*, edited by William Sturtevant. Vol. 9, *Southwest*, edited by Alfonzo Ortiz, 14–21. Washington, D.C.: Smithsonian Institution Press.

Beaglehole, Ernest
    1937    *Notes on Hopi Economic Life.* Yale University Publications in Anthropology, no. 15, 88 pp. New Haven, Conn.

Bourke, John G.
    1886    "The Urine Dance of the Zuni." *Proceedings of the American Association for the Advancement of Science* 34: 400–403.

Bunting, Bainbridge
    1976    *Early Architecture in New Mexico.* Albuquerque: University of New Mexico Press.

Cushing, Frank Hamilton
    1886    "A Study of Pueblo Pottery as Illustrative of Zuni Culture-Growth." In *Fourth Annual Report of the Bureau of Ethnology to the Secretary of the Smithsonian Institution, 1882–83*, edited by J. W. Powell, 467–521. Washington, D.C.: U.S. Government Printing Office.

    1922    "Oraibi in 1883." Part 1 of "Contributions to Hopi History," *American Anthropologist* 24(3):253–68.

Dockstader, Frederick J.
    1979    "Hopi History, 1850–1940." In *Handbook of North American Indians*, edited by William Sturtevant. Vol. 9, *Southwest*, edited by Alfonso Ortiz, 524–32. Washington, D.C.: Smithsonian Institution Press.

Eggan, Fred
1950    *Social Organization of the Western Pueblos.* Chicago: University of Chicago Press.

1964    "Alliance and Descent in Western Pueblo Society." In *Process and Pattern in Culture: Essays in Honor of Julian H. Steward,* edited by Robert A. Manners, 175–84. Chicago: Aldine Co.

Ferguson, T. J., and Barbara J. Mills
1978    "The Built Environment of Zuni Pueblo: The Bounding, Use, and Classification of Space." Paper presented at the 77th annual meeting of the American Anthropological Association. Zuni Archeology Program, Pueblo of Zuni.

Fewkes, J. Walter
1906    "The Sun's Influence on the Form of Hopi Pueblos." *American Anthropologist* 8:88–100.

Fowler, Don D.
1972    *"Photographed All the Best Scenery": Jack Hillers's Diary of the Powell Expeditions, 1871–1875.* Salt Lake City: University of Utah Press.

Goetzmann, William H.
1966    *Exploration and Empire: The Explorer and the Scientist in the Winning of the West.* New York: Alfred A. Knopf.

Hammond, George Peter, and Agapito Rey, eds.
1940    *Narratives of the Coronado Expedition 1540–1542.* Coronado Cuarto Centennial Publications, no. 2. Albuquerque: University of New Mexico Press.

Hinsley, Curtis M.
1981    *Savages and Scientists: The Smithsonian Institution and the Development of American Anthropology, 1846–1910.* Washington, D.C.: Smithsonian Institution Press.

Hodge, Frederick Webb
n.d.    "Oral History of F. W. Hodge." Manuscript C-D 4016, 264 pp. Oral History Collections, General Library, University of California, Berkeley.

Holmes, William Henry
1846–   *Random Records of a Lifetime Devoted to Science and Art.* 20 vols.
1931    Washington, D.C.: National Anthropological Archives.

Ives, Lt. Joseph C.
[1861]  *Report Upon the Colorado River of the West.* New York: Da Capo
1969    Press.

Judd, Neil M.
1967    *The Bureau of American Ethnology: A Partial History.* Norman: University of Oklahoma Press.

Kroeber, A. L.
  1919   *Zuni Kin and Clan.* Anthropological Papers of the American
         Museum of Natural History, vol. 18, part 2. New York: American
         Museum of Natural History.

Lekson, Stephen H.
  [1984]  *Great Pueblo Architecture of Chaco Canyon, New Mexico.* Origi-
  1986    nally published as *Chaco Canyon Studies*, Publications in Archeol-
          ogy 18B, National Park Service, United States Department of the
          Interior. Albuquerque: University of New Mexico Press.

Mark, Joan
  1980   *Four Anthropologists: An American Science in its Early Years.*
         New York: Science History Publications.

McIntire, Elliot G.
  1971   "Changing Patterns of Hopi Indian Settlement." *Annals of the
         Association of American Geographers* 61:510–21.

Mindeleff, Cosmos
  1897a  "The Influence of Geographic Environment." *American Geographic
         Society Journal* 29:1–12.
  1897b  "Pueblo Architecture." *The American Architect and Building News*,
         vol. 56, part 1 (April 17), 19–21; vol. 56, part 2 (May 22), 59–61;
         vol. 57, part 3 (June 24), 31–33; vol. 57, part 4 (Sept. 11), 87–88.
  1898a  "Aboriginal Architecture in the United States." *American Geo-
         graphic Society Bulletin* 30:414–27.
  1898b  "Navajo Houses." In *Seventeenth Annual Report of the Bureau of
         American Ethnology to the Secretary of the Smithsonian Institu-
         tion, 1895–96,* edited by J. W. Powell, 469–517. Washington, D.C.:
         U.S. Government Printing Office.
  1900   "Localization of Tusayan Clans." In *Nineteenth Annual Report of
         the Bureau of American Ethnology to the Secretary of the Smith-
         sonian Institution, 1897–98,* edited by J. W. Powell, 638–53.
         Washington, D.C.: U.S. Government Printing Office. Reprinted in
         this edition.

Montgomery, Ross G., Watson Smith, and John O. Brew
  1949   *Franciscan Awatovi: The Excavation and Conjectural Reconstruc-
         tion of a Seventeenth-Century Spanish Mission Establishment at
         a Hopi Indian Town in Northeastern Arizona.* Papers of the
         Peabody Museum of American Archeology and Ethnology, Harvard
         University, no. 36. Cambridge, Mass.

Morgan, Lewis Henry
  [1881]  *Houses and House-Life of the American Aborigines.* Originally
  1965    published as Contributions to North American Ethnology, vol. 4.
          Washington, D.C.: U.S. Government Printing Office. Introduction
          by Paul Bohannon. Chicago and London: University of Chicago
          Press.

Morris, Edwin Bateman, ed. and comp.
1951   *A History of the Washington-Metropolitan Chapter of the American Institute of Architects.* Washington, D.C.: The Washington-Metropolitan Chapter of the American Institute of Architects.

Parezo, Nancy J.
1985   "Cushing as Part of the Team: The Collecting Activities of the Smithsonian Institution." *American Ethnologist* 12(4):763–74.

Parsons, Elsie Clews
1936   "The House-Clan Complex of the Pueblos." In *Essays in Anthropology, Presented to A. L. Kroeber on his Sixtieth Birthday.* Berkeley: University of California Press.

Powell, John Wesley
1883   "Report of the Director." In *Second Annual Report of the Bureau of Ethnology to the Secretary of the Smithsonian Institution, 1880–81,* xv-xxxvii. Washington, D.C.: U.S. Government Printing Office.

Saile, David G.
1977   "Making a House in the Pueblo Indian World." *Architectural Association Quarterly* 9(2–3).

Smith, Delos
1948   "Obituary of Victor Mindeleff (1861–1948)." *Journal of the American Institute of Architects* 9(5):219–20.

Stephen, Alexander M.
1893   *The Navajo.* Washington, D.C.: Judd and Detweiler.
1936   *Hopi Journal of Alexander M. Stephen.* Edited by Elsie C. Parsons. 2 vols. Columbia University Contributions to Anthropology, no. 23. New York.

Titiev, Mischa
1944   *Old Oraibi: A Study of the Hopi Indians of Third Mesa.* Papers of the Peabody Museum of American Archeology and Ethnology, Harvard University, vol. 22, no. 1. Cambridge, Mass.

White, Leslie A., ed.
1942   "Lewis H. Morgan's Journal of a Trip to Southwestern Colorado and New Mexico, June 21 to August 7, 1878." *American Antiquity* 8(1).

Whiteley, Peter
1987   *Deliberate Acts: Changing Hopi Culture Through the Oraibi Split.* Tucson: University of Arizona Press.

Whorf, Benjamin Lee
1953   "Linguistic Factors in the Terminology of Hopi Architecture." *International Journal of American Linguistics* 19:141–45.

# A STUDY

OF

# PUEBLO ARCHITECTURE:

## TUSAYAN AND CIBOLA.

BY

### VICTOR MINDELEFF.

# CONTENTS.

5

# ILLUSTRATIONS.

―――――――

# A STUDY OF PUEBLO ARCHITECTURE IN TUSAYAN AND CIBOLA.

## By Victor Mindeleff.

### INTRODUCTION.

The remains of pueblo architecture are found scattered over thousands of square miles of the arid region of the southwestern plateaus. This vast area includes the drainage of the Rio Pecos on the east and that of the Colorado on the west, and extends from central Utah on the north beyond the limits of the United States southward, in which direction its boundaries are still undefined.

The descendants of those who at various times built these stone villages are few in number and inhabit about thirty pueblos distributed irregularly over parts of the region formerly occupied. Of these the greater number are scattered along the upper course of the Rio Grande and its tributaries in New Mexico; a few of them, comprised within the ancient provinces of Cibola and Tusayan, are located within the drainage of the Little Colorado. From the time of the earliest Spanish expeditions into the country to the present day, a period covering more than three centuries, the former province has been often visited by whites, but the remoteness of Tusayan and the arid and forbidding character of its surroundings have caused its more complete isolation. The architecture of this district exhibits a close adherence to aboriginal practices, still bears the marked impress of its development under the exacting conditions of an arid environment, and is but slowly yielding to the influence of foreign ideas.

The present study of the architecture of Tusayan and Cibola embraces all of the inhabited pueblos of those provinces, and includes a number of the ruins traditionally connected with them. It will be observed by reference to the map that the area embraced in these provinces comprises but a small portion of the vast region over which pueblo culture once extended.

This study is designed to be followed by a similar study of two typical groups of ruins, viz, that of Canyon de Chelly, in northeastern Arizona, and that of the Chaco Canyon, of New Mexico; but it has been necessary for the writer to make occasional reference to these ruins in the present

13

paper, both in the discussion of general arrangement and characteristic ground plans, embodied in Chapters II and III and in the comparison by constructional details treated in Chapter IV, in order to define clearly the relations of the various features of pueblo architecture. They belong to the same pueblo system illustrated by the villages of Tusayan and Cibola, and with the Canyon de Chelly group there is even some trace of traditional connection, as is set forth by Mr. Stephen in Chapter I. The more detailed studies of these ruins, to be published later, together with the material embodied in the present paper, will, it is thought, furnish a record of the principal characteristics of an important type of primitive architecture, which, under the influence of the arid environment of the southwestern plateaus, has developed from the rude lodge into the many-storied house of rectangular rooms. Indications of some of the steps of this development are traceable even in the architecture of the present day.

The pueblo of Zuñi was surveyed by the writer in the autumn of 1881 with a view to procuring the necessary data for the construction of a large-scale model of this pueblo. For this reason the work afforded a record of external features only.

The modern pueblos of Tusayan were similarly surveyed in the following season (1882–'83), the plans being supplemented by photographs, from which many of the illustrations accompanying this paper have been drawn. The ruin of Awatubi was also included in the work of this season.

In the autumn of 1885 many of the ruined pueblos of Tusayan were surveyed and examined. It was during this season's work that the details of the kiva construction, embodied in the last chapter of this paper, were studied, together with interior details of the dwellings. It was in the latter part of this season that the farming pueblos of Cibola were surveyed and photographed.

The Tusayan farming pueblo of Moen-kopi and a number of the ruins in the province were surveyed and studied in the early part of the season of 1887–'88, the latter portion of which season was principally devoted to an examination of the Chaco ruins in New Mexico.

In the prosecution of the field work above outlined the author has been greatly indebted to the efficient assistance and hearty coöperation of Mr. Cosmos Mindeleff, by whom nearly all the pueblos illustrated, with the exception of Zuñi, have been surveyed and platted.

The plans obtained have involved much careful work with surveying instruments, and have all been so platted as faithfully to record the minute variations from geometric forms which are so characteristic of the pueblo work, but which have usually been ignored in the hastily prepared sketch plans that have at times appeared. In consequence of the necessary omission of just such information in hastily drawn plans, erroneous impressions have been given regarding the degree of skill to which the pueblo peoples had attained in the planning and building of their villages. In the general distribution of the houses, and in the alignment and arrangement of their walls, as indicated in the plans shown in Chapters II and III, an absence of high architectural attainment is found, which is entirely in keeping with the lack of skill apparent in many of the constructional devices shown in Chapter IV.

In preparing this paper for publication Mr. Cosmos Mindeleff has rendered much assistance in the revision of manuscript, and in the preparation of some of the final drawings of ground plans; on him has also fallen the compilation and arrangement of Mr. A. M. Stephen's traditionary material from Tusayan, embraced in the first chapter of the paper.

This latter material is of special interest in a study of the pueblos as indicating some of the conditions under which this architectural type was developed, and it appropriately introduces the more purely architectural study by the author.

Such traditions must be used as history with the utmost caution, and only for events that are very recent. Time relations are often hopelessly confused and the narratives are greatly incumbered with mythologic details. But while so barren in definite information, these traditions are of the greatest value, often through their merely incidental allusions, in presenting to our minds a picture of the conditions under which the repeated migrations of the pueblo builders took place.

The development of architecture among the Pueblo Indians was comparatively rapid and is largely attributable to frequent changes, migrations, and movements of the people as described in Mr. Stephen's account. These changes were due to a variety of causes, such as disease, death, the frequent warfare carried on between different tribes and branches of the builders, and the hostility of outside tribes; but a most potent factor was certainly the inhospitable character of their environment. The disappearance of some venerated spring during an unusually dry season would be taken as a sign of the disfavor of the gods, and, in spite of the massive character of the buildings, would lead to the migration of the people to a more favorable spot. The traditions of the Zuñis, as well as those of the Tusayan, frequently refer to such migrations. At times tribes split up and separate, and again phratries or distant groups meet and band together. It is remarkable that the substantial character of the architecture should persist through such long series of compulsory removals, but while the builders were held together by the necessity for defense against their wilder neighbors or against each other, this strong defensive motive would perpetuate the laborious type of construction. Such conditions would contribute to the rapid development of the building art.

# CHAPTER I.

## TRADITIONAL HISTORY OF TUSAYAN.

### EXPLANATORY.

In this chapter [1] is presented a summary of the traditions of the Tusayan, a number of which were collected from old men, from Walpi on the east to Moen-kopi on the west. A tradition varies much with the tribe and the individual; an authoritative statement of the current tradition on any point could be made only with a complete knowledge of all traditions extant. Such knowledge is not possessed by any one man, and the material included in this chapter is presented simply as a summary of the traditions secured.

The material was collected by Mr. A. M. Stephen, of Keam's Canyon, Arizona, who has enjoyed unusual facilities for the work, having lived for a number of years past in Tusayan and possessed the confidence of the principal priests—a very necessary condition in work of this character. Though far from complete, this summary is a more comprehensive presentation of the traditionary history of these people than has heretofore been published.

### SUMMARY OF TRADITIONS.

The creation myths of the Tusayan differ widely, but none of them designate the region now occupied as the place of their genesis. These people are socially divided into family groups called wi′ngwu, the descendants of sisters, and groups of wi′ngwu tracing descent from the same female ancestor, and having a common totem called my′umu. Each of these totemic groups preserves a creation myth, carrying in its details special reference to themselves; but all of them claim a common origin in the interior of the earth, although the place of emergence to the surface is set in widely separated localities. They all agree in maintaining this to be the fourth plane on which mankind has existed. In the beginning all men lived together in the lowest depths, in a region of darkness and moisture; their bodies were misshaped and horrible, and they suffered great misery, moaning and bewailing continually. Through the intervention of Myúingwa (a vague conception known as the god of the interior) and of Baholikonga (a crested serpent of enormous size, the genius of water), the "old men" obtained a seed from which sprang a magic growth of cane. It penetrated through a crevice

---

[1] This chapter is compiled by Cosmos Mindeleff from material collected by A. M. Stephen.

16

in the roof overhead and mankind climbed to a higher plane. A dim light appeared in this stage and vegetation was produced. Another magic growth of cane afforded the means of rising to a still higher plane on which the light was brighter; vegetation was reproduced and the animal kingdom was created. The final ascent to this present, or fourth plane, was effected by similar magic growths and was led by mythic twins, according to some of the myths, by climbing a great pine tree, in others by climbing the cane, *Phragmites communis*, the alternate leaves of which afforded steps as of a ladder, and in still others it is said to have been a rush, through the interior of which the people passed up to the surface. The twins sang as they pulled the people out, and when their song was ended no more were allowed to come; and hence, many more were left below than were permitted to come above; but the outlet through which mankind came has never been closed, and Myu'ingwa sends through it the germs of all living things. It is still symbolized by the peculiar construction of the hatchway of the kiva and in the designs on the sand altars in these underground chambers, by the unconnected circle painted on pottery and by devices on basketry and other textile fabrics.

All the people that were permitted to come to the surface were collected and the different families of men were arranged together. This was done under the direction of twins, who are called Pekónghoya, the younger one being distinguished by the term Balíngahoya, the Echo. They were assisted by their grandmother, Kóhkyang wúhti, the Spider woman, and these appear in varying guises in many of the myths and legends. They instructed the people in divers modes of life to dwell on mountain or on plain, to build lodges, or huts, or windbreaks. They distributed appropriate gifts among them and assigned each a pathway, and so the various families of mankind were dispersed over the earth's surface.

The Hopituh,[1] after being taught to build stone houses, were also divided, and the different divisions took separate paths. The legends indicate a long period of extensive migrations in separate communities; the groups came to Tusayan at different times and from different directions, but the people of all the villages concur in designating the Snake people as the first occupants of the region. The eldest member of that nyumu tells a curious legend of their migration from which the following is quoted:

At the general dispersal my people lived in snake skins, each family occupying a separate snake skin bag, and all were hung on the end of a rainbow, which swung around until the end touched Navajo Mountain, where the bags dropped from it; and wherever a bag dropped, there was their house. After they arranged their bags they came out from them as men and women, and they then built a stone house which had five sides. [The story here relates the adventures of a mythic Snake Youth, who brought back a strange woman who gave birth to rattlesnakes; these bit the people and compelled them to migrate.] A brilliant star arose in the southeast,

---

[1] The term by which the Tusayan Indians proper designate themselves. This term does not include the inhabitants of the village of Tewa or Hano, who are called Hanomuh.

which would shine for a while and then disappear. The old men said, "Beneath that star there must be people," so they determined to travel toward it. They cut a staff and set it in the ground and watched till the star reached its top, then they started and traveled as long as the star shone; when it disappeared they halted. But the star did not shine every night, for sometimes many years elapsed before it appeared again. When this occurred, our people built houses during their halt; they built both round and square houses, and all the ruins between here and Navajo Mountain mark the places where our people lived. They waited till the star came to the top of the staff again, then they moved on, but many people were left in those houses and they followed afterward at various times. When our people reached Wipho (a spring a few miles north from Walpi) the star disappeared and has never been seen since. They built a house there and after a time Másauwu (the god of the face of the earth) came and compelled them to move farther down the valley, to a point about half way between the East and Middle Mesa, and there they stayed many plantings. One time the old men were assembled and Másauwu came among them, looking like a horrible skeleton, and his bones rattling dreadfully. He menaced them with awful gestures, and lifted off his fleshless head and thrust it into their faces; but he could not frighten them. So he said, "I have lost my wager; all that I have is yours; ask for anything you want and I will give it to you." At that time our people's house was beside the water course, and Másauwu said, "Why are you sitting here in the mud? Go up yonder where it is dry." So they went across to the low, sandy terrace on the west side of the mesa, near the point, and built a house and lived there. Again the old men were assembled and two demons came among them and the old men took the great Baho and the nwelas and chased them away. When they were returning, and were not far north from their village, they met the Lenbaki (Cane-Flute, a religious society still maintained) of the Horn family. The old men would not allow them to come in until Másauwu appeared and declared them to be good Hopituh. So they built houses adjoining ours and that made a fine, large village. Then other Hopituh came in from time to time, and our people would say, "Build here, or build there," and portioned the land among the new comers.

The site of the first Snake house in the valley, mentioned in the foregoing legend, is now barely to be discerned, and the people refuse to point out the exact spot. It is held as a place of votive offerings during the ceremony of the Snake dance, and, as its name, Bátni, implies, certain rain-fetiches are deposited there in small jars buried in the ground. The site of the village next occupied can be quite easily distinguished, and is now called Kwetcap tutwi, ash heap terrace, and this was the village to which the name Walpi was first applied—a term meaning the place at the notched mesa, in allusion to a broad gap in the stratum of sandstone on the summit of the mesa, and by which it can be distinguished from a great distance. The ground plan of this early Walpi can still be partly traced, indicating the former existence of an extensive village of clustering, little-roomed houses, with thick walls constructed of small stones.

The advent of the Lenbaki is still commemorated by a biennial ceremony, and is celebrated on the year alternating with their other biennial ceremony, the Snake dance.

The Horn people, to which the Lenbaki belonged, have a legend of coming from a mountain range in the east.

Its peaks were always snow covered, and the trees were always green. From the hillside the plains were seen, over which roamed the deer, the antelope, and the bison, feeding on never-failing grasses. Twining through these plains were streams of bright water, beautiful to look upon. A place where none but those who were of our people ever gained access.

This description suggests some region of the headwaters of the Rio Grande. Like the Snake people, they tell of a protracted migration, not of continuous travel, for they remained for many seasons in one place, where they would plant and build permanent houses. One of these halting places is described as a canyon with high, steep walls, in which was a flowing stream; this, it is said, was the Tségi (the Navajo name for Canyon de Chelly). Here they built a large house in a cavernous recess, high up in the canyon wall. They tell of devoting two years[1] to ladder making and cutting and pecking shallow holes up the steep rocky side by which to mount to the cavern, and three years more were employed in building the house. While this work was in progress part of the men were planting gardens, and the women and children were gathering stones. But no adequate reason is given for thus toiling to fit this impracticable site for occupation; the footprints of Másauwu, which they were following, led them there.

The legend goes on to tell that after they had lived there for a long time a stranger happened to stray in their vicinity, who proved to be a Hopituh, and said that he lived in the south. After some stay he left and was accompanied by a party of the "Horn," who were to visit the land occupied by their kindred Hopituh and return with an account of them; but they never came back. After waiting a long time another band was sent, who returned and said that the first emissaries had found wives and had built houses on the brink of a beautiful canyon, not far from the other Hopituh dwellings. After this many of the Horns grew dissatisfied with their cavern home, dissensions arose, they left their home, and finally they reached Tusayan. They lived at first in one of the canyons east of the villages, in the vicinity of Keam's Canyon, and some of the numerous ruins on its brink mark the sites of their early houses. There seems to be no legend distinctly attaching any particular ruin to the Horn people, although there is little doubt that the Snake and the Horn were the two first peoples who came to the neighborhood of the present villages. The Bear people were the next, but they arrived as separate branches, and from opposite directions, although of the same Hopituh stock. It has been impossible to obtain directly the legend of the Bears from the west. The story of the Bears from the east tells of encountering the Fire people, then living about 25 miles east from Walpi; but these are now extinct, and nearly all that is known of them is told in the Bear legend, the gist of which is as follows:

The Bears originally lived among the mountains of the east, not far distant from the Horns. Continual quarrels with neighboring villages

---

[1] The term yasuna, translated here as "year," is of rather indefinite significance; it sometimes means thirteen moons and in other instances much longer periods.

brought on actual fighting, and the Bears left that region and traveled westward. As with all the other people, they halted, built houses, and planted, remaining stationary for a long while; this occurred at different places along their route.

A portion of these people had wings, and they flew in advance to survey the land, and when the main body were traversing an arid region they found water for them. Another portion had claws with which they dug edible roots, and they could also use them for scratching hand and foot holes in the face of a steep cliff. Others had hoofs, and these carried the heaviest burdens; and some had balls of magic spider web, which they could use on occasion for ropes, and they could also spread the web and use it as a mantle, rendering the wearer invisible when he apprehended danger.

They too came to the Tségi (Canyon de Chelly), where they found houses but no people, and they also built houses there. While living there a rupture occurred, a portion of them separating and going far to the westward. These seceding bands are probably that branch of the Bears who claim their origin in the west. Some time after this, but how long after is not known, a plague visited the canyon, and the greater portion of the people moved away, but leaving numbers who chose to remain. They crossed the Chinli valley and halted for a short time at a place a short distance northeast from Great Willow water ("Eighteen Mile Spring"). They did not remain there long, however, but moved a few miles farther west, to a place occupied by the Fire people who lived in a large oval house. The ruin of this house still stands, the walls from 5 to 8 feet high, and remarkable from the large-sized blocks of stone used in their construction; it is still known to the Hopituh as Tebvwúki, the Fire-house. Here some fighting occurred, and the Bears moved westward again to the head of Antelope (Jeditoh) Canyon, about 4 miles from Keam's Canyon and about 15 miles east from Walpi. They built there a rambling cluster of small-roomed houses, of which the ground plan has now become almost obliterated. This ruin is called by the Hopituh "the ruin at the place of wild gourds." They seem to have occupied this neighborhood for a considerable period, as mention is made of two or three segregations, when groups of families moved a few miles away and built similar house clusters on the brink of that canyon.

The Fire-people, who, some say, were of the Horn people, must have abandoned their dwelling at the Oval House or must have been driven out at the time of their conflict with the Bears, and seem to have traveled directly to the neighborhood of Walpi. The Snakes allotted them a place to build in the valley on the east side of the mesa, and about two miles north from the gap. A ridge of rocky knolls and sand dunes lies at the foot of the mesa here, and close to the main cliff is a spring. There are two prominent knolls about 400 yards apart and the summits of these are covered with traces of house walls; also portions of walls can be discerned on all the intervening hummocks. The place is known as Sikyátki, the yellow-house, from the color of the sandstone of which the houses were built. These and other fragmentary bits have walls not over a foot thick, built of small stones dressed by rubbing, and all laid in mud; the inside of the walls also show a smooth coating of mud plaster. The dimensions of the rooms are very small, the largest measuring 9½ feet long, by 4½ feet wide. It is improbable that any of these structures were over two stories high, and many of them were built in excavated places around the rocky summits of the knolls. In these instances no rear wall was built; the partition walls, radiating at irregular angles, abut against the rock itself. Still, the great numbers of these houses, small as they were, must have been far more than the Fire-people could have required, for the oval house which they abandoned measures not more than a hundred feet by fifty. Probably other incoming gentes, of whom no story has been preserved, had also the ill fate to build there, for the Walpi people afterward slew all its inhabitants.

There is little or no detail in the legends of the Bear people as to their life in Antelope Canyon; they can now distinguish only one ruin with certainty as having been occupied by their ancestors, while to all the other ruins fanciful names have been applied. Nor is there any special cause mentioned for abandoning their dwellings there; probably, however, a sufficient reason was the cessation of springs in their vicinity. Traces of former large springs are seen at all of them, but no water flows from them at the present time. Whatever their motive, the Bears left Antelope Cañyon, and moved over to the village of Walpi, on the terrace below the point of the mesa. They were received kindly there, and were apparently placed on an equal footing with the Walpi, for it seems the Snake, Horn, and Bear have always been on terms of friendship. They built houses at that village, and lived there for some considerable time; then they moved a short distance and built again almost on the very point of the mesa. This change was not caused by any disagreement with their neighbors; they simply chose that point as a suitable place on which to build all their houses together. The site of this Bear house is called Kisákobi, the obliterated house, and the name is very appropriate, as there is merely the faintest trace here and there to show where a building stood, the stones having been used in the construction of the modern Walpi. These two villages were quite close together, and the subsequent construction of a few additional groups of rooms almost connected them, so that they were always considered and spoken of as one.

It was at this period, while Walpi was still on this lower site, that the Spaniards came into the country. They met with little or no opposition, and their entrance was marked by no great disturbances. No special tradition preserves any of the circumstances of this event; these first coming Spaniards being only spoken of as the " Kast'ilumuh who wore iron garments, and came from the south," and this brief mention may be accounted for by the fleeting nature of these early visits.

The zeal of the Spanish priests carried them everywhere throughout their newly acquired territory, and some time in the seventeenth century a band of missionary monks found their way to Tusayan. They were accompanied by a few troops to impress the people with a due regard for Spanish authority, but to display the milder side of their mission, they also brought herds of sheep and cattle for distribution. At first these were herded at various springs within a wide radius around the villages, and the names still attaching to these places memorize the introduction of sheep and cattle to this region. The Navajo are first definitely mentioned in tradition as occupants of this vicinity in connection with these flocks and herds, in the distribution of which they gave much undesirable assistance by driving off the larger portion to their own haunts.

The missionaries selected Awatubi, Walpi, and Shumopavi as the sites for their mission buildings, and at once, it is said, began to introduce a system of enforced labor. The memory of the mission period is held in great detestation, and the onerous toil the priests imposed is still adverted to as the principal grievance. Heavy pine timbers, many of which are now pointed out in the kiva roofs, of from 15 to 20 feet in length and a foot or more in diameter, were cut at the San Francisco Mountain, and gangs of men were compelled to carry and drag them to the building sites, where they were used as house beams. This necessitated prodigious toil, for the distance by trail is a hundred miles, most of the way over a rough and difficult country. The Spaniards are said to have employed a few ox teams in this labor, but the heaviest share was performed by the impressed Hopituh, who were driven in gangs by the Spanish soldiers, and any who refused to work were confined in a prison house and starved into submission.

The "men with the long robes," as the missionaries were called, are said to have lived among these people for a long time, but no trace of their individuality survives in tradition.

Possibly the Spanish missionaries may have striven to effect some social improvement among these people, and by the adoption of some harsh measures incurred the jealous anger of the chiefs. But the system of labor they enforced was regarded, perhaps justly, as the introduction of serfdom, such as then prevailed in the larger communities in the Rio Grande valleys. Perhaps tradition belies them; but there are many stories of their evil, sensual lives—assertions that they violated women, and held many of the young girls at their mission houses, not as pupils, but as concubines.

In any case, these hapless monks were engaged in a perilous mission in seeking to supplant the primitive faith of the Tusayan, for among the native priests they encountered prejudices even as violent as their own. With too great zeal they prohibited the sacred dances, the votive offerings to the nature-deities, and similar public observances, and strove to suppress the secret rites and abolish the religious orders and societies. But these were too closely incorporated with the system of gentes and other family kinships to admit of their extinction. Traditionally, it is said that, following the discontinuance of the prescribed ceremonies, the favor of the gods was withdrawn, the clouds brought no rain, and the fields yielded no corn. Such a coincidence in this arid region is by no means improbable, and according to the legends, a succession of dry seasons resulting in famine has been of not infrequent occurrence. The superstitious fears of the people were thus aroused, and they cherished a mortal hatred of the monks.

In such mood were they in the summer of 1680, when the village Indians rose in revolt, drove out the Spaniards, and compelled them to retreat to Mexico. There are some dim traditions of that event still existing among the Tusayan, and they tell of one of their own race coming from the river region by the way of Zuñi to obtain their cooperation in the proposed revolt. To this they consented.

Only a few Spaniards being present at that time, the Tusayan found courage to vent their enmity in massacre, and every one of the hated invaders perished on the appointed day. The traditions of the massacre center on the doom of the monks, for they were regarded as the embodiment of all that was evil in Spanish rule, and their pursuit, as they tried to escape among the sand dunes, and the mode of their slaughter, is told with grim precision; they were all overtaken and hacked to pieces with stone tomahawks.

It is told that while the monks were still in authority some of the Snake women urged a withdrawal from Walpi, and, to incite the men to action, carried their mealing-stones and cooking vessels to the summit of the mesa, where they desired the men to build new houses, less accessible to the domineering priests. The men followed them, and two or three small house groups were built near the southwest end of the present village, one of them being still occupied by a Snake family, but the others have been demolished or remodeled. A little farther north, also on the west edge, the small house clusters there were next built by the families of two women called Tji-vwó-wati and Si-kya-tcí-wati. Shortly after the massacre the lower village was entirely abandoned, and the building material carried above to the point which the Snakes had chosen, and on which the modern Walpi was constructed. Several beams of the old mission houses are now pointed out in the roofs of the kivas.

There was a general apprehension that the Spaniards would send a force to punish them, and the Shumopavi also reconstructed their village in a stronger position, on a high mesa overlooking its former site. The other villages were already in secure positions, and all the smaller agricultural settlements were abandoned at this period, and excepting at one or two places on the Moen-kopi, the Tusayan have ever since confined themselves to the close vicinity of their main villages.

The house masses do not appear to bear any relation to division by phratries. It is surprising that even the social division of the phratries

GENERAL MAP
OF THE
PUEBLO REGION
OF
ARIZONA AND NEW MEXICO,
SHOWING RELATIVE POSITION OF THE PROVINCES
OF
TUSAYAN AND CIBOLA.
BY
VICTOR MINDELEFF.

*Shaded area represents the Provinces of*
*Tusayan and Cibola.*

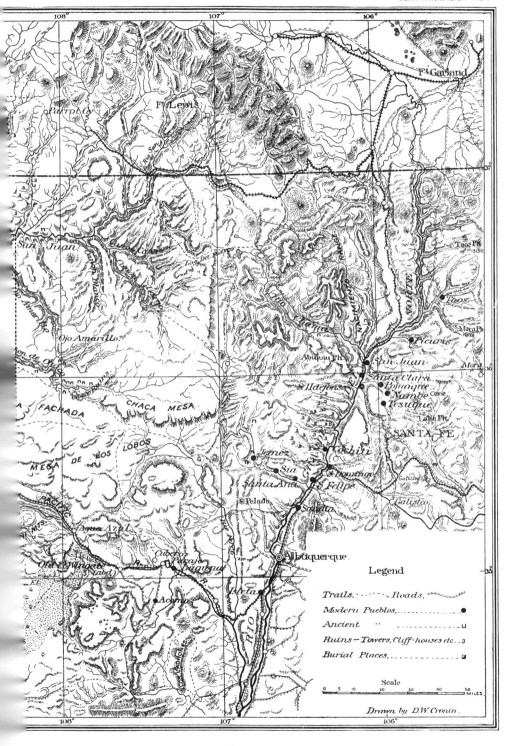

Legend

Trails. ....---....   Roads, ~~~~~~

Modern Pueblos,.......... ●

Ancient      "      .............∪

Ruins — Towers, Cliff-houses etc...◘

Burial Places,.............◙

Scale

0   5   10        20        30        40        50
MILES

Drawn by D.W. Cronin.

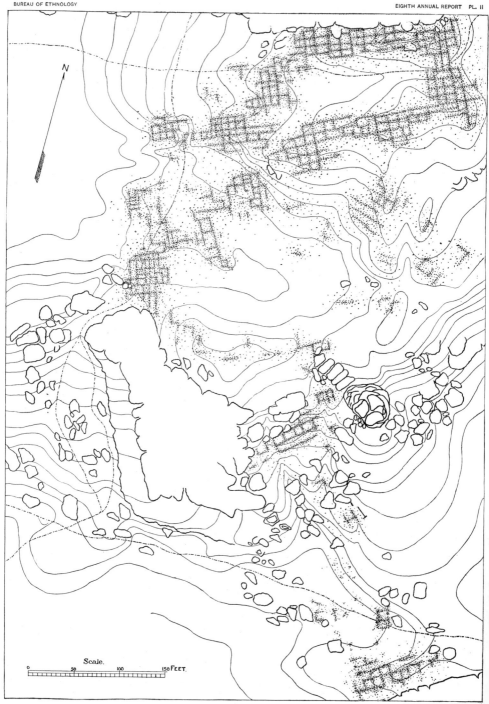

N

Scale.
0    50    100    150 FEET.

OLD MASHONGNAVI.

GENERAL VIEW OF AWATUBI.

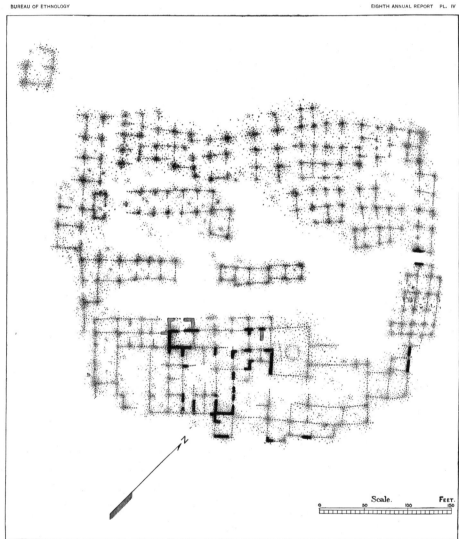

Scale.          Feet.
0          50          100          150

AWATUBI (TALLA-HOGAN).

STANDING WALLS OF AWATUBI.

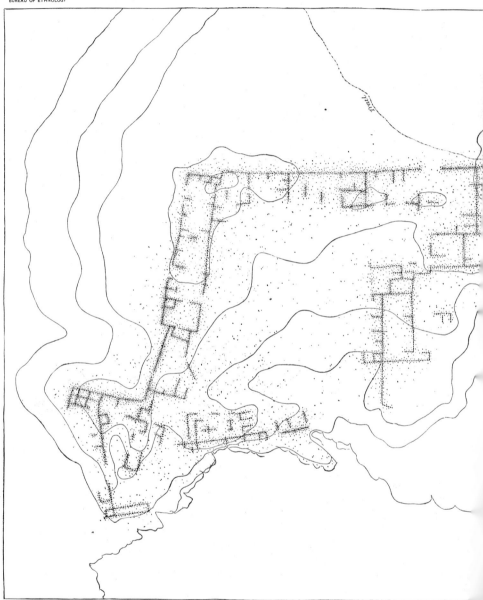

HORN HOUSE.

Scale.

0      50      100      150 FEET

ADOBE FRAGMENT IN AWATUBI.

BAT HOUSE·

MISHIPTONGA (JEDITOH).

Scale

0    50    100    150 FEET.

A SMALL RUIN NEAR MOEN-KOPI.

MASONRY ON THE OUTER WALL OF THE FIRE-HOUSE.

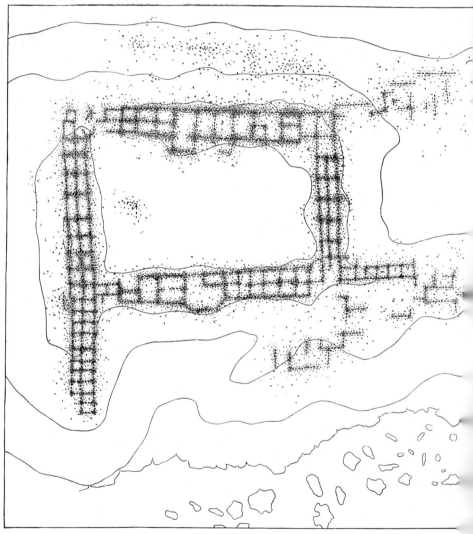

CHUKUBI.

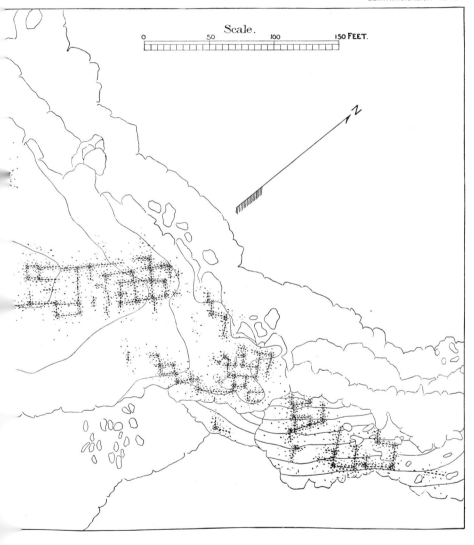

Scale.

0    50    100    150 FEET.

is preserved. The Hopituh certainly marry within phratries, and occasionally with the same gens. There is no doubt, however, that in the earlier villages each gens, and where practicable, the whole of the phratry, built their houses together. To a certain extent the house of the priestess of a gens is still regarded as the home of the gens. She has to be consulted concerning proposed marriages, and has much to say in other social arrangements.

While the village of the Walpi was still upon the west side of the mesa point, some of them moved around and built houses beside a spring close to the east side of the mesa. Soon after this a dispute over planting ground arose between them and the Sikyátki, whose village was also on that side of the mesa and but a short distance above them. From this time forward bad blood lay between the Sikyátki and the Walpi, who took up the quarrel of their suburb. It also happened about that time, so tradition says, more of the Coyote people came from the north, and the Pikyás nyu-mu, the young cornstalk, who were the latest of the Water people, came in from the south. The Sikyátki, having acquired their friendship, induced them to build on two mounds, on the summit of the mesa overlooking their village. They had been greatly harrassed by the young slingers and archers of Walpi, who would come across to the edge of the high cliff and assail them with impunity, but the occupation of these two mounds by friends afforded effectual protection to their village. These knolls are about 40 yards apart, and about 40 feet above the level of the mesa which is something over 400 feet above Sikyátki. Their roughly leveled summits measure 20 by 10 feet and are covered with traces of house walls; and it is evident that groups of small-roomed houses were clustered also around the sloping sides. About a hundred yards south from their dwellings the people of the mounds built for their own protection a strong wall entirely across the mesa, which at that point is contracted to about 200 feet in width, with deep vertical cliffs on either side. The base of the wall is still quite distinct, and is about 3 feet thick.

But no reconciliation was ever effected between the Walpi and the Sikyátki and their allies, and in spite of their defensive wall frequent assaults were made upon the latter until they were forced to retreat. The greater number of them retired to Oraibi and the remainder to Sikyátki, and the feud was still maintained between them and the Walpi.

Some of the incidents as well as the disastrous termination of this feud are still narrated. A party of the Sikyátki went prowling through Walpi one day while the men were afield, and among other outrages one of them shot an arrow through a window and killed a chief's daughter while she was grinding corn. The chief's son resolved to avenge the death of his sister, and some time after this went to Sikyátki, professedly to take part in a religious dance, in which he joined until just before the close of the ceremony. Having previously observed where the handsomest girl was seated among the spectators on the house terraces, he ran up the ladder as if to offer her a prayer emblem, but instead he drew out a sharp flint knife from his girdle and cut her throat. He threw the body down where all could see it, and ran along the adjoining terraces till he cleared the village. A little way up the mesa was a large flat rock, upon which he sprang and took off his dancer's mask so that all might recognize him, then turning again to the mesa he sped swiftly up the trail and escaped.

And so foray and slaughter continued to alternate between them until the planting season of some indefinite year came around. All the Sikyátki men were to begin the season by planting the fields of their chief on a certain day, which was announced from the housetop by the Second Chief as he made his customary evening proclamations, and the Walpi, becoming aware of this, planned a fatal onslaught. Every man and woman able to draw a bow or wield a weapon were got in readiness and at night they crossed the mesa and concealed themselves along its edge, overlooking the doomed village. When the day came they waited until the men had gone to the field and then rushed down upon the houses. The chief, who was too old to go afield, was the first one killed, and then followed the indiscriminate slaughter of women and children, and the destruction of the houses. The wild tumult in the village alarmed the Sikyátki and they came rushing back, but too late to defend their homes. Their struggles were hopeless, for they had only their planting sticks to use as weapons, which availed but little against the Walpi with their bows and arrows, spears, slings, and war clubs. Nearly all of the Sikyátki men were killed, but some of them escaped to Oraibi and some to Awatubi. A number of the girls and younger women were spared, and distributed among the different villages, where they became wives of their despoilers.

It is said to have been shortly after the destruction of Sikyátki that the first serious inroad of a hostile tribe occurred within this region, and all the stories aver that these early hostiles were from the north, the Ute being the first who are mentioned, and after them the Apache, who made an occasional foray.

While these families of Hopituh stock had been building their straggling dwellings along the canyon brinks, and grouping in villages around the base of the East Mesa, other migratory bands of Hopituh had begun to arrive on the Middle Mesa. As already said, it is admitted that the Snake were the first occupants of this region, but beyond that fact the traditions are contradictory and confused. It is probable, however, that not long after the arrival of the Horn, the Squash people came from the south and built a village on the Middle Mesa, the ruin of which is called Chukubi. It is on the edge of the cliff on the east side of the neck of that mesa, and a short distance south of the direct trail leading from Walpi to Oraibi. The Squash people say that they came from Palát Kwabi, the Red Land in the far South, and this vague term expresses nearly all their knowledge of that traditional land. They say they lived for a long time in the valley of the Colorado Chiquito, on the south side of that stream and not far from the point where the railway crosses it. They still distinguish the ruin of their early village there, which was built as usual on the brink of a canyon, and call it Etípsíkya, after a shrub that grows there profusely. They crossed the river opposite that place, but built no permanent houses until they reached the vicinity of Chukubi, near which two smaller clusters of ruins, on knolls, mark the sites of dwellings which they claim to have been theirs. Three groups (nyumu) traveling together were the next to follow them; these were the Bear, the Bear-skin-rope, and the Blue Jay. They are said to have been very numerous, and to have come from the vicinity of San Francisco Mountain. They did not move up to Chukubi, but built a large village on the summit, at the south end of the mesa, close to the site of the present Mashongnavi. Soon afterward came the Burrowing Owl, and the Coyote, from the vicinity of Navajo Mountains in the north, but they were not very numerous. They also built upon the Mashongnavi summit.

After this the Squash people found that the water from their springs was decreasing, and began moving toward the end of the mesa, where the other people were. But as there was then no suitable place left on the summit, they built a village on the sandy terrace close below it, on the west side; and as the springs at Chukubi ultimately ceased entirely, the rest of the Squash people came to the terrace and were again united in one village. Straggling bands of several other groups, both wingwu and nyumu, are mentioned as coming from various directions. Some built on the terrace and some found house room in Mashongnavi. This name is derived as follows: On the south side of the terrace on which the Squash village was built is a high column of sandstone which is vertically split in two, and formerly there was a third pillar in line, which has long since fallen. These three columns were called Tútu-walha, the guardians, and both the Squash village and the one on the summit were so named. On the north side of the terrace, close to the present village, is another irregular massy pillar of sandstone called Mashóniniptu, meaning "the other which remains erect," having reference to the one on the south side, which had fallen. When the Squash withdrew to the summit the village was then called Mashóniniptuovi, "at the place of the other which remains erect;" now that term is never used, but always its syncopated form, Mashongnavi.

The Squash village, on the south end of the Middle Mesa, was attacked by a fierce band that came from the north, some say the Ute, others say the Apache; but whoever the invaders were, they completely overpowered the people, and carried off great stores of food and other plunder. The village was then evacuated, the houses dismantled, and the material removed to the high summit, where they reconstructed their dwellings around the village which thenceforth bore its present name of Mashongnavi. Some of the Squash people moved over to Oraibi, and portions of the Katchina and Paroquet people came from

there to Mashongnavi about the same time, and a few of these two
groups occupied some vacant houses also in Shupaulovi; for this village
even at that early date had greatly diminished in population, having
sustained a disastrous loss of men in the canyon affrays east of Walpi.

Shumopavi seems to have been built by portions of the same groups
who went to the adjacent Mashongnavi, but the traditions of the two
villages are conflicting. The old traditionists at Shumopavi hold that
the first to come there were the Paroquet, the Bear, the Bear-skin-rope,
and the Blue Jay. They came from the west—probably from San Francisco Mountain. They claim that ruins on a mesa bluff about 10 miles
south from the present village are the remains of a village built by these
groups before reaching Shumopavi, and the Paroquets arrived first, it
is said, because they were perched on the heads of the Bears, and, when
nearing the water, they flew in ahead of the others. These groups built
a village on a broken terrace, on the east side of the cliff, and just below
the present village. There is a spring close by called after the Shun-
óhu, a tall red grass, which grew abundantly there, and from which the
town took its name. This spring was formerly very large, but two years
ago a landslide completely buried it; lately, however, a small outflow
is again apparent.

The ruins of the early village cover a hillocky area of about 800 by
250 feet, but it is impossible to trace much of the ground plan with
accuracy. The corner of an old house still stands, some 6 or 8 feet high,
extending about 15 feet on one face and about 10 feet on the other. The
wall is over 3 feet in thickness, but of very clumsy masonry, no care
having been exercised in dressing the stones, which are of varying sizes
and laid in mud plaster. Interest attaches to this fragment, as it is one
of the few tangible evidences left of the Spanish priests who engaged in
the fatal mission to the Hopituh in the sixteenth century. This bit of
wall, which now forms part of a sheep-fold, is pointed out as the remains
of one of the mission buildings.

Other groups followed—the Mole, the Spider, and the "Wíksrun."
These latter took their name from a curious ornament worn by the men.
A piece of the leg-bone of a bear, from which the marrow had been
extracted and a stopper fixed in one end, was attached to the fillet binding the hair, and hung down in front of the forehead. This gens and
the Mole are now extinct.

Shumopavi received no further accession of population, but lost to
some extent by a portion of the Bear people moving across to Walpi.
No important event seems to have occurred among them for a long period
after the destruction of Sikyátki, in which they bore some part, and
only cursory mention is made of the ingress of "enemies from the north;"
but their village, apparently, was not assailed.

The Oraibi traditions tend to confirm those of Shumopavi, and tell
that the first houses there were built by Bears, who came from the latter
place. The following is from a curious legend of the early settlement:

The Bear people had two chiefs, who were brothers; the elder was called Vwen-ti-só-mo, and the younger Ma-tcí-to. They had a desperate quarrel at Shumopavi, and their people divided into two factions, according as they inclined to one or other of the contestants. After a long period of contention Ma-tcí-to and his followers withdrew to the mesa where Oraibi now stands, about 8 miles northwest from Shumopavi, and built houses a little to the southwest of the limits of the present town. These houses were afterwards destroyed by "enemies from the north," and the older portion of the existing town, the southwest ends of the house rows, were built with stones from the demolished houses. Fragments of these early walls are still occasionally unearthed.

After Ma-tcí-to and his people were established there, whenever any of the Shumopavi people became dissatisfied with that place they built at Oraibi, Ma-tcí-to placed a little stone monument about halfway between these two villages to mark the boundary of the land. Vwen-ti-so'-mo objected to this, but it was ultimately accepted with the proviso that the village growing the fastest should have the privilege of moving it toward the other village. The monument still stands, and is on the direct Oraibi trail from Shumopavi, 3 miles from the latter. It is a well dressed, rectangular block of sandstone, projecting two feet above the ground, and measures 8½ by 7 inches. On the end is carved the rude semblance of a human head, or mask, the eyes and mouth being merely round shallow holes, with a black line painted around them. The stone is pecked on the side, but the head and front are rubbed quite smooth, and the block, tapering slightly to the base, suggests the ancient Roman Termini.

There are Eagle people living at Oraibi, Mashongnavi, and Walpi, and it would seem as if they had journeyed for some time with the later Snake people and others from the northwest. Vague traditions attach them to several of the ruins north of the Moen-kopi, although most of these are regarded as the remains of Snake dwellings.

The legend of the Eagle people introduces them from the west, coming in by way of the Moen-kopi water course. They found many people living in Tusayan, at Oraibi, the Middle Mesa, and near the East Mesa, but the Snake village was yet in the valley. Some of the Eagles remained at Oraibi, but the main body moved to a large mound just east of Mashongnavi, on the summit of which they built a village and called it Shi-tái-mu. Numerous traces of small-roomed houses can be seen on this mound and on some of the lower surroundings. The uneven summit is about 300 by 200 feet, and the village seems to have been built in the form of an irregular ellipse, but the ground plan is very obscure.

While the Eagles were living at Shi-tái-mu, they sent "Yellow Foot" to the mountain in the east (at the headwaters of the Rio Grande) to obtain a dog. After many perilous adventures in caverns guarded by bear, mountain lion, and rattlesnake, he got two dogs and returned.

They were wanted to keep the coyotes out of the corn and the gardens. The dogs grew numerous, and would go to Mashongnavi in search of food, and also to some of the people of that village, which led to serious quarrels between them and the Eagle people. Ultimately the Shi-tái-mu chief proclaimed a feast, and told the people to prepare to leave the village forever. On the feast day the women arranged the food basins on the ground in a long line leading out of the village. The people passed along this line, tasting a mouthful here or there, but without stopping, and when they reached the last basin they were beyond the limits of the village. Without turning around they continued on down into the valley until they were halted by the Snake people. An arrangement was effected with the latter, and the Eagles built their houses in the Snake village. A few of the Eagle families who had become attached to Mashongnavi chose to go to that village, where their descendants still reside, and are yet held as close relatives by the Eagles of Walpi. The land around the East Mesa was then portioned out, the Snakes, Horns, Bears, and Eagles each receiving separate lands, and these old allotments are still approximately maintained.

According to the Eagle traditions the early occupants of Tusayan came in the following succession: Snake, Horn, Bear, Middle Mesa, Oraibi, and Eagle, and finally from the south came the Water families. This sequence is also recognized in the general tenor of the legends of the other groups.

Shupaulovi, a small village quite close to Mashongnavi, would seem to have been established just before the coming of the Water people. Nor does there seem to have been any very long interval between the arrival of the earliest occupants of the Middle Mesa and this latest colony. These were the Sun people, and like the Squash folk, claim to have come from Palátkwabi, the Red Land, in the south. On their northward migration, when they came to the valley of the Colorado Chiquito, they found the Water people there, with whom they lived for some time. This combined village was built upon Homólobi, a round terraced mound near Sunset Crossing, where fragmentary ruins covering a wide area can yet be traced.

Incoming people from the east had built the large village of Awatubi, high rock, upon a steep mesa about nine miles southeast from Walpi. When the Sun people came into Tusayan they halted at that village and a few of them remained there permanently, but the others continued west to the Middle Mesa. At that time also they say Chukubi, Shi-taimu, Mashongnavi, and the Squash village on the terrace were all occupied, and they built on the terrace close to the Squash village also. The Sun people were then very numerous and soon spread their dwellings over the summit where the ruin now stands, and many indistinct lines of house walls around this dilapidated village attest its former size. Like the neighboring village, it takes its name from a rock near by, which is used as a place for the deposit of votive offerings, but the etymology of the term can not be traced.

Some of the Bear people also took up their abode at Shupaulovi, and later a nyumu of the Water family called Batni, moisture, built with them; and the diminished families of the existing village are still composed entirely of these three nyumu.

The next arrivals seem to have been the Asanyumu, who in early days lived in the region of the Chama, in New Mexico, at a village called Kaékibi, near the place now known as Abiquiu. When they left that region they moved slowly westward to a place called Túwii (Santo Domingo), where some of them are said to still reside. The next halt was at Kaiwáika (Laguna) where it is said some families still remain, and they staid also a short time at A'ikoka (Acoma); but none of them remained at that place. From the latter place they went to Sióki (Zuñi), where they remained a long time and left a number of their people there, who are now called Aiyáhokwi by the Zuñi. They finally reached Tusayan by way of Awatubi. They had been preceded from the same part of New Mexico by the Honan nyumu (the Badger people), whom they found living at the last-named village. The Magpie, the Putc Kóhu (Boomerang-shaped hunting stick), and the Field-mouse families of the Asa remained and built beside the Badger, but the rest of its groups continued across to the Walpi Mesa. They were not at first permitted to come up to Walpi, which then occupied its present site, but were allotted a place to build at Coyote Water, a small spring on the east side of the mesa, just under the gap. They had not lived there very long, however, when for some valuable services in defeating at one time a raid of the Ute (who used to be called the Tcingawúptuh) and of the Navajo at another, they were given for planting grounds all the space on the mesa summit from the gap to where Sichumovi now stands, and the same width, extending across the valley to the east. On the mesa summit they built the early portion of the house mass on the north side of the village, now known as Hano. But soon after this came a succession of dry seasons, which caused a great scarcity of food almost amounting to a famine, and many moved away to distant streams. The Asa people went to Túpkabi (Deep Canyon, the de Chelly), about 70 miles northeast from Walpi, where the Navajo received them kindly and supplied them with food. The Asa had preserved some seeds of the peach, which they planted in the canyon nooks, and numerous little orchards still flourish there. They also brought the Navajo new varieties of food plants, and their relations grew very cordial. They built houses along the base of the canyon walls, and dwelt there for two or three generations, during which time many of the Asa women were given to the Navajo, and the descendants of these now constitute a numerous clan among the Navajo, known as the Kiáini, the High-house people.

The Navajo and the Asa eventually quarreled and the latter returned to Walpi, but this was after the arrival of the Hano, by whom they found their old houses occupied. The Asa were taken into the village of Walpi, being given a vacant strip on the east edge of the mesa, just where the main trail comes up to the village. The Navajo, Ute, and Apache had frequently gained entrance to the village by this trail, and to guard it the Asa built a house group along the edge of the cliff at that point, immediately overlooking the trail, where some of the people still live; and the kiva there, now used by the Snake order, belongs to them. There was a crevice in the rock, with a smooth bottom extending to the edge of the cliff and deep enough for a ki'koli. A wall was built to close the outer edge and it was at first intended to build a dwelling house there, but it was afterward excavated to its present size and made into a kiva, still called the wikwálhobi, the kiva of the Watchers of the High Place. The Walpi site becoming crowded, some of the Bear and Lizard people moved out and built houses on the site of the present Sichumovi; several Asa families followed them, and after them came some of the Badger people. The village grew to an extent considerably beyond its present size, when it was abandoned on account of a malignant plague. After the plague, and within the present generation, the village was rebuilt—the old houses being torn down to make the new ones.

After the Asa came the next group to arrive was the Water family. Their chief begins the story of their migration in this way:

In the long ago the Snake, Horn, and Eagle people lived here (in Tusayan), but their corn grew only a span high, and when they sang for rain the cloud god sent only a thin mist. My people then lived in the distant Pa-lát Kwá-bi in the South. There was a very bad old man there, who, when he met any one, would spit in his face, blow his nose upon him, and rub ordure upon him. He ravished the girls and did all manner of evil. Baholikonga got angry at this and turned the world upside down, and water spouted up through the kivas and through the fireplaces in the houses. The earth was rent in great chasms, and water covered everything except one narrow ridge of mud; and across this the serpent deity told all the people to travel. As they journeyed across, the feet of the bad slipped and they fell into the dark water, but the good, after many days, reached dry land. While the water was rising around the village the old people got on the tops of the houses, for they thought they could not struggle across with the younger people; but Baholikonga clothed them with the skins of turkeys, and they spread their wings out and floated in the air just above the surface of the water, and in this way they got across. There were saved of our people Water, Corn, Lizard, Horned Toad, Sand, two families of Rabbit, and Tobacco. The turkey tail dragged in the water—hence the white on the turkey tail now. Wearing these turkey-skins is the reason why old people have dewlaps under the chin like a turkey; it is also the reason why old people use turkey-feathers at the religious ceremonies.

In the story of the wandering of the Water people, many vague references are made to various villages in the South, which they constructed or dwelt in, and to rocks where they carved their totems at temporary halting places. They dwelt for a long time at Homólobi, where the Sun people joined them; and probably not long after the latter left the Water people followed on after them. The largest number of this family seem to have made their dwellings first at Mashongnavi and Shupaulovi; but like the Sun people they soon spread to all the villages.

The narrative of part of this journey is thus given by the chief before quoted:

It occupied 4 years to cross the disrupted country. The kwakwanti (a warrior order) went ahead of the people and carried seed of corn, beans, melons, squashes, and cotton. They would plant corn in the mud at early morning and by noon it was ripe and thus the people were fed. When they reached solid ground they rested, and then they built houses. The kwakwanti were always out exploring—sometimes they were gone as long as four years. Again we would follow them on long journeys, and halt and build houses and plant. While we were traveling if a woman became heavy with child we would build her a house and put plenty of food in it and leave her there, and from these women sprang the Pima, Maricopa, and other Indians in the South.

Away in the South, before we crossed the mountains (south of the Apache country) we built large houses and lived there a long while. Near these houses is a large rock on which was painted the rain-clouds of the Water phratry, also a man carrying corn in his arms; and the other phratries also painted the Lizard and the Rabbit upon it. While they were living there the kwakwanti made an expedition far to the north and came in conflict with a hostile people. They fought day after day, for days and days—they fought by day only and when night came they separated, each party retiring to its own ground to rest. One night the cranes came and each crane took a kwakwanti on his back and brought them back to their people in the South.

Again all the people traveled north until they came to the Little Colorado, near San Francisco Mountains, and there they built houses up and down the river. They also made long ditches to carry the water from the river to their gardens. After living there a long while they began to be plagued with swarms of a kind of gnat called the sand-fly, which bit the children, causing them to swell up and die. The place becoming unendurable, they were forced again to resume their travels. Before starting, one of the Rain-women, who was big with child, was made comfortable in one of the houses on the mountain. She told her people to leave her, because she knew this was the place where she was to remain forever. She also told them that hereafter whenever they should return to the mountain to hunt she would provide them with plenty of game. Under her house is a spring and any sterile woman who drinks of its water will bear children. The people then began a long journey to reach the summit of the table land on the north. They camped for rest on one of the terraces, where there was no water, and they were very tired and thirsty. Here the women celebrated the rain-feast—they danced for three days, and on the fourth day the clouds brought heavy rain and refreshed the people. This event is still commemorated by a circle of stones at that place. They reached a spring southeast from Káibitho (Kumás Spring) and there they built a house and lived for some time. Our people had plenty of rain and cultivated much corn and some of the Walpi people came to visit us. They told us that their rain only came here and there in fine misty sprays, and a basketful of corn was regarded as a large crop. So they asked us to come to their land and live with them and finally we consented. When we got there we found some Eagle people living near the Second Mesa; our people divided, and part went with the Eagle and have ever since remained there; but we camped near the First Mesa. It was planting time and the Walpi celebrated their rain-feast but they brought only a mere misty drizzle. Then we celebrated our rain-feast and planted. Great rains and thunder and lightning immediately followed and on the first day after planting our corn was half an arm's length high; on the fourth day it was its full height, and in one moon it was ripe. When we were going up to the village (Walpi was then north of the gap, probably), we were met by a

Bear man who said that our thunder frightened the women and we must not go near
the village. Then the kwakwanti said, "Let us leave these people and seek a land
somewhere else," but our women said they were tired of travel and insisted upon
our remaining. Then "Fire-picker" came down from the village and told us to come
up there and stay, but after we had got into the village the Walpi women screamed
out against us—they feared our thunder—and so the Walpi turned us away. Then
our people, except those who went to the Second Mesa, traveled to the northeast as
far as the Tsegi (Canyon de Chelly), but I can not tell whether our people built the
houses there. Then they came back to this region again and built houses and had
much trouble with the Walpi, but we have lived here ever since.

Groups of the Water people, as already stated, were distributed
among all the villages, although the bulk of them remained at the Middle Mesa; but it seems that most of the remaining groups subsequently
chose to build their permanent houses at Oraibi. There is no special tradition of this movement; it is only indicated by this circumstance, that
in addition to the Water families common to every village, there are
still in Oraibi several families of that people which have no representatives in any of the other villages. At a quite early day Oraibi became
a place of importance, and they tell of being sufficiently populous to
establish many outlying settlements. They still identify these with
ruins on the detached mesas in the valley to the south and along the
Moen-kopi ("place of flowing water") and other intermittent streams in
the west. These sites were occupied for the purpose of utilizing cultivable tracts of land in their vicinity, and the remotest settlement, about
45 miles west, was especially devoted to the cultivation of cotton, the
place being still called by the Navajo and other neighboring tribes, the
"cotton planting ground." It is also said that several of the larger
ruins along the course of the Moen-kopi were occupied by groups of the
Snake, the Coyote, and the Eagle who dwelt in that region for a long
period before they joined the people in Tusayan. The incursions of
foreign bands from the north may have hastened that movement, and
the Oraibi say they were compelled to withdraw all their outlying colonies. An episode is related of an attack upon the main village when
a number of young girls were carried off, and 2 or 3 years afterward
the same marauders returned and treated with the Oraibi, who paid a
ransom in corn and received all their girls back again. After a quiet
interval the pillaging bands renewed their attacks and the settlements
on the Moen-kopi were vacated. They were again occupied after another peace was established, and this condition of alternate occupancy
and abandonment seems to have existed until within quite recent time.

While the Asa were still sojourning in Canyon de Chelly, and before
the arrival of the Hano, another bloody scene had been enacted in
Tusayan. Since the time of the Antelope Canyon feuds there had been
enmity between Awatubi and some of the other villages, especially
Walpi, and some of the Sikyatki refugees had transmitted their feudal
wrongs to their descendants who dwelt in Awatubi. They had long
been perpetrating all manner of offenses; they had intercepted hunting

parties from the other villages, seized their game, and sometimes killed the hunters; they had fallen upon men in outlying corn fields, maltreating and sometimes slaying them, and threatened still more serious outrage. Awatubi was too strong for Walpi to attack single-handed, so the assistance of the other villages was sought, and it was determined to destroy Awatubi at the close of a feast soon to occur. This was the annual "feast of the kwakwanti," which is still maintained and is held during the month of November by each village, when the youths who have been qualified by certain ordeals are admitted to the councils. The ceremonies last several days, and on the concluding night special rites are held in the kivas. At these ceremonies every man must be in the kiva to which he belongs, and after the close of the rites they all sleep there, no one being permitted to leave the kiva until after sunrise on the following day.

There was still some little intercourse between Awatubi and Walpi, and it was easily ascertained when this feast was to be held. On the day of its close, the Walpi sent word to their allies "to prepare the war arrow and come," and in the evening the fighting bands from the other villages assembled at Walpi, as the foray was to be led by the chief of that village. By the time night had fallen something like 150 marauders had met, all armed, of course; and of still more ominous import than their weapons were the firebrands they carried—shredded cedar bark loosely bound in rolls, resinous splinters of piñon, dry greasewood (a furze very easily ignited), and pouches full of pulverized red peppers.

Secure in the darkness from observation, the bands followed the Walpi chief across the valley, every man with his weapons in hand and a bundle of inflammables on his back. Reaching the Awatubi mesa they cautiously crept up the steep, winding trail to the summit, and then stole round the village to the passages leading to the different courts holding the kivas, near which they hid themselves. They waited till just before the gray daylight came, then the Walpi chief shouted his war cry and the yelling bands rushed to the kivas. Selecting their positions, they were at them in a moment, and quickly snatching up the ladders through the hatchways, the only means of exit, the doomed occupants were left as helpless as rats in a trap. Fire was at hand in the numerous little cooking pits, containing the jars of food prepared for the celebrants, the inflammable bundles were lit and tossed into the kivas, and the piles of firewood on the terraced roofs were thrown down upon the blaze, and soon each kiva became a furnace. The red pepper was then cast upon the fire to add its choking tortures, while round the hatchways the assailants stood showering their arrows into the mass of struggling wretches. The fires were maintained until the roofs fell in and buried and charred the bones of the victims. It is said that every male of Awatubi who had passed infancy perished in the slaughter, not one escaping. Such of the women and children as were spared were taken out, and all the houses were destroyed, after which the captives were divided among the different villages.

The date of this last feudal atrocity can be made out with som
of exactness, because in 1692, Don Diego Vargas with a milita
visited Tusayan and mentions Awatubi as a populous village a., w..ucn
he made some halt. The Hano (Tewa) claim that they have lived in
Tusayan for five or six generations, and that when they arrived there
was no Awatubi in existence; hence it must have been destroyed not
long after the close of the seventeenth century.

Since the destruction of Awatubi only one other serious affray has
occurred between the villages; that was between Oraibi and Walpi.
It appears that after the Oraibi withdrew their colonies from the south
and west they took possession of all the unoccupied planting grounds to
the east of the village, and kept reaching eastward till they encroached
upon some land claimed by the Walpi. This gave rise to intermittent
warfare in the outlying fields, and whenever the contending villagers
met a broil ensued, until the strife culminated in an attack upon Walpi.
The Oraibi chose a day when the Walpi men were all in the field on the
east side of the mesa, but the Walpi say that their women and dogs
held the Oraibi at bay until the men came to the rescue. A severe bat-
tle was fought at the foot of the mesa, in which the Oraibi were routed
and pursued across the Middle Mesa, where an Oraibi chief turned and
implored the Walpi to desist. A conciliation was effected there, and
harmonious relations have ever since existed between them. Until
within a few years ago the spot where they stayed pursuit was marked
by a stone, on which a shield and a dog were depicted, but it was a source
of irritation to the Oraibi and it was removed by some of the Walpi.

In the early part of the eighteenth century the Ute from the north,
and the Apache from the south made most disastrous inroads upon the
villages, in which Walpi especially suffered. The Navajo, who then
lived upon their eastern border, also suffered severely from the same
bands, but the Navajo and the Tusayan were not on the best terms and
never made any alliance for a common defense against these invaders.

Hano was peopled by a different linguistic stock from that of the other
villages—a stock which belongs to the Rio Grande group. According
to Polaka, the son of the principal chief, and himself an enterprising
trader who has made many journeys to distant localities—and to others,
the Hano once lived in seven villages on the Rio Grande, and the village
in which his forefathers lived was called Tceewáge. This, it is said, is
the same as the present Mexican village of Peña Blanca.

The Hano claim that they came to Tusayan only after repeated solici-
tation by the Walpi, at a time when the latter were much harassed by
the Ute and Apache. The story, as told by Kwálakwai, who lives in
Hano, but is not himself a Hano, begins as follows:

"Long ago the Hopi'tuh were few and were continually harassed by the Yútamo
(Ute), Yuíttcemo (Apache), and Dacábimo (Navajo). The chiefs of the Tcuin nyumu (Snake people) and the Hónin nyumu (Bear people) met together and made the
ba'ho (sacred plume stick) and sent it with a man from each of these people to the
house of the Tewa, called Tceewádigi, which was far off on the Múina (river)
near Alavia (Sante Fé).

The messengers did not succeed in persuading the Tewa to come and the embassy was sent three times more. On the fourth visit the Tewa consented to come, as the Walpi had offered to divide their land and their waters with them, and set out for Tusayan, led by their own chief, the village being left in the care of his son. This first band is said to have consisted of 146 women, and it was afterwards followed by another and perhaps others.

Before the Hano arrived there had been a cessation of hostile inroads, and the Walpi received them churlishly and revoked their promises regarding the division of land and waters with them. They were shown where they could build houses for themselves on a yellow sand mound on the east side of the mesa just below the gap. They built there, but they were compelled to go for their food up to Walpi. They could get no vessels to carry their food in, and when they held out their hands for some the Walpi women mockingly poured out hot porridge and scalded the fingers of the Hano.

After a time the Ute came down the valley on the west side of the mesa, doing great harm again, and drove off the Walpi flocks. Then the Hano got ready for war; they tied buckskins around their loins, whitened their legs with clay, and stained their body and arms with dark red earth (ocher). They overtook the Ute near Wípho (about 3 miles north from Hano), but the Ute had driven the flocks up the steep mesa side, and when they saw the Tewa coming they killed all the sheep and piled the carcasses up for a defense, behind which they lay down. They had a few firearms also, while the Hano had only clubs and bows and arrows; but after some fighting the Ute were driven out and the Tewa followed after them. The first Ute was killed a short distance beyond, and a stone heap still (?) marks the spot. Similar heaps marked the places where other Ute were killed as they fled before the Hano, but not far from the San Juan the last one was killed.

Upon the return of the Hano from this successful expedition they were received gratefully and allowed to come up on the mesa to live—the old houses built by the Asa, in the present village of Hano, being assigned to them. The land was then divided, an imaginary line between Hano and Sichumovi, extending eastward entirely across the valley, marked the southern boundary, and from this line as far north as the spot where the last Utah was killed was assigned to the Hano as their possession.

When the Hano first came the Walpi said to them, "let us spit in your mouths, and you will learn our tongue," and to this the Hano consented. When the Hano came up and built on the mesa they said to the Walpi, "let us spit in your mouths and you will learn our tongue," but the Walpi would not listen to this, saying it would make them vomit. This is the reason why all the Hano can talk Hopí, and none of the Hopítuh can talk Hano.

The Asa and the Hano were close friends while they dwelt in New Mexico, and when they came to this region both of them were called Hánomuh by the other people of Tusayan. This term signifies the mode in which the women of these people wear their hair, cut off in front on a line with the mouth and carelessly parted or hanging over the face, the back hair rolled up in a compact queue at the nape of the neck. This uncomely fashion prevails with both matron and maid, while among the other Tusayan the matron parts her hair evenly down the head and wears it hanging in a straight queue on either side, the maidens wearing theirs in a curious discoid arrangement over each temple.

Although the Asa and the Hano women have the same peculiar fashion of wearing the hair, still there is no affinity of blood claimed between them. The Asa speak the same language as the other Tusayan, but the Tewa (Hano) have a quite distinct language which belongs to the Tañoan stock. They claim that the occupants of the following pueblos, in the same region of the Rio Grande, are of their people and speak the same tongue.

| Kótite | Cochití (?). | | Kápung | Santa Clara (?) |
|--------|--------------|---|--------|-----------------|
| Númi | Nambé. | | Pokwádi | Pojoaque. |
| Ohke | San Juan. | | Tetsógi | Tesuque. |
| Posówe | (Doubtless extinct.) | | Also half of Taos. | |

Pleasant relations existed for some time, but the Walpi again grew ill-tempered; they encroached upon the Hano planting grounds and stole their property. These troubles increased, and the Hano moved away from the mesa; they crossed the west valley and built temporary shelters. They sent some men to explore the land on the westward to find a suitable place for a new dwelling. These scouts went to the Moen-kopi, and on returning, the favorable story they told of the land they had seen determined the Tewa to go there.

Meanwhile some knowledge of these troubles had reached Tceewá-digi, and a party of the Tewa came to Tusayan to take their friends back. This led the Hopituh to make reparation, which restored the confidence of the Hano, and they returned to the mesa, and the recently arrived party were also induced to remain. Yet even now, when the Hano (Tewa) go to visit their people on the river, the latter beseech them to come back, but the old Tewa say, "we shall stay here till our breath leaves us, then surely we shall go back to our first home to live forever."

The Walpi for a long time frowned down all attempts on the part of the Hano to fraternize; they prohibited intermarriages, and in general tabued the Hano. Something of this spirit was maintained until quite recent years, and for this reason the Hano still speak their own language, and have preserved several distinctive customs, although now the most friendly relations exist among all the villages. After the Hano were quietly established in their present position the Asa returned, and the Walpi allotted them a place to build in their own village. As before mentioned, the house mass on the southeast side of Walpi, at the head of the trail leading up to the village at that point, is still occupied by Asa families, and their tenure of possession was on the condition that they should always defend that point of access and guard the south end of the village. Their kiva is named after this circumstance as that of "the Watchers of the High Place."

Some of the Bear and Lizard families being crowded for building space, moved from Walpi and built the first houses on the site of the present village of Sichumovi, which is named from the Sivwapsi, a shrub which formerly grew there on some mounds (chumo).

This was after the Asa had been in Walpi for some time; probably about 125 years ago. Some of the Asa, and the Badger, the latter descendants of women saved from the Awatubi catastrophe, also moved to Sichumovi, but a plague of smallpox caused the village to be aban-doned shortly afterward. This pestilence is said to have greatly re-duced the number of the Tusayan, and after it disappeared there were many vacant houses in every village. Sichumovi was again occupied by a few Asa families, but the first houses were torn down and new ones constructed from them.

### LIST OF TRADITIONARY GENTES.

In the following table the early phratries (nyu-mu) are arranged in the order of their arrival, and the direction from which each came is given, except in the case of the Bear people. There are very few represent-atives of this phratry existing now, and very little tradition extant con-cerning its early history. The table does not show the condition of these organizations in the present community but as they appear in the tra-ditional accounts of their coming to Tusayan, although representatives of most of them can still be found in the various villages. There are, moreover, in addition to these, many other gentes and sub-gentes of more recent origin. The subdivision, or rather the multiplication of gentes may be said to be a continuous process; as, for example, in "corn" can be found families claiming to be of the root, stem, leaf, ear, blossom, etc., all belonging to corn; but there may be several families of each of these components constituting district sub-gentes. At present there are really but four phratries recognized among the Hopituh, the Snake, Horn, Eagle, and Rain, which is indifferently designated as Water or Corn:

1. Ho'-nan—Bear.

    Ho'-nan .......... Bear.
    Ko'-kyañ-a ....... Spider.
    Tco'-zir .......... Jay.
    He'k-pa.......... Fir.

2. Tcu'-a — Rattlesnake — from the west and north.

    Tcu'-a ........... Rattlesnake.
    Yu'ñ-ya......... Cactus—opuntia.
    Pü'n-e............ Cactus, the spe-
    cies that grows
    in dome-like
    masses.

2. Tcu'-a—Rattlesnake—from the west and north—Continued.

    Ü'-se............. Cactus, candela-
    bra, or branch-
    ing stemmed
    species.
    He'-wi .......... Dove.
    Pi-vwa'ni ........ Marmot.
    Pi'h-tca.......... Skunk.
    Ka-la'-ci-au-u ....Raccoon.

3. A'-la—Horn—from the east.

    So'-wiñ-wa....... Deer.
    Tc'ib-io .......... Antelope.
    Pa'ñ-wa ......... Mountain sheep.

4. Kwa′-hü—Eagle—from the west and south.

    Kwa′-hü .........Eagle.
    Kwa′-yo .........Hawk.
    Mas-si′ kwa′-yo ..Chicken hawk.
    Tda′-wa .........Sun.
    Ka-ha′-bi ........Willow.
    Te′-bi............Greasewood.

5. Ka-tci′-na—Sacred dancer—from the east.

    Ka-tci′-na........Sacred dancer.
    Gya′-zro .........Parroquet.
    Uñ-wu′-si ........Raven.
    Si-kya′-tci .......Yellow bird.
    Si-he′-bi .........Cottonwood.
    Sa-la′-bi .........Spruce.

6. A′sa—a plant (unknown) — from the Chama.

    A′sa .............
    Tca′-kwai-na .....Black earth Kat-cina.
    Pu′tc-ko-hu ......B o o m e r a n g hunting stick.
    Pi′-ca ............Field mouse.

6. A′sa—a plant (unknown)—from the Chama—Continued.

    Hoc′-bo-a ........Road runner, or c h a p a r r a l cock.
    Po-si′-o ..........Magpie.
    Kwi′ñobi ........Oak.

7. Ho-na′-ni—Badger—from the east.

    Ho-na′-ni ........Badger.
    Müñ-ya′u-wu .....Porcupine.
    Wu-so′-ko........Vulture.
    Bu′-li ............Butterfly.
    Bu-li′-so .........Evening p r i m-rose.
    Na′-hü ...........Medicine of all kinds; generic.

8. Yo′-ki—Rain—from the south.

    Yo′-ki............Rain.
    O′-mau ..........Cloud.
    Ka′-i-e...........Corn.
    Mu′r-zi-bu-si .....Bean.
    Ka-wa′i-ba-tuñ-a .Watermelon.
    Si-vwa′-pi........Bigelovia gra-veolens.

The foregoing is the Water or Rain phratry proper, but allied to them are the two following phratries, who also came to this region with the Water phratry.

LIZARD.

Kü′-kü-tci...... ⎫
Ba-tci′p-kwa-si . ⎪ Species of liz-
Na′-nan-a-wi ... ⎬ ards.
Mo′-mo-bi ...... ⎭
Pi′-sa ............White sand.
Tdu′-wa .........Red sand.
Tcu′-kai .........Mud.

RABBIT.

So′-wi ...........Jackass rabbit.
Tda′-bo ..........Cottontail r a b-bit.
Pi′-ba............Tobacco.
Tcoñ-o ...........Pipe.

Polaka gives the following data:

Te′-wa gentes and phratries.

| Tewa | | Hopi′tuh | | Navajo | |
|---|---|---|---|---|---|
| Ko′ⁿ-lo .............. | ⎱ | Ka′-ai ..........| Nata′ⁿ............ | Corn. | |
| Cä ................. | ⎰ | Pi′-ba .........| Na′-to .............. | Tobacco. | |
| Ke .................. | ⎱ | Ho′-nau .......| Cac ............... | Bear. | |
| Tce′-li .............. | ⎰ | Ca′-la-bi .........| Ts′-co .............. | Spruce. | |
| Ke′gi .............. | ⎱ | Ki′-hu .........| Ki-a′-ni .......... | House. | |
| Tuñ................. | ⎰ | Tda′-wu ........| Tjon-a-ai′ ........ | Sun. | |
| O′-ku-wuñ ......... | ⎱ | O′-mau..........| Kus .............. | Cloud. | |
| Nuñ ............... | ⎰ | Tcu′-kai ........| Huc-klic ......... | Mud. | |

The gentes bracketed are said to "belong together," but do not seem to have distinctive names—as phratries.

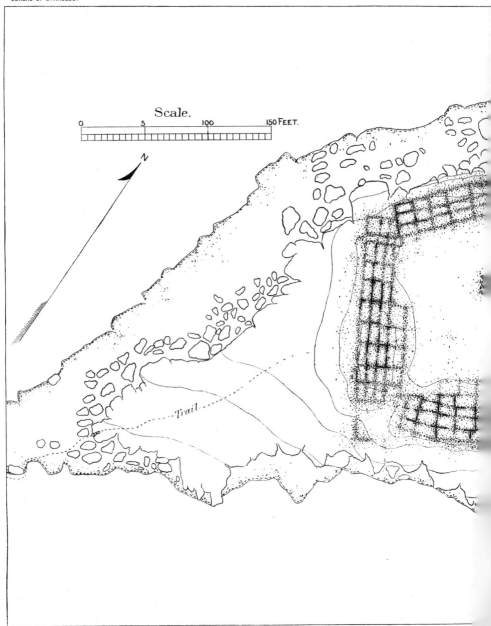

Scale.

PAYUPKI.

H. Hobart Nichols, '89.

GENERAL VIEW OF PAYUPKI.

STANDING WALLS OF PAYUPKI.

HANO.

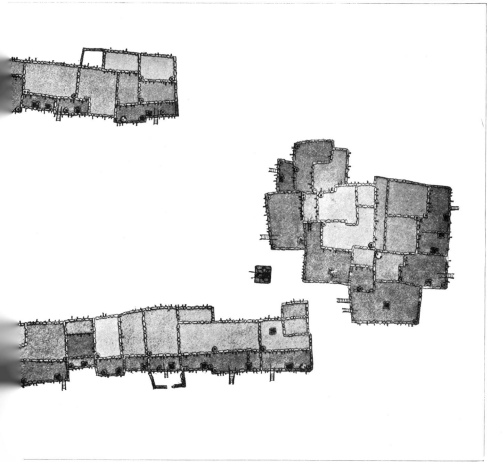

VIEW OF HANO.

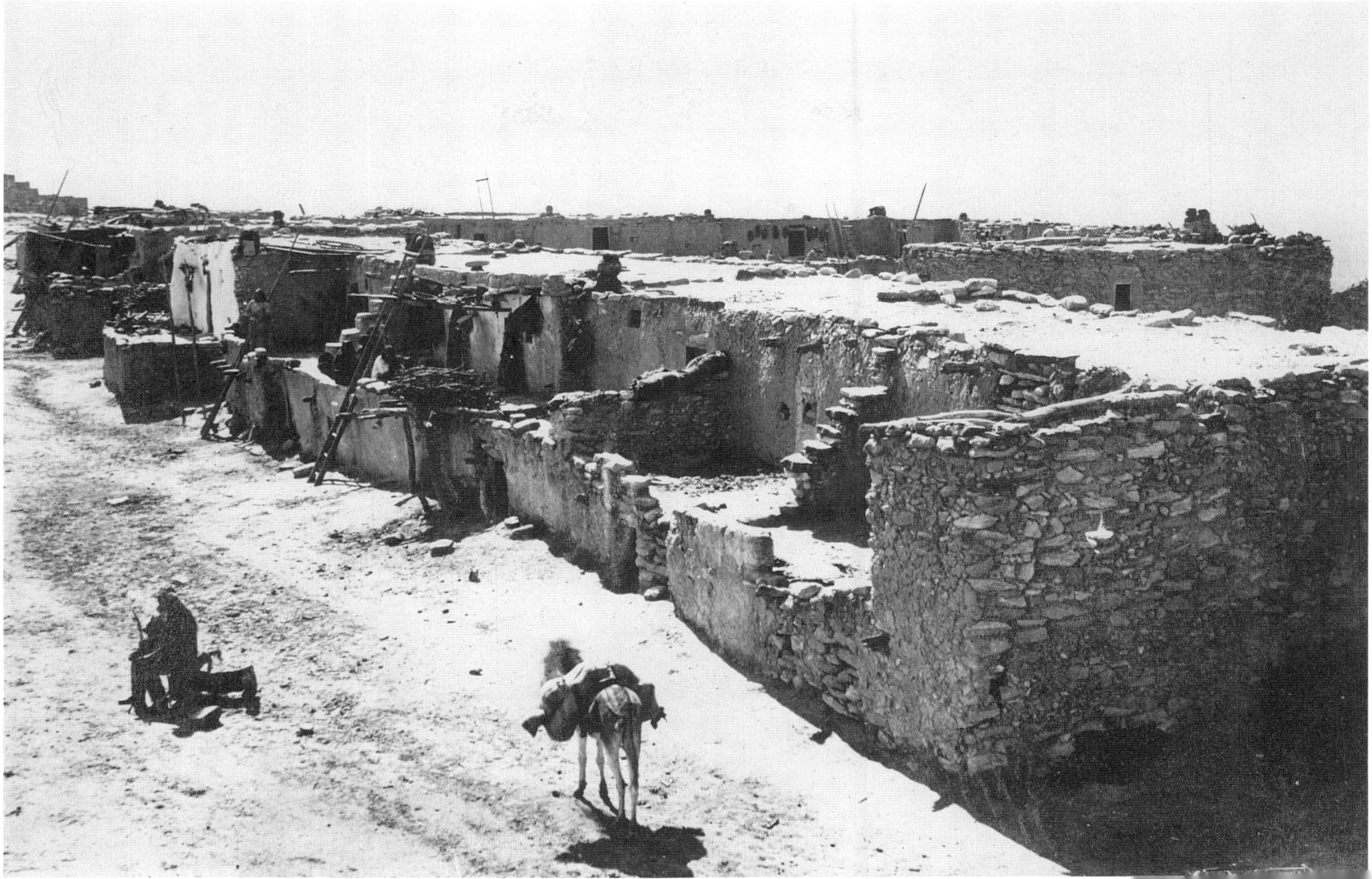

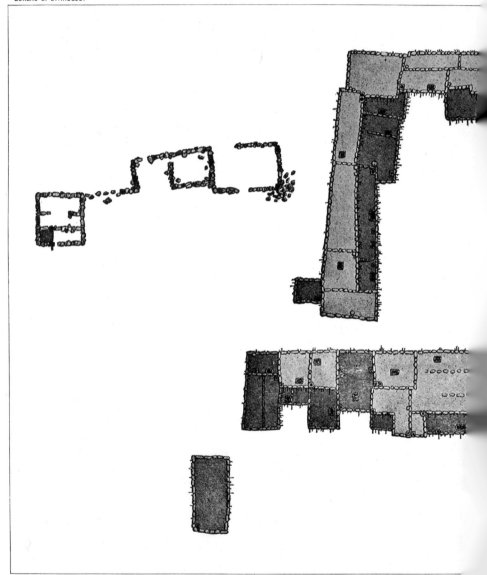

SICHUMOVI.

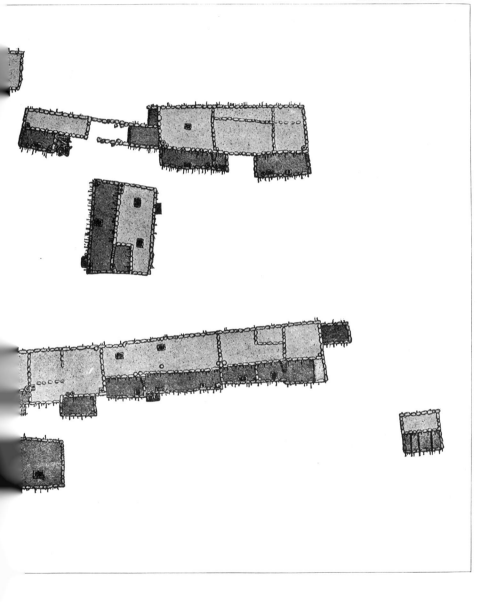

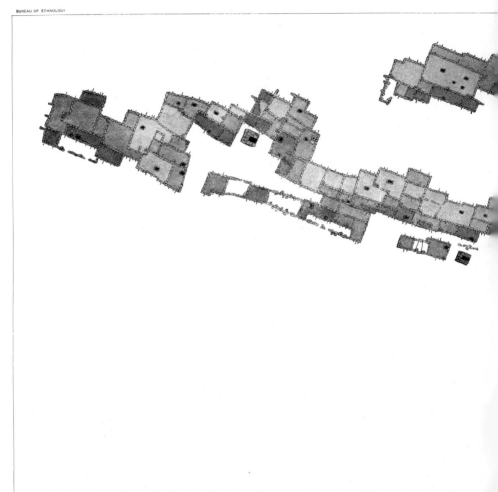

WALPI.

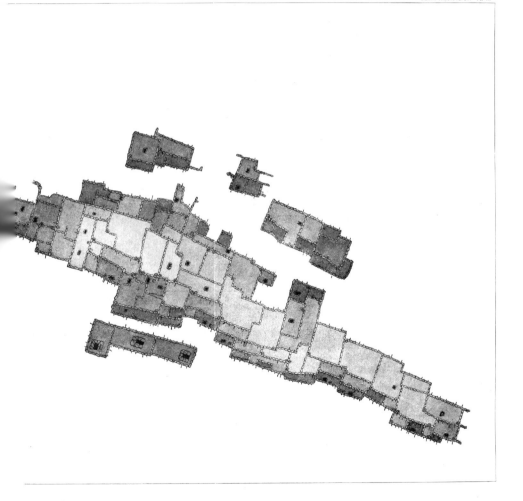

VIEW OF WALPI.

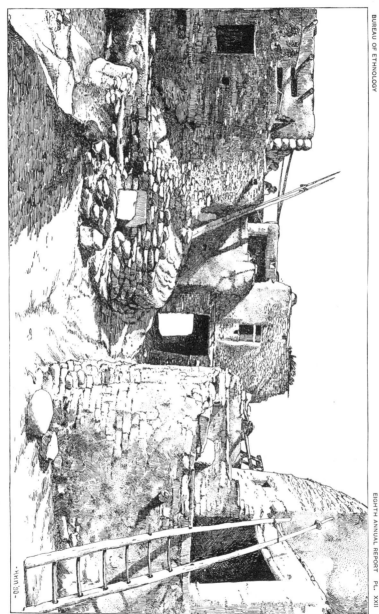

SOUTH PASSAGEWAY OF WALPI.

HOUSES BUILT OVER IRREGULAR SITES, WALPI.

DANCE ROCK AND KIVA, WALPI.

An interesting ruin which occurs on a mesa point a short distance north of Mashongnavi is known to the Tusayan under the name of Payupki. There are traditions and legends concerning it among the Tusayan, but the only version that could be obtained is not regarded by the writer as being up to the standard of those incorporated in the "Summary" and it is therefore given separately, as it has some suggestive value. It was obtained through Dr. Jeremiah Sullivan, then resident in Tusayan.

The people of Payupki spoke the same language as those on the first mesa (Walpi). Long ago they lived in the north, on the San Juan, but they were compelled to abandon that region and came to a place about 20 miles northwest from Oraibi. Being compelled to leave there, they went to Canyon de Chelly, where a band of Indians from the southeast joined them, with whom they formed an alliance. Together the two tribes moved eastward toward the Jemez Mountains, whence they drifted into the valley of the Rio Grande. There they became converts to the fire-worship then prevailing, but retained their old customs and language. At the time of the great insurrection (of 1680) they sheltered the native priests that were driven from some of the Rio Grande villages, and this action created such distrust and hatred among the people that the Payupki were forced to leave their settlement. Their first stop was at Old Laguna (12 miles east of the modern village) and they had with them then some 35 or 40 of the priests. After leaving Laguna they came to Bear Spring (Fort Wingate) and had a fight there with the Apache, whom they defeated. They remained at Bear Spring for several years, until the Zuñi compelled them to move. They then attempted to reach the San Juan, but were deceived in the trail, turned to the west and came to where Pueblo Colorado is now (the present post-office of Ganado, between Fort Defiance and Keam's Canyon). They remained there a long time, and through their success in farming became so favorably known that they were urged to come farther west. They refused, in consequence of which some Tusayan attacked them. They were captured and brought to Walpi (then on the point) and afterwards they were distributed among the villages. Previous to this capture the priests had been guiding them by feathers, smoke, and signs seen in the fire. When the priest's omens and oracles had proved false the people were disposed to kill them, but the priests persuaded them to let it depend on a test case—offering to kill themselves in the event of failure. So they had a great feast at Awatubi. The priests had long, hollow reeds inclosing various substances—feathers, flour, corn-pollen, sacred water, native tobacco (piba), corn, beans, melon seeds, etc., and they formed in a circle at sunrise on the plaza and had their incantations and prayers. As the sun rose a priest stepped forth before the people and blew through his reed, desirous of blowing that which was therein away from him, to scatter it abroad. But the wind would not blow and the contents of the reed fell to the ground. The priests were divided into groups, according to what they carried. In the evening all but two groups had blown. Then the elder of the twain turned his back eastward, and the reed toward the setting sun, and he blew, and the wind caught the feather and carried it to the west. This was accepted as a sign and the next day the Tusayan freed the slaves, giving each a blanket with corn in it. They went to the mesa where the ruin now stands and built the houses there. They asked for planting grounds, and fields were given them; but their crops did not thrive, and they stole corn from the Mashongnavi. Then, fearful lest they should be surprised at night, they built a wall as high as a man's head about the top of their mesa, and they had big doorways, which they closed and fastened at night. When they were compelled to plant corn for themselves they planted it on the ledges of the mesa, but it grew only as high as a man's knees; the leaves were very small and the grains grew only on one side of it. After a time they became friendly with the Mashongnavi again, and a boy from that village conceived a passion for a Payupki girl. The latter tribe objected to a marriage but the Mashongnavi were very desirous for it and some warriors of that village proposed if the boy could persuade the girl to fly with him, to aid and protect him. On an appointed day, about sundown, the girl came down from the mesa into the valley, but she was discovered by some old women who were baking pottery, who gave the alarm. Hearing the noise a party of the Mashongnavi, who were lying in wait, came up, but they encountered a party of the Payupki who had come out and a fight ensued. During the fight the young man was killed; and this caused so much bitterness of feeling that the Payupki were frightened, and remained quietly in their pueblo for several days. One morning, however, an old woman came over to Mashongnavi to borrow some tobacco, saying that they were going to have a dance in her village in five days. The next day the Payupki quietly departed. Seeing no smoke from the village the Mashongnavi at first thought that the Payupki were preparing for their dance, but on the third day a band of warriors was sent over to inquire and they found the village abandoned. The estufas and the houses of the priests were pulled down.

The narrator adds that the Payupki returned to San Felipe whence they came.

# CHAPTER II.

## RUINS AND INHABITED VILLAGES OF TUSAYAN.

### PHYSICAL FEATURES OF THE PROVINCE.

That portion of the southwestern plateau country comprised in the Province of Tusayan has usually been approached from the east, so that the easternmost of the series of mesas upon which the villages are situated is called the "First Mesa." The road for 30 or 40 miles before reaching this point traverses the eastern portion of the great plateau whose broken margin, farther west, furnishes the abrupt mesa-tongues upon which the villages are built. The sandstone measures of this plateau are distinguished from many others of the southwest by their neutral colors. The vegetation consisting of a scattered growth of stunted piñon and cedar, interspersed with occasional stretches of dull-gray sage, imparts an effect of extreme monotony to the landscape. The effect is in marked contrast to the warmth and play of color frequently seen elsewhere in the plateau country.

The plateaus of Tusayan are generally diversified by canyons and buttes, whose precipitous sides break down into long ranges of rocky talus and sandy foothills. The arid character of this district is especially pronounced about the margin of the plateau. In the immediate vicinity of the villages there are large areas that do not support a blade of grass, where barren rocks outcrop through drifts of sand or lie piled in confusion at the bases of the cliffs. The canyons that break through the margins of these mesas often have a remarkable similarity of appearance, and the consequent monotony is extremely embarrassing to the traveler, the absence of running water and clearly defined drainage confusing his sense of direction.

The occasional springs which furnish scanty water supply to the inhabitants of this region are found generally at great distances apart, and there are usually but few natural indications of their location. They often occur in obscure nooks in the canyons, reached by tortuous trails winding through the talus and foothills, or as small seeps at the foot of some mesa. The convergence of numerous Navajo trails, however, furnishes some guide to these rare water sources.

The series of promontories upon which the Tusayan villages are built are exceptionally rich in these seeps and springs. About the base of the " First Mesa" (Fig. 1), within a distance of 4 or 5 miles from the villages located upon it, there are at least five places where water can be obtained. One of these is a mere surface reservoir, but the others appear to be permanent springs. The quantity of water, however, is so small that it produces no impression on the arid and sterile effect of the surroundings, except in its immediate vicinity. Here small patches of green, standing out in strong relief against their sandy back-grounds, mark the position of clusters of low, stunted peach trees that have obtained a foothold on the steep sand dunes.

Fig. 1. View of the First Mesa.

In the open plains surrounding the mesa rim (6,000 feet above the sea), are seen broad stretches of dusty sage brush and prickly greasewood. Where the plain rises toward the base of the mesa a scattered growth of scrub cedar and piñon begins to appear. But little of this latter growth is seen in the immediate vicinity of the villages; it is, however, the characteristic vegetation of the mesas, while, in still higher altitudes, toward the San Juan, open forests of timber are met with. This latter country seems scarcely to have come within the ancient builder's province; possibly on account of its coldness in winter and for the reason that it is open to the incursions of warlike hunting tribes. Sage brush and greasewood grow abundantly near the villages, and these curious gnarled and twisted shrubs furnish the principal fuel of the Tusayan.

Occasionally grassy levels are seen that for a few weeks in early summer are richly carpeted with multitudes of delicate wild flowers. The beauty of these patches of gleaming color is enhanced by contrast with the forbidding and rugged character of the surroundings; but in a very short time these blossoms disappear from the arid and parched desert that they have temporarily beautified.   These beds of bloom are not seen in the immediate vicinity of the present villages, but are unexpectedly met with in portions of the neighboring mesas and canyons.

After crossing the 6 or 7 miles of comparatively level country that intervenes between the mouth of Keam's Canyon and the first of the occupied mesas, the toilsome ascent begins; at first through slopes and dunes and then over masses of broken talus, as the summit of the mesa is gradually approached.   Near the top the road is flanked on one side by a very abrupt descent of broken slopes, and on the other by a precipitous rocky wall that rises 30 or 40 feet above.   The road reaches the brink of the promontory by a sharp rise at a point close to the village of Hano.

### METHODS OF SURVEY.

Before entering upon a description of the villages and ruins, a few words as to the preparation of the plans accompanying this paper will not be amiss.   The methods pursued in making the surveys of the inhabited pueblos were essentially the same throughout.   The outer wall of each separate cluster was run with a compass and a tape measure, the lines being closed and checked upon the corner from which the beginning was made, so that the plan of each group stands alone, and no accumulation of error is possible.   The stretched tapeline afforded a basis for estimating any deviations from a straight line which the wall presented, and as each sight was plotted on the spot these deviations are all recorded on the plan, and afford an indication of the degree of accuracy with which the building was carried out.   Upon the basis thus obtained, the outlines of the second stories were drawn by the aid of measurements from the numerous jogs and angles; the same process being repeated for each of the succeeding stories.   The plan at this stage recorded all the stories in outline.   The various houses and clusters were connected by compass sights and by measurements.   A tracing of the outline plan was then made, on which the stories were distinguished by lines of different colors, and upon this tracing were recorded all the vertical measurements.   These were generally taken at every corner, although in a long wall it was customary to make additional measurements at intervening points.

Upon the original outline were then drawn all such details as coping stones, chimneys, trapdoors, etc., the tapeline being used where necessary to establish positions.   The forms of the chimneys as well as their position and size were also indicated on this drawing, which was finally tinted to distinguish the different terraces.   Upon this colored sheet were located all openings.   These were numbered, and at the same time described in a notebook, in which were also recorded the necessary vertical measurements, such as their height and elevation above the ground.   In the same notebook the openings were also fully described. The ladders were located upon the same sheet, and were consecutively lettered and described in the notebook. This description furnishes a record of the ladder, its projection above the coping, if any, the difference in the length of its poles, the character of the tiepiece, etc. Altogether these notebooks furnish a mass of statistical data which has been of great service in the elaboration of this report and in the preparation of models. Finally, a level was carried over the whole village, and the height of each corner and jog above an assumed base was determined. A reduced tracing was then made of the plan as a basis for sketching in such details of topography, etc., as it was thought advisable to preserve.

These plans were primarily intended to be used in the construction of large scale models, and consequently recorded an amount of information that could not be reproduced upon the published drawings without causing great confusion.

The methods followed in surveying the ruins underwent some changes from time to time as the work progressed. In the earlier work the lines of the walls, so far as they could be determined, were run with a compass and tapeline and gone over with a level. Later it was found more convenient to select a number of stations and connect them by crosssights and measurements. These points were then platted, and the walls and lines of débris were carefully drawn in over the framework of lines thus obtained, additional measurements being taken when necessary. The heights of standing walls were measured from both sides, and openings were located on the plan and described in a notebook, as was done in the survey of the inhabited villages. The entire site was then leveled, and from the data obtained contour lines were drawn with a 5-foot interval. Irregularities in the directions of walls were noted. In the later plans of ruins a scale of symbols, seven in number, were employed to indicate the amount and distribution of the débris. The plans, as published, indicate the relative amounts of débris as seen upon the ground. Probable lines of wall are shown on the plan by dotted lines drawn through the dots which indicate débris. With this exception, the plans show the ruins as they actually are. Standing walls, as a rule, are drawn in solid black; their heights appear on the field sheets, but could not be shown upon the published plans without confusing the drawing. The contour lines represent an interval of 5 feet; the few cases in which the secondary or negative contours are used will not produce confusion, as their altitude is always given in figures.

PLANS AND DESCRIPTIONS OF RUINS.

The ruins described in this chapter comprise but a few of those found within the province of Tusayan. These were surveyed and recorded on account of their close traditional connection with the present villages, and for the sake of the light that they might throw upon the relation of the modern pueblos to the innumerable stone buildings of unknown date so widely distributed over the southwestern plateau country. Such traditional connection with the present peoples could probably be established for many more of the ruins of this country by investigations similar to those conducted by Mr. Stephen in the Tusayan group; but this phase of the subject was not included in our work. In the search for purely architectural evidence among these ruins it must be confessed that the data have proved disappointingly meager. No trace of the numerous constructive details that interest the student of pueblo architecture in the modern villages can be seen in the low mounds of broken down masonry that remain in most of the ancient villages of Tusayan. But little masonry remains standing in even the best preserved of these ruins, and villages known to have been occupied within two centuries are not distinguishable from the remains to which distinct tradition (save that they were in the same condition when the first people of the narrators' gens came to this region) no longer clings. Though but little architectural information is to be derived from these ruins beyond such as is conveyed by the condition and character of the masonry and the general distribution of the plan, the plans and relation to the topography are recorded as forming, in connection with the traditions, a more complete account than can perhaps be obtained later.

In our study of architectural details, when a comparison is suggested between the practice at Tusayan and that of the ancient builders, our illustrations for the latter must often be drawn from other portions of the builders' territory where better preserved remains furnish the necessary data.

### WALPI RUINS.

In the case of the pueblo of Walpi, a portion of whose people seem to have been the first comers in this region, a number of changes of sites have taken place, at least one of which has occurred within the historic period. Of the various sites occupied one is pointed out north of the gap on the first mesa. At the present time this site is only a low mound of sand-covered débris with no standing fragment of wall visible. The present condition of this early Walpi is illustrated in Fig. 2. In the absence of foundation walls or other definite lines, the character of the site is expressed by the contour lines that define its relief. Another of the sites occupied by the Walpi is said to have been in the open valley separating the first from the second mesa, but here no trace of the remains of a stone village has been discovered. This traditional location is referred to by Mr. Stephen in his account of Walpi. The last site occupied previous to the present one on the mesa summit was on a lower bench of the first mesa promontory at its southern extremity. Here the houses are said to have been distributed over quite a large area, and occasional fragments of masonry are still seen at widely separated points; but the ground plan can not now be traced. This was the site of a Spanish mission, and some of the Tusayan point out the position formerly occupied by mission buildings, but no architectural evidence of such structures is visible. It seems to be fairly certain, however, that this was the site of Walpi at a date well within the historic period, although now literally there is not one stone upon another. The destruction in this instance has probably been more than usually complete on account of the close proximity of the succeeding pueblo, making the older remains a very convenient stone quarry for the construction of the houses on the mesa summit. Of the three abandoned sites of Walpi referred to, not one furnishes sufficient data for a suggestion of a ground plan or of the area covered.

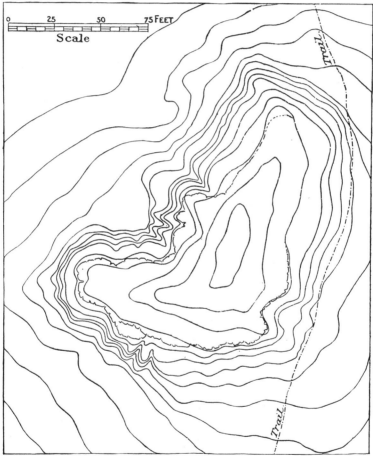

FIG. 2. Ruins, Old Walpi mound.

OLD MASHONGNAVI.

In the case of Mashongnavi we have somewhat more abundant material. It will be desirable to quote a few lines of narrative from the account of a Mashongnavi Indian of the name of Nuvayauma, as indicating the causes that led to the occupation of the site illustrated.

We turned and came to the north, meeting the Apache and "Beaver Indians," with whom we had many battles, and being few we were defeated, after which we came up to Mashongnavi [the ruin at the "Giant's Chair"] and gave that rock its name [name not known], and built our houses there. The Apache came upon us again, with the Comanche, and then we came to [Old Mashóngnavi]. We lived there in peace many years, having great success with crops, and our people increased in numbers, and the Apache came in great numbers and set fire to the houses and burned our corn, which you will find to-day there burnt and charred. After they had destroyed our dwellings we came upon the mesa, and have lived here since.

The ruins referred to as having been the first occupied by the Mashongnavi at a large isolated rock known as the "Giant's Chair," have not been examined. The later village from which they were driven by the attacks of the Apache to their present site has been surveyed. The plan of the fallen walls and lines of débris by which the form of much of the old pueblo can still be traced is given in Pl. II. The plan of the best preserved portion of the pueblo towards the north end of the sheet clearly indicates a general adherence to the inclosed court arrangement with about the same degree of irregularity that characterizes the modern village. Besides the clearly traceable portions of the ruin that bear such resemblance to the present village in arrangement, several small groups and clusters appear to have been scattered along the slope of the foothills, but in their present state of destruction it is not clear whether these clusters were directly connected with the principal group, or formed part of another village. Occasional traces of foundation walls strongly suggest such connection, although from the character of the site this intervening space could hardly have been closely built over. With the exception of the main cluster above described the houses occupy very broken and irregular sites. As indicated on the plan, the slope is broken by huge irregular masses of sandstone protruding from the soil, while much of the surface is covered by scattered fragments that have fallen from neighboring pinnacles and ledges. The contours indicate the general character of the slopes over which these irregular features are disposed. The fragment of ledge shown on the north end of the plate, against which a part of the main cluster has been built, is a portion of a broad massive ledge of sandstone that supports the low buttes upon which the present villages of Mashongnavi and Shupaúlovi are built, and continues as a broad, level shelf of solid rock for several miles along the mesa promontory. Its continuation on the side opposite that shown in the plate may be seen in the general view of Shupaulovi (Pl. XXXI).

### SHITAIMUVI.

The vestiges of another ruined village, known as Shitaimuvi, are found in the vicinity of Mashongnavi, occupying and covering the crown of a rounded foothill on the southeast side of the mesa. No plan of this ruin could be obtained on account of the complete destruction of the walls. No line of foundation stones even could be found, although the whole area is more or less covered with the scattered stones of former masonry. An exceptional quantity of pottery fragments is also strewn

over the surface.  These bear a close resemblance to the fine class of
ware characteristic of "Talla Hogan" or "Awatubi," and would suggest that this pueblo was contemporaneous with the latter.  Some
reference to this ruin will be found in the traditionary material in
Chapter I.

AWATUBI.

The ruin of Awatubi is known to the Navajo as Talla Hogan, a term
interpreted as meaning "singing house" and thought to refer to the
chapel and mission that at one time flourished here, as described by
Mr. Stephen in Chapter I.  Tradition ascribes great importance to this
village.  At the time of the Spanish conquest it was one of the most
prosperous of the seven "cities" of Tusayan, and was selected as the
site of a mission, a distinction shared by Walpi, which was then on a
lower spur of the first mesa, and by Shumopavi, which also was built
on a lower site than the present village of that name.  Traditions referring to this pueblo have been collected from several sources and,
while varying somewhat in less important details, they all concur in
bringing the destruction of the village well within the period of Spanish
occupation.

On the historical site, too, we know that Cruzate on the occasion of
the attempted reconquest of the country visited this village in 1692,
and the ruin must therefore be less than two centuries old, yet the completeness of destruction is such that over most of its area no standing
wall is seen, and the outlines of the houses and groups are indicated
mainly by low ridges and masses of broken-down masonry, partly covered by the drifting sands.  The group of rooms that forms the south
east side of the pueblo is an exception to the general rule.  Here fragmentary walls of rough masonry stand to a height, in some cases, of 8
feet above the débris.  The character of the stonework, as may be seen
from Pl. V, is but little better than that of the modern villages.  This
better preserved portion of the village seems to have formed part of a
cluster of mission buildings.  At the points designated A on the
ground plan may be seen the remnants of walls that have been built of
straw adobe in the typical Spanish manner.  These rest upon foundations of stone masonry.  See Pl. VI.  The adobe fragments are probably part of the church or associated buildings.  At two other points on
the ground plan, both on the northeast side, low fragments of wall are
still standing, as may be seen from the plate.  At one of these points
the remains indicate that the village was provided with a gateway near
the middle of the northeast side.

The general plan of this pueblo is quite different from that of the present villages, and approaches the older types in symmetry and compact-
ness.  There is a notable absence of the arrangement of rooms into long
parallel rows.  This typical Tusayan feature is only slightly approximated in some subordinate rows within the court.  The plan suggests
that the original pueblo was built about three sides of a rectangular

court, the fourth or southeast side—later occupied by the mission build-ings—being left open, or protected only by a low wall. Outside the rectangle of the main pueblo, on the northeast side, are two fragments of rude masonry, built by Navajo sheep herders. Near the west corner of the pueblo are the vestiges of two rooms, outside the pueblo proper, which seem to belong to the original construction.

Awatubi is said to have had excavated rectangular kivas, situated in the open court, similar to those used in the modern village. The peo-ple of Walpi had partly cleared out one of these chambers and used it as a depository for ceremonial plume-sticks, etc., but the Navajo came and carried off their sacred deposits, tempted probably by their market value as ethnologic specimens. No trace of these kivas was visible at the time the ruins were surveyed.

The Awatubi are said to have had sheep at the time the village was destroyed. Some of the Tusayan point out the remains of a large sheep corral near the spring, which they say was used at that time, but it is quite as likely to have been constructed for that purpose at a much later date.

#### HORN HOUSE.

The Horn House is so called because tradition connects this village with some of the people of the Horn phratry of the Hopituh or Tusayan. The ruin is situated on a projecting point of the mesa that forms the western flank of Jeditoh Valley, not far from where the Holbrook road to Keam's Canyon ascends the brink of the mesa. The village is almost completely demolished, no fragment of standing wall remaining in place. Its general plan and distribution are quite clearly indicated by the usual low ridges of fallen masonry partly covered by drifted sand. There is but little loose stone scattered about, the sand having filled in all the smaller irregularities.

It will be seen from the plan, Pl. VII, that the village has been built close to the edge of the mesa, following to some extent the irregularities of its outline. The mesa ruin at this point, however, is not very high, the more abrupt portion having a height of 20 or 30 feet. Near the north end of the village the ground slopes very sharply toward the east and is rather thickly covered with the small stones of fallen masonry, though but faint vestiges of rooms remain. In plan the ruin is quite elongated, following the direction of the mesa. The houses were quite irregularly disposed, particularly in the northern portion of the ruin. But here the indications are too vague to determine whether the houses were originally built about one long court or about two or more smaller ones. The south end of the pueblo, however, still shows a well defined court bounded on all sides by clearly traceable rooms. At the extreme south end of the ruin the houses have very irregular outlines, a result of their adaptation to the topography, as may be seen in the illustration.

The plan shows the position of a small group of cottonwood trees, just below the edge of the mesa and nearly opposite the center of the village. These trees indicate the proximity of water, and mark the probable site of the spring that furnished this village with at least part of its water supply.

There are many fragments of pottery on this spot, but they are not so abundant as at Awatubi.

Two partly excavated rooms were seen at this ruin, the work of some earlier visitors who hoped to discover ethnologic or other treasure.

These afforded no special information, as the character of the masonry exposed differed in no respect from that seen at other of the Tusayan ruins. No traces of adobe construction or suggestions of foreign influence were seen at this ruin.

### SMALL RUIN BETWEEN HORN HOUSE AND BAT HOUSE.

On a prolongation of the mesa occupied by the Horn House, midway between it and another ruined pueblo known as the Bat House, occur the remains of a small and compact cluster of houses (Fig. 3). It is situated on the very mesa edge, here about 40 feet high, at the head of a small canyon which opens into the Jeditoh Valley, a quarter of a mile below.

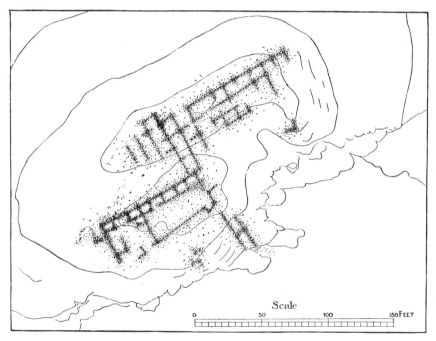

Scale

0　　　　　　50　　　　　　100　　　　　150 FEET

FIG. 3. Ruin between Bat House and Horn House.

The site affords an extended outlook to the south over a large part of Jeditoh Valley. The topography about this point, which receives the drainage of a considerable area of the mesa top, would fit it especially for the establishment of a reservoir. This fact probably had much to do with its selection as a dwelling site. The masonry is in about the same state of preservation as that of the Horn House, and some of the stones of the fallen walls seem to have been washed down from the mesa edge to the talus below.

BAT HOUSE.

The Bat House is a ruin of nearly the same size as the Horn House, although in its distribution it does not follow the mesa edge so closely as the latter, and is not so elongated in its general form. The northern portion is quite irregular, and the rooms seem to have been somewhat crowded. The southern half, with only an occasional room traceable, as indicated on the plan, Pl. VIII, still shows that the rooms were distributed about a large open court.

The Bat House is situated on the northwest side of the Jeditoh Valley, on part of the same mesa occupied by the two ruins described above. It occupies the summit of a projecting spur, overlooking the main valley for an extent of more than 5 miles. The ruin lies on the extreme edge of the cliff, here about 200 feet high, and lying beneath it on the east and south are large areas of arable land. Altogether it forms an excellent defensive site, combined with a fair degree of convenience to fields and water from the Tusayan point of view.

This ruin, near its northeastern extremity, contains a feature that is quite foreign to the architecture of Tusayan, viz, a defensive wall. It is the only instance of the use by the Hopituh of an inclosing wall, though it is met with again at Payupki (Pl. XIII), which, however, was built by people from the Rio Grande country.

MISHIPTONGA.

Mishiptonga is the Tusayan name for the southernmost, and by far the largest, of the Jeditoh series of ruins (Pl. IX). It occurs quite close to the Jeditoh spring which gives its name to the valley along whose northern and western border are distributed the ruins above described, beginning with the Horn house.

This village is rather more irregular in its arrangement than any other of the series. There are indications of a number of courts inclosed by large and small clusters of rooms, very irregularly disposed, but with a general trend towards the northeast, being roughly parallel with the mesa edge. In plan this village approaches somewhat that of the inhabited Tusayan villages. At the extreme southern extremity of the mesa promontory is a small secondary bench, 20 feet lower than the site of the main village. This bench has also been occupied by a number of houses. On the east side the pueblo was built to the very edge of the bluff, where small fragments of masonry are still standing. The whole village seems so irregular and crowded in its arrangement that it suggests a long period of occupancy and growth, much more than do the other villages of this (Jeditoh) group.

The pueblo may have been abandoned or destroyed prior to the advent of the Spaniards in this country, as claimed by the Indians, for no traditional mention of it is made in connection with the later feuds and wars that figure so prominently in the Tusayan oral history of the last three centuries. The pueblo was undoubtedly built by some of the ancient gentes of the Tusayan stock, as its plan, the character of the site chosen, and, where traceable, the quality of workmanship link it with the other villages of the Jeditoh group.

### MOEN-KOPI RUINS.

A very small group of rooms, even smaller than the neighboring farming pueblo of Moen-kopi, is situated on the western edge of the mesa summit about a quarter of a mile north of the modern village of Moen-kopi. As the plan shows (Fig. 4), the rooms were distributed in

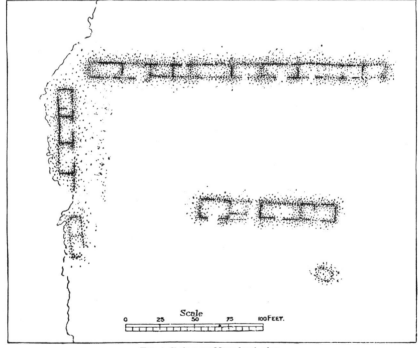

FIG. 4. Ruin near Moen-kopi, plan.

three rows around a small court. This ruin also follows the general northeastern trend which has been noticed both in the ruined and in the occupied pueblos of Tusayan. The rows here were only one room deep and not more than a single story high at any point, as indicated by the very small amount of débris. As the plate shows, nearly the entire plan is clearly defined by fragments of standing walls. The walls are built of thin tablets of the dark-colored sandstone which caps the mesa. Where the walls have fallen the débris is comparatively free from earth, indicating that adobe has been sparingly used. The walls, in places standing to a height of 2 or 3 feet, as may be seen in the illustration, Pl. x, show unusual precision of workmanship and finish, resembling in this respect some of the ancient pueblos farther north. This is to some extent due to the exceptional suitability of the tabular stones of the mesa summit. The almost entire absence of pottery fragments and other objects of art which are such a constant accompaniment of the ruins throughout this region strongly suggest that it was occupied for a very short time. In Chapter III it will be shown that a similar order of occupation took place at Ojo Caliente, one of the Zuñi farming villages. This ruin is probably of quite recent origin, as is the present village of Moen-kopi, although it may possibly have belonged to an earlier colony of which we have no distinct trace. This fertile and well watered valley, a veritable garden spot in the Tusayan deserts, must have been one of the first points occupied. Some small cliff-dwellings, single rooms in niches of a neighboring canyon wall, attest the earlier use of the valley for agricultural purposes, although it is doubtful whether these rude shelters date back of the Spanish invasion of the province.

A close scrutiny of the many favorable sites in this vicinity would probably reveal the sand-encumbered remains of some more important settlement than any of those now known.

RUINS ON THE ORAIBI WASH.

The wagon road from Keam's Canyon to Tuba City crosses the Oraibi wash at a point about 7 miles above the village of Oraibi. As it enters a branch canyon on the west side of the wash it is flanked on each side by rocky mesas and broken ledges. On the left or west side a bold promontory, extending southward, is quite a conspicuous feature of the landscape. The entire flat mesa summit, and much of the slope of a rocky butte that rises from it, are covered with the remains of a small pueblo, as shown on the plan, Fig. 5. All of this knoll except its eastern side is lightly covered with scattered débris. On the west and north sides there are many large masses of broken rock distributed over the slope. There is no standing wall visible from below, but on closer approach several interesting specimens of masonry are seen. On the north side, near the west end, there is a fragment of curved wall which follows the margin of the rock on which it is built. It is about 8 or 10 feet long and 3 feet high on the outer side. The curve is carefully executed and the workmanship of the masonry good. Farther east, and still on the north side, there is a fragment of masonry exhibiting a reversed curve. This piece of wall spans the space between two adjoining rocks, and the top of the wall is more than 10 feet above the rock on which it stands. The shape of this wall and its relation to the surroundings are indicated on the plan, Fig. 5. On the south side of the ruin on the mesa surface, and near an outcropping rock, are the re-

FOOT TRAIL TO WALPI.

MASHONGNAVI.

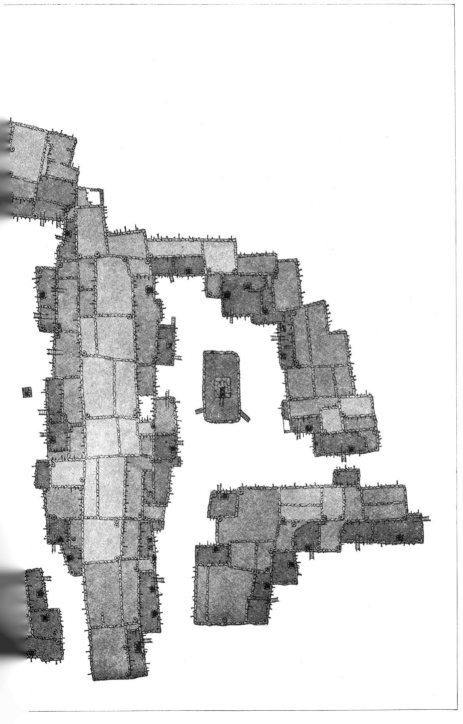

MASHONGNAVI, WITH SHUPAULOVI IN DISTANCE.

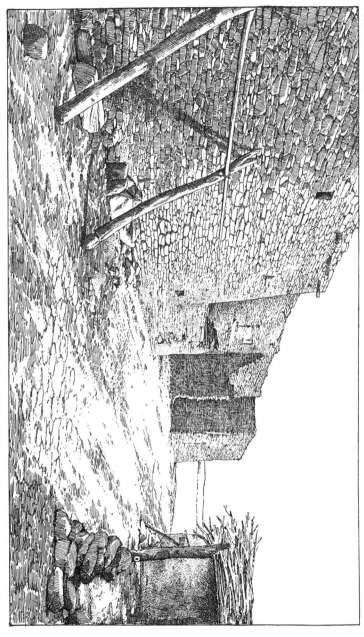

BACK WALL OF A MASHONGNAVI HOUSE ROW.

WEST SIDE OF A PRINCIPAL ROW IN MASHONGNAVI.

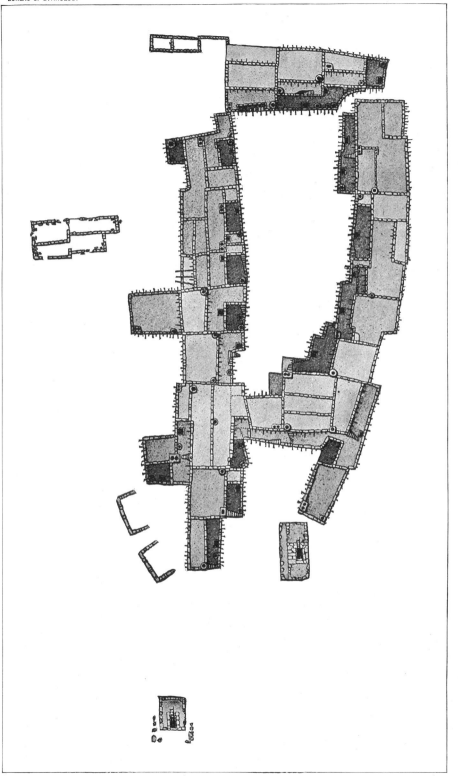

SHUPAULOVI.

SHUPAULOVI.

A COVERED PASSAGEWAY OF SHUPAULOVI.

H.Hobart Nichols, 90.

THE CHIEF KIVA OF SHUPAULOVI.

SHUMOPAVI.

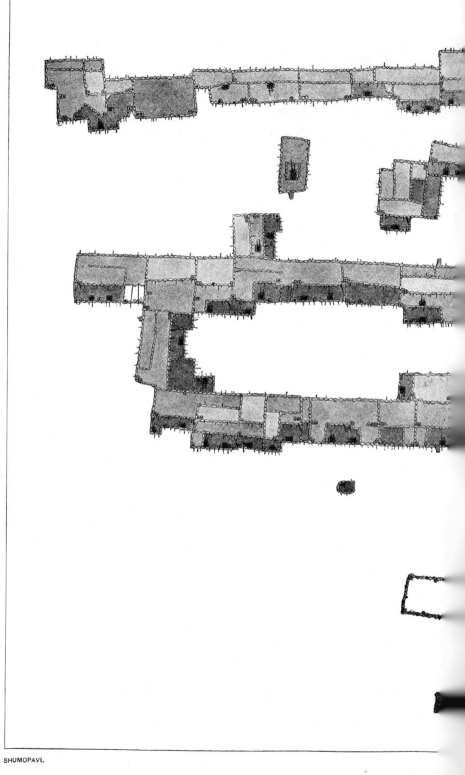

SHUMOPAVI.

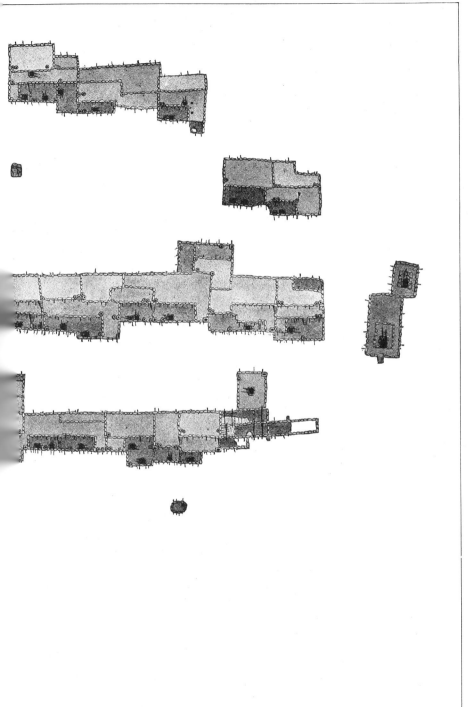

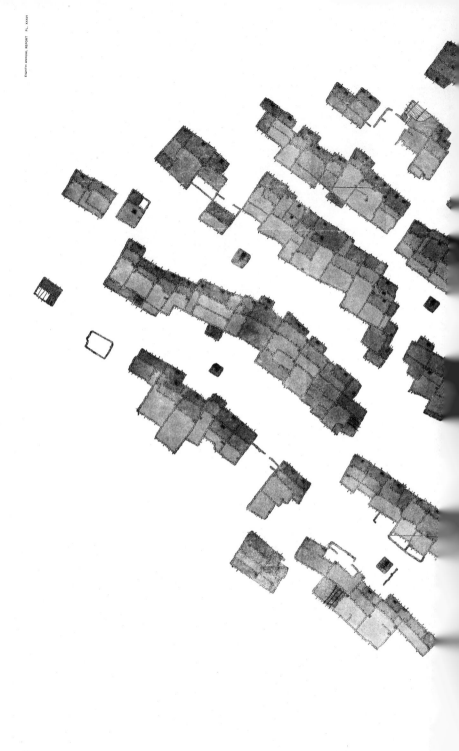

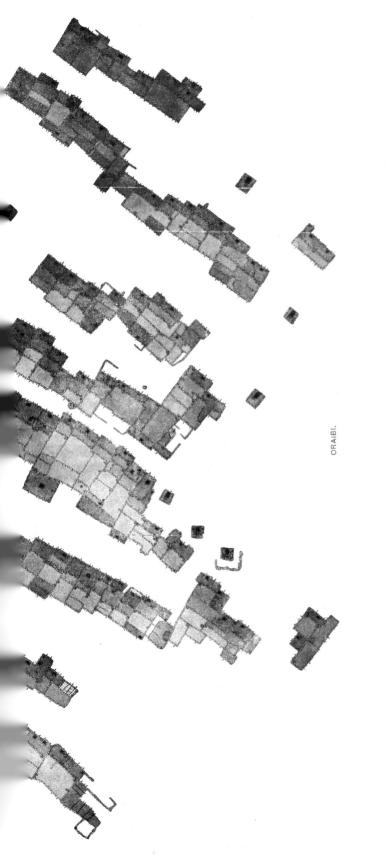

ORAIBI.

KEY TO ORAIBI PLAN, ALSO SHOWING LOCALIZATION OF GENTES.

mains of what appears to have been a circular room, perhaps 8 or 10 feet in diameter, though it is too much broken down to determine this accurately. Only a small portion of the south wall can be definitely traced. On the south slope of the mesa are indications of walls, too vaguely defined to admit of the determination of their direction. Similar vestiges of masonry are found on the north and west, but not extending to as great a distance from the knoll as those on the south.

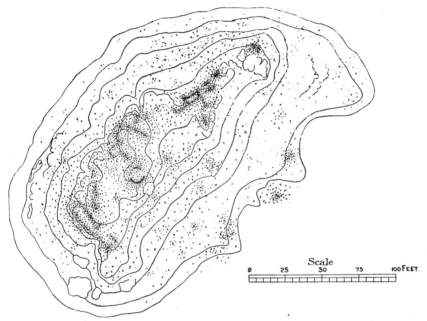

Fig. 5. Ruin 7 miles north of Oraibi.

In that portion of the ruin which lies on top of the knoll, the walls so far as traced conform to the shape of the site. The ground plan of the buildings that once occupied the slopes can not be traced, and it is impossible to determine whether its walls were carried through continuously.

The masonry exhibited in the few surviving fragments of wall is of unusually good quality, resembling somewhat that of the Fire House, Fig. 7, and other ruins of that class. The stones are of medium size, not dressed, and are rather rougher and less flat than is usual, but the wall has a good finish. The stone, however, is of poor quality. Most of the débris about the ruin consists of small stone fragments and sand, comparatively few stones of the size used in the walls being seen. The material evidently came from the immediate vicinity of the ruin.

Pottery fragments were quite abundant about this ruin, most of the ware represented being of exceptional quality and belonging to the older types; red ware with black lines and black and white ware were especially abundant.

There is quite an extensive view from the ruin, the top of the butte commanding an outlook down the valley past Oraibi, and about 5 miles north. There is also an extended outlook up the valley followed by the wagon road above referred to, and over two branch valleys, one on the east and another of much less extent on the west. The site was well adapted for defense, which must have been one of the principal motives for its selection.

KWAITUKI.

The ruin known to the Tusayan as Kwaituki (Fig. 6) is also on the west side of the Oraibi wash, 14 miles above Oraibi, and about 7 miles above the ruin last described. Its general resemblance to the latter is very striking. The builders have apparently been actuated by

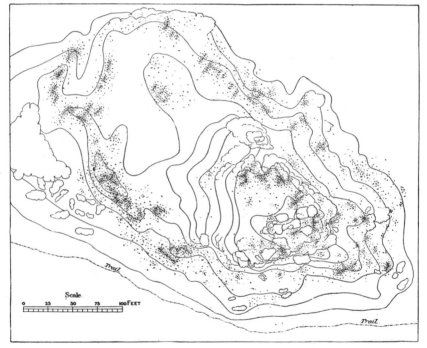

FIG. 6. Ruin 14 miles north of Oraibi (Kwaituki).

the same motives in their choice of a site, and their manner of utilizing it corresponds very closely. The crowning feature of the rocky knoll in this case is a picturesque group of rectangular masses of sandstone, somewhat irregularly distributed. The bare summit of a large block-like mass still retains the vestiges of rooms, and probably most of the groups were at one time covered with buildings, forming a prominent citadel-like group in the midst of the village. To the north of this rocky butte a large area seems to have been at one time inclosed by buildings, form-ing a court of unusual dimensions. Along the outer margin of the pueblo occasional fragments of walls define former rooms, but the amount and character of the débris indicate that the inner area was almost completely inclosed with buildings. The remains of masonry extend on the south a little beyond the base of the central group of rocks, but here the vestiges of stonework are rather faint and scattered.

In the nearly level tops of some of the rocks forming the central pile are many smoothly worn depressions or cavities, which have evidently been used for the grinding and shaping of stone implements.

A remarkable feature occurring within this village is a cave or underground fissure in the rocks, which evidently had been used by the inhabitants. The mouth or entrance to this cavern, partly obstructed and concealed at the time of our visit, occurs at the point A on the plan. On clearing away the rubbish at the mouth and entering it was found so obstructed with broken rock and fine dust that but little progress could be made in its exploration; but the main crevice in the rock could be seen by artificial light to extend some 10 feet back from the mouth, where it became very shallow. It could be seen that the original cavern had been improved by the pueblo-builders, as some of the timbers that had been placed inside were still in position, and a low wall of masonry on the south side remained intact. Some Navajos stated that they had discovered this small cave a couple of years before and had taken from it a large unbroken water jar of ancient pottery and some other specimens. The place was probably used by the ancient occupants simply for storage.

Fragments of pottery of excellent quality were very abundant about this ruin and at the foot of the central rocks the ground was thickly strewn with fragments, often of large size.

The defensive character of this site parallels that of the ruin 7 miles farther south in quite a remarkable manner, and the villages were apparently built and occupied at the same time.

### TEBUGKIHU, OR FIRE HOUSE.

About 15 miles northeast of Keam's Canyon, and about 25 miles from Walpi, is a small ruin called by the Tusayan " Tebugkihu," built by people of the Fire gens (now extinct). As the plan (Fig. 7) clearly shows, this pueblo is very different from the typical Tusayan villages that have been previously described. The apparent unity of the plan, and the skillful workmanship somewhat resembling the pueblos of the Chaco are in marked contrast to the irregularity and careless construction of most of the Tusayan ruins. Its distance from the center of the province, too, suggests outside relationship; but still the Tusayan traditions undoubtedly connect the place with some of the ancestral gentes, as seen in Chapter I.

The small and compact cluster of rooms is in a remarkable state of preservation, especially the outside wall. This wall was carefully and massively constructed, and stands to the height of several feet around the entire circumference of the ruin, except along the brink of the cliff, as the plan shows.

This outer wall contains by far the largest stones yet found incorporated in pueblo masonry. A fragment of this masonry is illustrated in Pl. XI. The largest stone shown measures about 5 feet in length, and the one adjoining on the right measures about 4 feet. These dimensions are quite remarkable in pueblo masonry, which is distinguished by the use of very small stones.

The well defined outer wall of this cluster to the unaided eye appears to be elliptical, but it will be seen from the plan that the ellipse is somewhat pointed on the side farthest from the cliff. As in other cases of ancient pueblos with curved outlines, the outer wall seems to have been built first, and the inner rooms, while kept as rectangular as possible, were adjusted to this curve. This arrangement often led to a cumulating divergence from radial lines in some of the partitions, which irregularity was taken up in one room, as in this instance, in the space near the gate. The outer wall is uniform in construction so far as preserved. Many irregularities appear, however, in the construction of the inner or partition walls, and some of the rooms show awkward attempts at adjustment to the curve of the outer wall.

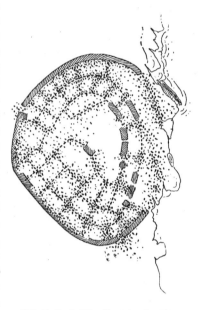

FIG. 7. Oval (Fire House) ruin, plan (Tebugkihu).

The ruin is situated on the very brink of a small canyon, which probably contained a spring at the foot of the cliff close under the ruin site, as the vegetation there has an unusual appearance of freshness, suggesting the close proximity of water to the surface. A steep trail evidently connected the village with the bottom of the canyon. Some of the rocks of the mesa rim were marked by numerous cup-like cavities similar to those seen at Kwaituki, and used in the polishing and forming of stone implements. The type of pueblo here illustrated belonged to a people who relied largely on the architecture for defense, differing in this respect from the spirit of Tusayan architecture generally, where the inaccessible character of the site was the chief dependence.

### CHUKUBI.

The ruin called Chukubi by the Tusayan (Pl. XII) is situated on the Middle Mesa, about 3 miles northeast of Mashongnavi. It occupies a promontory above the same broad sandstone ledge that forms such a conspicuous feature in the vicinity of Mashongnavi and Shupaulovi, and which supports the buttes upon which these villages are built.

Little masonry now remains on this site, but here and there a fragment aids in defining the general plan of the pueblo. In general form the village was a large rectangle with a line of buildings across its center, dividing it into two unequal courts, and a projecting wing on the west side. As may be seen from the illustration, one end of the ruin forms a clearly defined rectangular court, composed of buildings mostly two rooms deep. Here, as in other ruins of Tusayan, the arrangement about inclosed courts is in contrast with the parallelism of rows, so noticeable a feature in the occupied villages. At the east end of the ruin are several curious excavations. The soft sandstone has been hollowed out to a depth of about 10 inches, in prolongation of the outlines of adjoining rooms. Such excavation to obtain level floors is quite unusual among the pueblo builders; it was practiced to a very small extent, and only where it could be done with little trouble. Any serious inequality of surface was usually incorporated in the construction, as will be noticed at Walpi (Pl. XXIII). Vestiges of masonry indicating detached rooms were seen in each of the courts of the main rectangle.

On the slope of the hill, just above the broad ledge previously described, there is a fine spring, but no trace of a trail connecting it with the pueblo could be found.

This village was advantageously placed for defense, but not to the same degree as Payupki, illustrated in Pl. XIII.

PAYUPKI.

The ruin called Payupki (Pl. XIII) occupies the summit of a bold promontory south of the trail, from Walpi to Oraibi, and about 6 miles northwest from Mashongnavi. The outer extremity of this promontory is separated from the mesa by a deep notch. The summit is reached from the mesa by way of the neck, as the outer point itself is very abrupt, much of the sandstone ledge being vertical. A bench, 12 or 15 feet below the summit and in places quite broad, encircles the promontory. This bench also breaks off very abruptly.

As may be seen from the plan, the village is quite symmetrically laid out and well arranged for defense. It is placed at the mesa end of the promontory cap, and for greater security the second ledge has also been fortified. All along the outer margin of this ledge are the remains of a stone wall, in some places still standing to a height of 1 or 2 feet. This wall appears to have extended originally all along the ledge around three sides of the village. The steepness of the cliff on the remaining side rendered a wall superfluous. On the plain below this promontory, and immediately under the overhanging cliff, are two corrals, and also the remains of a structure that resembles a kiva, but which appears to be of recent construction.

In the village proper (Pl. XIV) are two distinctly traceable kivas. One of these, situated in the court, is detached and appears to have been partly underground. The other, located in the southeast end of the village, has also, like the first, apparently been sunk slightly below the surface. There is a jog in the standing wall of this kiva which corresponds to that usually found in the typical Tusayan kivas (see Figs. 22 and 25). On the promontory and east of the village is a single room of more than average length, with a well formed door in the center of one side. This room has every appearance of being contemporary with the rest of the village, but its occurrence in this entirely isolated position is very unusual. Still farther east there is a mass of débris that may have belonged to a cluster of six or eight rooms, or it may possibly be the remains of temporary stone shelters for outlooks over crops, built at a later date than the pueblo. As may be seen from the illustration (Pl. XV), the walls are roughly built of large slabs of sandstone of various sizes. The work is rather better than that of modern Tusayan, but much inferior to that seen in the skillfully laid masonry of the ruins farther north. In many of these walls an occasional sandstone slab of great length is introduced. This peculiarity is probably due to the character of the local material, which is more varied than usual. All of the stone here used is taken from ledges in the immediate vicinity. It is usually light in color and of loose texture, crumbling readily, and subject to rapid decay, particularly when used in walls that are roughly constructed.

Much of the pottery scattered about this ruin has a very modern appearance, some of it having the characteristic surface finish and color of the Rio Grande ware. A small amount of ancient pottery also occurs here, some of the fragments of black and white ware displaying intricate fret patterns. The quantity of these potsherds is quite small, and they occur mainly in the refuse heaps on the mesa edge.

This ruin combines a clearly defined defensive plan with utilization of one of the most inaccessible sites in the vicinity, producing altogether a combination that would seem to have been impregnable by any of the ordinary methods of Indian warfare.

## PLANS AND DESCRIPTIONS OF THE INHABITED VILLAGES.

### HANO.

The village of Hano, or Tewa, is intrusive and does not properly belong to the Tusayan stock, as appears from their own traditions. It is somewhat loosely planned (Pl. XVI) and extends nearly across the mesa tongue, which is here quite narrow, and in general there is no appreciable difference between the arrangement here followed and that of the other villages. One portion of the village, however, designated as House No. 5 on the plan, differs somewhat from the typical arrangement in long irregular rows, and approaches the pyramidal form found among the more eastern pueblos, notably at Taos and in portions of Zuñi. As has been seen, tradition tells us that this site was taken up by the Tewa at a late date and subsequent to the Spanish conquest; but some houses, formerly belonging to the Asa people, formed a nucleus about which the Tewa village of Hano was constructed. The pyramidal house occupied by the old governor, is said to have been built over such remains of earlier houses.

The largest building in the village appears to have been added to from time to time as necessity for additional space arose, resulting in much the same arrangement as that characterizing most of the Tusayan houses, viz, a long, irregular row, not more than three stories high at any point. The small range marked No. 4 on the plan contains a section three stories high, as does the long row and also the pyramidal cluster above referred to. (Pl. XVII.)

The kivas are two in number, one situated within the village and the other occupying a position in the margin of the mesa. These ceremonial chambers, so far as observed, appear to be much like those in the other villages, both in external and internal arrangement.

Within the last few years the horse trail that afforded access to Hano and Sichumovi has been converted into a wagon road, and during the progress of this work, under the supervision of an American, considerable blasting was done. Among other changes the marginal kiva, which was nearly in line with the proposed improvements, was removed. This was done despite the protest of the older men, and their predictions of dire calamity sure to follow such sacrilege. A new site was selected close by and the newly acquired knowledge of the use of powder was utilized in blasting out the excavation for this subterranean chamber. It is altogether probable that the sites of all former kivas were largely determined by accident, these rooms being built at points where natural fissures or open spaces in the broken mesa edge furnished a suitable depression or cavity. The builders were not capable of working the stone to any great extent, and their operations were probably limited to trimming out such natural excavations and in part lining them with masonry.

There is a very noticeable scarcity of roof-holes, aside from those of the first terrace. As a rule the first terrace has no external openings on the ground and is entered from its roof through large trap-doors, as shown on the plans. The lower rooms within this first terrace are not inhabited, but are used as storerooms.

At several points ruined walls are seen, remains of abandoned rooms that have fallen into decay. Occasionally a rough, buttress-like projection from a wall is the only vestige of a room or a cluster of rooms, all traces on the ground having been obliterated.

The mesa summit, that forms the site of this village, is nearly level, with very little earth on its surface. A thin accumulation of soil and rubbish lightly covers the inner court, but outside, along the face of the long row, the bare rock is exposed continuously. Where the rooms have been abandoned and the walls have fallen, the stones have all been utilized in later constructions, leaving no vestige of the former wall on the rocky site, as the stones of the masonry have always been set upon the surface of the rock, with no excavation or preparation of footings of any kind.

SICHUMOVI.

According to traditional accounts this village was founded at a more recent date than Walpi. It has, however, undergone many changes since its first establishment.

The principal building is a long irregular row, similiar to that of Hano (Pl. XVIII). A portion of an L-shaped cluster west of this row, and a small row near it parallel to the main building, form a rude approximation to the inclosed court arrangement. The terracing here, however, is not always on the court side, whereas in ancient examples such arrangement was an essential defensive feature, as the court furnished the only approach to upper terraces. In all of these villages there is a noticeable tendency to face the rows eastward instead of toward the court. The motive of such uniformity of direction in the houses must have been strong, to counteract the tendency to adhere to the ancient arrangement. The two kivas of the village are built side by side, in contact, probably on account of the presence at this point of a favorable fissure or depression in the mesa surface.

On the south side of the village are the remains of two small clusters of rooms that apparently have been abandoned a long time. A portion of a room still bounded by standing walls has been utilized as a corral for burros (Pl. XIX).

At this village are three small detached houses, each composed of but a single room, a feature not at all in keeping with the spirit of pueblo construction. In this instance it is probably due to the selection of the village as the residence of whites connected with the agency or school. Of these single-room houses, one, near the south end of the long row, was being built by an American, who was living in another such house near the middle of this row. The third house, although fairly well preserved at the time of the survey, was abandoned and falling into ruin. Adjoining the middle one of these three buildings on the south side are the outlines of two small compartments, which were evidently built as corrals for burros and are still used for that purpose.

This village, though limited to two stories in height, has, like the others of the first mesa, a number of roof holes or trapdoors in the upper story, an approach to the Zuñi practice. This feature among the Tusayan villages is probably due to intercourse with the more eastern pueblos, for it seems to occur chiefly among those having such communication most frequently. Its presence is probably the result simply of borrowing a convenient feature from those who invented it to meet a necessity. The conditions under which the houses were built have hardly been such as to stimulate the Tusayan to the invention of such a device. The uniform height of the second-story roofs seen in this village, constituting an almost unbroken level, is a rather exceptional feature in pueblo architecture. Only one depression occurs in the whole length of the main row.

WALPI.

Of all the pueblos, occupied or in ruins, within the provinces of Tusayan and Cibola, Walpi exhibits the widest departure from the typical pueblo arrangement (Pl. xx).

The carelessness characteristic of Tusayan architecture seems to have reached its culmination here. The confused arrangement of the rooms, mainly due to the irregularities of the site, contrasts with the work at some of the other villages, and bears no comparison with much of the ancient work. The rooms seem to have been clustered together with very little regard to symmetry, and right angles are very unusual. (See Fig. 8.)

The general plan of the village of to-day confirms the traditional accounts of its foundation. According to these its growth was gradual, beginning with a few small clusters, which were added to from time to time as the inhabitants of the lower site upon the spur of the mesa, where the mission was established, moved up and joined the pioneers on the summit. It is probable that some small rooms or clusters were built on this conspicuous promontory soon after the first occupation of this region, on account of its exceptionally favorable position as an outlook over the fields (Pl. xxi).

Though the peculiar conformation of the site on which the village has been built has produced an unusual irregularity of arrangement, yet even here an imperfect example of the typical inclosed court may be found, at one point containing the principal kiva or ceremonial chamber of the village. It is probable that the accidental occurrence of a suitable break or depression in the mesa top determined the position of this kiva at an early date and that the first buildings clustered about this point.

A unique feature in this kiva is its connection with a second subterranean chamber, reached from the kiva through an ordinary doorway. The depression used for the kiva site must have been either larger than was needed or of such form that it could not be thrown into one rectangular chamber. It was impossible to ascertain the form of this second room, as the writer was not permitted to approach the connecting doorway, which was closed with a slab of cottonwood. This chamber, used as a receptacle for religious paraphernalia, was said to connect with an upper room within the cluster of dwellings close by, but this could not be verified at the time of our visit. The plan indicates that such an adjoining chamber, if of average size, could easily extend partly under the dwellings on either the west or south side of the court. The rocky mesa summit is quite irregular in this vicinity, with rather an abrupt ascent to the passageway on the south as shown in Pl. XXII. Southeast from the kiva there is a large mass of rocks projecting above the general level, which has been incorporated into a cluster of dwelling rooms. Its character and relation to the architecture may be seen in Pl. XXIII. So irregular a site was not likely to be built upon until most of the available level surface had been taken up, for even in masonry of much higher development than can be found in Tusayan the builders, unable to overcome such obstacles as a large mass of protruding rock, have accommodated their buildings to such irregularities. This is very noticeable in the center cluster of Mummy Cave (in Canyon del Muerto, Arizona), where a large mass of sandstone, fallen from the roof of the rocky niche in which the houses were built, has been incorporated into the house cluster. Between this and another kiva to the north the mesa top is nearly level. The latter kiva is

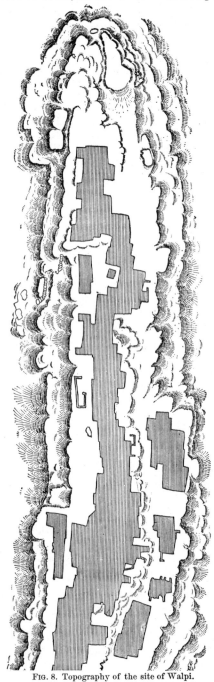

FIG. 8. Topography of the site of Walpi.

also subterranean and was built in an accidental break in sandstone. On the very margin of this fissure stands a curious isolated rock that has survived the general erosion of the mesa. It is near this rock that the celebrated Snake-dance takes place, although the kiva from which the dancers emerge to perform the open air ceremony is not adjacent to this monument (Pl. XXIV).

A short distance farther toward the north occur a group of three more kivas. These are on the very brink of the mesa, and have been built in recesses in the crowning ledge of sandstone of such size that they could conveniently be walled up on the outside, the outer surface of rude walls being continuous with the precipitous rock face of the mesa.

The positions of all these ceremonial chambers seem to correspond with exceptionally rough and broken portions of the mesa top, showing that their location in relation to the dwelling clusters was due largely to accident and does not possess the significance that position does in many ancient pueblos built on level and unencumbered sites, where the adjustment was not controlled by the character of the surface.

The Walpi promontory is so abrupt and difficult of access that there is no trail by which horses can be brought to the village without passing through Hano and Sichumovi, traversing the whole length of the mesa tongue, and crossing a rough break or depression in the mesa summit close to the village. Several foot trails give access to the village, partly over the nearly perpendicular faces of rock. All of these have required to be artificially improved in order to render them practicable. Plate XXV, from a photograph, illustrates one of these trails, which, a portion of the way, leads up between a huge detached slab of sandstone and the face of the mesa. It will be seen that the trail at this point consists to a large extent of stone steps that have been built in. At the top of the flight of steps where the trail to the mesa summit turns to the right the solid sandstone has been pecked out so as to furnish a series of footholes, or steps, with no projection or hold of any kind alongside. There are several trails on the west side of the mesa leading down both from Walpi and Sichúmovi to a spring below, which are quite as abrupt as the example illustrated. All the water used in these villages, except such as is caught during showers in the basin-like water pockets of the mesa top, is laboriously brought up these trails in large earthenware canteens slung over the backs of the women.

Supplies of every kind, provisions, harvested crops, fuel, etc., are brought up these steep trails, and often from a distance of several miles, yet these conservative people tenaciously cling to the inconvenient situation selected by their fathers long after the necessity for so doing has passed away. At present no argument of convenience or comfort seems sufficient to induce them to abandon their homes on the rocky heights and build near the water supply and the fields on which they depend for subsistence.

One of the trails referred to in the description of Hano has been converted into a wagon road, as has been already described. The Indians preferred to expend the enormous amount of labor necessary to convert this bridle path into a wagon road in order slightly to overcome the inconvenience of transporting every necessary to the mesa upon their own backs or by the assistance of burros. This concession to modern ideas is at best but a poor substitute for the convenience of homes built in the lower valleys.

MASHONGNAVI.

Mashongnavi, situated on the summit of a rocky knoll, is a compact though irregular village, and the manner in which it conforms to the

FIG. 9. Mashongnavi and Shupaulovi from Shumopavi.

general outline of the available ground is shown on the plan. Convenience of access to the fields on the east and to the other villages probably prompted the first occupation of the east end of this rocky butte (Pl. XXVI).

In Mashongnavi of to-day the eastern portion of the village forms a more decided court than do the other portions. The completeness in itself of this eastern end of the pueblo, in connection with the form of the adjoining rows, strongly suggests that this was the first portion of the pueblo built, although examination of the masonry and construction furnish but imperfect data as to the relative age of different portions of the village. One uniform gray tint, with only slight local variations in character and finish of masonry, imparts a monotonous effect of antiquity to the whole mass of dwellings. Here and there, at rare intervals, is seen a wall that has been newly plastered; but, ordinarily, masonry of 10 years' age looks nearly as old as that built 200 years earlier. Another feature that suggests the greater antiquity of the eastern court of the pueblo is the presence and manner of occurrence here of the kiva. The old builders may have been influenced to some extent in their choice of site by the presence of a favorable depression for the construction of a kiva, though this particular example of the ceremonial room is only partly subterranean. The other kivas are almost or quite below the ground level. Although a favorable depression might readily occur on the summit of the knoll, a deep cavity, suitable for the construction of the subterranean kiva, would not be likely to occur at such a distance from the margin of the sandstone ledge. The builders evidently preferred to adopt such half-way measures with their first kiva in order to

secure its inclosure within the court, thus conforming to the typical
pueblo arrangement. The numerous exceptions to this arrangement
seen in Tusayan are due to local causes. The general view of Mashong-

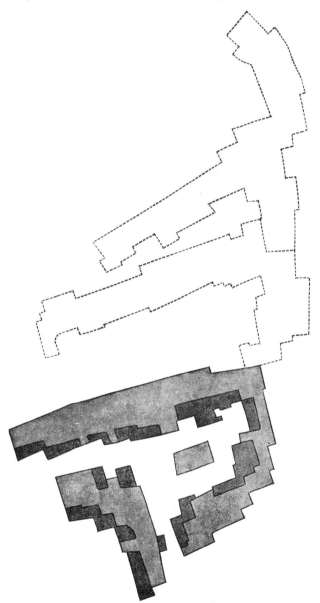

FIG. 10. Diagram showing growth of Mashongnavi.

navi given in Pl. XXVII shows that the site of this pueblo, as well as
that of its neighbor, Shupaulovi, was not particularly defensible, and
that this fact would have weight in securing adherence in the first por-

tion of the pueblo built to the defensive inclosed court containing the ceremonial chamber. The plan strongly indicates that the other courts of the pueblo were added as the village grew, each added row facing

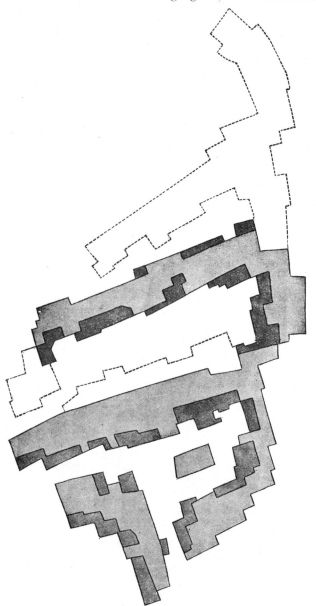

FIG. 11. Diagram showing growth of Mashongnavi.

toward the back of an older row, producing a series of courts, which, to the present time, show more terracing on their western sides. The eastern side of each court is formed, apparently, by a few additions of low rooms to what was originally an unbroken exterior wall, and which is still clearly traceable through these added rooms. Such an exterior wall is illustrated in Pl. XXVIII. This process continued until

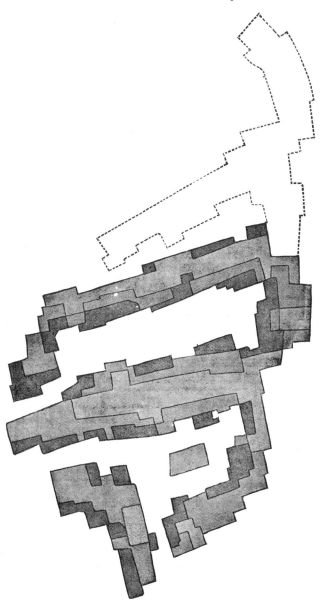

FIG. 12. Diagram showing growth of Mashongnavi.

the last cluster nearly filled the available site and a wing was thrown out corresponding to a tongue or spur of the knoll upon which it was built. Naturally the westernmost or newer portions show more clearly the evidence of additions and changes, but such evidence is not wholly wanting in the older portions. The large row that bounds the original eastern court on the west side may be seen on the plan to be of unusual width, having the largest number of rooms that form a terrace with western aspect; yet the nearly straight line once defining the original back wall of the court inclosing cluster on this side has not been obscured to any great extent by the later additions (Pl. XXVIII). This village furnishes the most striking example in the whole group of the manner in which a pueblo was gradually enlarged as increasing population demanded more space. Such additions were often carried out on a definite plan, although the results in Tusayan fall far short of the symmetry that characterizes many ruined pueblos in New Mexico and Arizona.

A few of these ancient examples, especially some of the smaller ruins of the Chaco group, are so symmetrical in their arrangement that they seem to be the result of a single effort to carry out a clearly fixed plan. By far the largest number of pueblos, however, built among the southwest tablelands, if occupied for any length of time, must have been subject to irregular enlargement. In some ancient examples, such additions to the first plan undoubtedly took place without marring the general symmetry. This was the case at Pueblo Bonito, on the Chaco, where the symmetrical and even curve of the exterior defensive wall, which was at least four stories high, remained unbroken, while the large inclosed court was encroached upon by wings added to the inner terraces. These additions comfortably provided for a very large increase of population after the first building of the pueblo, without changing its exterior appearance.

In order to make clearer this order of growth in Mashongnavi, a series of skeleton diagrams is added in Figs. 10, 11, and 12, giving the outlines of the pueblo at various supposed periods in the course of its enlargement. The larger plan of the village (Pl. XXVI) serves as a key to these terrace outlines.

The first diagram illustrates the supposed original cluster of the east court (Fig. 10), the lines of which can be traced on the larger plan, and it includes the long, nearly straight line that marks the western edge of the third story. This diagram shows also, in dotted lines, the general plan that may have guided the first additions to the west. The second diagram (Fig. 11) renders all the above material in full tint, again indicating further additions by dotted lines, and so on. (Fig. 12.) The portions of a terrace, which face westward in the newer courts of the pueblo, illustrated in Pl. XXIX, were probably built after the western row, completing the inclosure, and were far enough advanced to indicate definitely an inclosed court, upon which the dwelling rooms faced.

SHUPAULOVI.

This village, by far the smallest pueblo of the Tusayan group, illustrates a simple and direct use of the principle of the inclosed court.
The plan (Pl. XXX) shows that the outer walls are scarcely broken by
terraces, and nearly all the dwelling apartments open inwards upon the
inclosure, in this respect closely following the previously described
ancient type, although widely differing from it in the irregular disposition of the rooms. (Pl. XXXI.) A comparison with the first of the
series of diagrams illustrating the growth of Mashóngnavi, will show
how similar the villages may have been at one stage, and how suitable
a nucleus for a large pueblo this village would prove did space and
character of the site permit. Most of the available summit of the rocky
knoll has already been covered, as will be seen from the topographic
sketch of the site (Fig. 13). The plan shows also that some efforts at

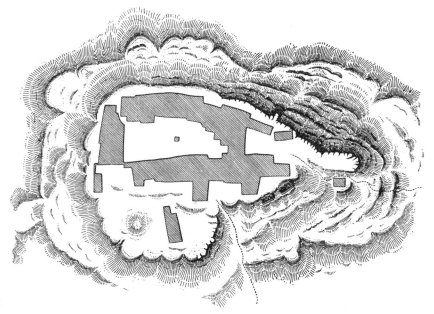

FIG. 13. Topography of the site of Shupaulovi.

extension of the pueblo have been made, but the houses outside of the
main cluster have been abandoned, and are rapidly going to ruin.
Several small rooms occur on the outer faces of the rows, but it can be
readily seen that they do not form a part of the original plan but were
added to an already complete structure.

In the inclosed court of this pueblo occurs a small box-like stone
inclosure, covered with a large slab, which is used as a sort of shrine or
depository for the sacred plume sticks and other ceremonial offerings.

A COURT OF ORAIBI.

MASONRY TERRACES OF ORAIBI.

ORAIBI HOUSE ROW, SHOWING COURT SIDE.

BACK OF ORAIBI HOUSE ROW.

THE SITE OF MOEN-KOPI.

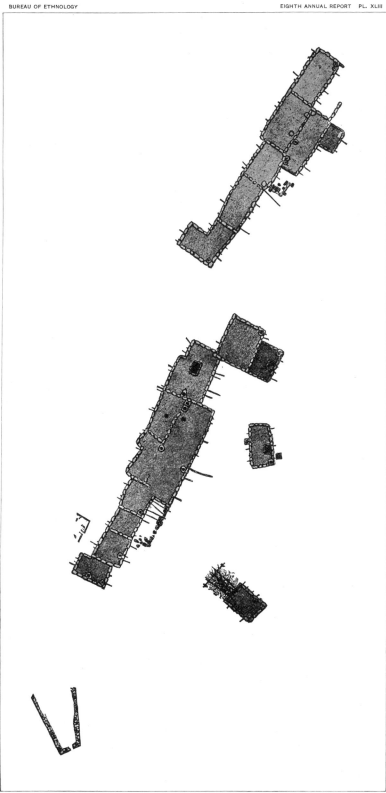

MOEN-KOPI.

MOEN-KOPI.

THE MORMON MILL AT MOEN-KOPI.

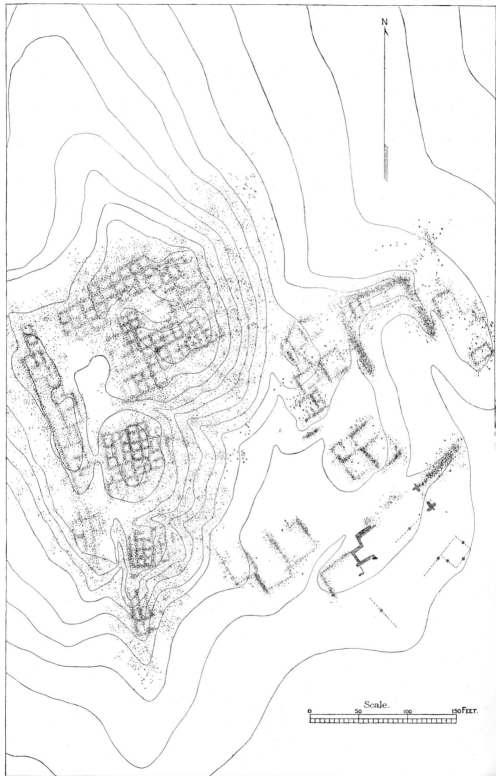

N

Scale.

0          50          100          150 FEET.

HAWIKUH.

HAWIKUH, VIEW.

ADOBE CHURCH AT HAWIKUH.

KETCHIPAUAN.

KETCHIPAUAN.

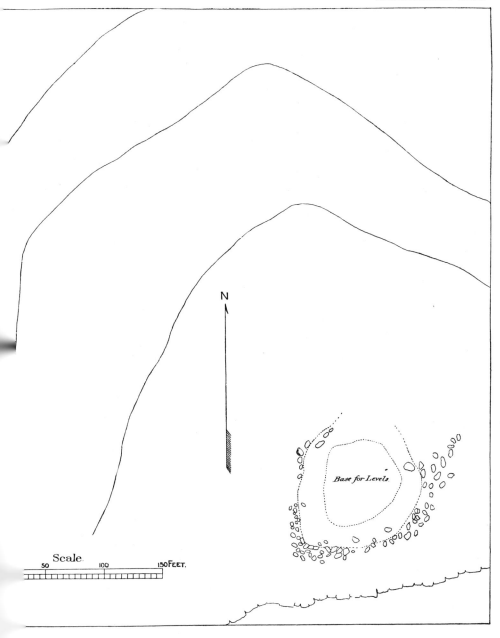

N

Base for Levels

Scale.
50        100        150 FEET.

STONE CHURCH AT KETCHIPAUAN.

EIGHTH ANNUAL REPORT    PL. LIII

SITE OF KIAKIMA, AT BASE OF TÁAAIYALANA.

This feature is found at some of the other villages, notably at Mashongnavi, in the central court, and at Hano, where it is located at some distance outside of the village, near the main trail to the mesa.

The plan of this small village shows three covered passageways similar to those noted in Walpi on the first mesa, though their presence
here can not be ascribed to the same motives that impelled the, Walpi
to build in this way; for the densely crowded site occupied by the latter compelled them to resort to this expedient. One of these is illustrated in Pl. xxxii. Its presence may be due in this instance to a determination to adhere to the protected court while seeking to secure convenient means of access to the inclosed area. It is remarkable that
this, the smallest of the group, should contain this feature.

This village has but two kivas, one of which is on the rocky summit
near the houses and the other on the lower ground near the foot of the
trail that leads to the village. The upper kiva is nearly subterranean,
the roof being but a little above the ground on the side toward the
village, but as the rocky site slopes away a portion of side wall is exposed. This was roughly built, with no attempt to impart finish to its
outer face, either by careful laying of the masonry or by plastering.
Pl. xxxiii illustrates this kiva in connection with the southeastern portion of the village. The plan shows how the prolongation of the side
rows of the village forms a suggestion of a second court. Its development into any such feature as the secondary or additional courts of
Mashóngnavi was prohibited by the restricted site.

As in other villages of this group, the desire to adhere to the subterranean form of ceremonial chamber outweighed the inducement to place
it within the village, or, in the case of the second kiva, even of placing it
on the same level as the houses, which are 30 feet above it with an
abrupt trail between them. It is curious and instructive to see a room,
the use of which is so intimately connected with the inner life of the
village, placed in such a comparatively remote and inaccessible position
through an intensely conservative adherence to ancient practice requir-
ing this chamber to be depressed.

The general view of the village given in Pl. xxxi strikingly illustrates the blending of the rectangular forms of the architecture with
the angular and sharply defined fractures of the surrounding rock.
This close correspondence in form between the architecture and its immediate surroundings is greatly heightened by the similarity in color.
Mr. Stephen has called attention to a similar effect on the western side
of Walpi and its adjacent mesa edge, which he thought indicates a distinct effort at concealment on the part of the builders, by blending the
architecture with the surroundings. This similarity of effect is often
accidental, and due to the fact that the materials of the houses and of
the mesas on which they are built are identical. Even in the case of
Walpi, cited by Mr. Stephen, where the buildings come to the very
mesa edge, and in their vertical lines appear to carry out the effect of

the vertical fissures in the upper benches of sandstone, there was no intentional concealment. It is more likely that, through the necessity of building close to the limits of the crowded sites, a certain degree of correspondence was unintentionally produced between the jogs and angles of the houses and those of the mesa edge.

Such correspondence with the surroundings, which forms a striking feature of many primitive types of construction where intention of concealment had no part, is doubtless mainly due to the use of the most available material, although the expression of a type of construction that has prevailed for ages in one locality would perhaps be somewhat influenced by constantly recurring forms in its environment. In the system of building under consideration, such influence would, however, be a very minute fraction in the sum of factors producing the type and could never account for such examples of special and detailed correspondence as the cases cited, nor could it have any weight in developing a rectangular type of architecture.

In the development of primitive arts the advances are slow and laborious, and are produced by adding small increments to current knowledge. So vague and undefined an influence as that exerted by the larger forms of surrounding nature are seldom recognized and acknowledged by the artisan; on the contrary, experiments, resulting in improvement, are largely prompted by practical requirements. Particularly is this the case in the art of house-building.

## SHUMOPAVI.

This village, although not so isolated as Oraibi, has no near neighbors and is little visited by whites or Indians. The inhabitants are rarely seen at the trading post to which the others resort, and they seem to be pretty well off and independent as compared with their neighbors of the other villages (Pl. XXXIV). The houses and courts are in keeping with the general character of the people and exhibit a degree of neatness and thrift that contrasts sharply with the tumble-down appearance of some of the other villages, especially those of the Middle Mesa and Oraibi. There is a general air of newness about the place, though it is questionable whether the architecture is more recent than that of the other villages of Tusayan. This effect is partly due to the custom of frequently renewing the coating of mud plaster. In most of the villages little care is taken to repair the houses until the owner feels that to postpone such action longer would endanger its stability. Many of the illustrations in this chapter indicate the proportion of rough masonry usually exposed in the walls. At Shumopavi (Pl. XXXV), however, most of the walls are smoothly plastered. In this respect they resemble Zuñi and the eastern pueblos, where but little naked masonry can be seen. Another feature that adds to the effect of neatness and finish in this village is the frequent use of a whitewash of gypsum on the outer face of the walls. This wash is used partly as an ornament and partly as protection against the rain. The material, called by the Mexicans "yeso," is very commonly used in the interior of their houses throughout this region, both by Mexicans and Indians. More rarely it is used among the pueblos as an external wash. Here, however, its external use forms quite a distinctive feature of the village. The same custom in several of the cliff houses of Canyon de Chelly attests the comparative antiquity of the practice, though not necessarily its pre-Columbian origin.

Shumopavi, compared with the other villages, shows less evidence of having been built on the open court idea, as the partial inclosures assume such elongated forms in the direction of the long, straight rows of the rooms; yet examination shows that the idea was present to a slight extent.

At the southeast corner of the pueblo there is a very marked approach to the open court, though it is quite evident that the easternmost row has its back to the court, and that the few rooms that face the other way are later additions. In fact, the plan of the village and the distribution of the terraces seem to indicate that the first construction consisted only of a single row facing nearly east, and was not an inclosed court, and that a further addition to the pueblo assumed nearly the same form, with its face or terraced side toward the back of the first row only partly adapting itself by the addition of a few small rooms later, to the court arrangement, the same operation being continued, but in a form not so clearly defined, still farther toward the west.

The second court is not defined on the west by such a distinct row as the others, and the smaller clusters that to some extent break the long, straight arrangement bring about an approximation to a court, though here again the terraces only partly face it, the eastern side being bounded by the long exterior wall of the middle row, two and three stories high, and almost unbroken throughout its entire length of 400 feet. The broken character of the small western row, in conjunction with the clusters near it, imparts a distinct effect to the plan of this portion, differentiating it in character from the masses of houses formed by the other two rows. The latter are connected at their southern end by a short cross row which converts this portion of the village practically into a single large house. Two covered passageways, however, which are designated on the plan, give access to the southeast portion of the court. This portion is partly separated from the north half of the inclosure by encroaching groups of rooms. This partial division of the original narrow and long court appears to be of later date.

The kivas are four in number, of which but one is within the village. The latter occupies a partly inclosed position in the southwest portion, and probably owes its place to some local facility for building a kiva on this spot in the nature of a depression in the mesa summit; but even with such aid the ceremonial chamber was built only partly under ground, as may be seen in Fig. 14. The remaining three kivas are more distinctly subterranean, and in order to obtain a suitable site one of these was located at a distance of more than 200 feet from the village, toward the mesa edge on the east. The other two are built very close together, apparently in contact, just beyond the northern extremity of the village. One of these is about 3 feet above the surface at one corner, but nearly on a level with the ground at its western side where it adjoins its neighbor. These two kivas are illustrated in Pl. LXXXVIII and Fig. 21.

Here again we find that the ceremonial chamber that forms so impor-

FIG. 14. Court kiva of Shumopavi.

tant a feature among these people, occupies no fixed relation to the dwellings, and its location is largely a matter of accident, a site that would admit of the partial excavation or sinking of the chamber below the surface being the main requisite. The northwest court contains another of the small inclosed shrines already described as occurring at Shupaulovi and elsewhere.

The stonework of this village also possesses a somewhat distinctive character. Exposed masonry, though comparatively rare in this well-plastered pueblo, shows that stones of suitable fracture were selected and that they were more carefully laid than in the other villages. In places the masonry bears a close resemblance to some of the ancient work, where the spaces between the longer tablets of stone were carefully chinked with small bits of stone, bringing the whole wall to a uniform face, and is much in advance of the ordinary slovenly methods of construction followed in Tusayan.

Shumopavi is the successor of an older village of that name, one of the cities of the ancient Tusayan visited by a detachment of Coronado's expedition in 1540. The ruins of that village still exist, and they formerly contained vestiges of the old church and mission buildings established by the monks. The squared beams from these buildings were considered valuable enough to be incorporated in the construction of ceremonial kivas in some of the Tusayan villages. This old site was not visited by the party.

## ORAIBI.

This is one of the largest modern pueblos, and contains nearly half the population of Tusayan; yet its great size has not materially affected the arrangement of the dwellings. The general plan (see Pl. XXXVI) simply shows an unusually large collection of typical Tusayan house-rows, with the general tendency to face eastward displayed in the other villages of the group. There is a remarkable uniformity in the direction of the rows, but there are no indications of the order in which the successive additions to the village were made, such as were found at Mashóngnavi.

The clusters of rooms do not surpass the average dimensions of those in the smaller villages. In five of the clusters in Oraibi a height of four stories is reached by a few rooms; a height seen also in Walpi.

At several points in Oraibi, notably on the west side of cluster No. 7, may be seen what appears to be low terraces faced with rough masonry. The same thing is also seen at Walpi, on the west side of the northern-most cluster. This effect is produced by the gradual filling in of abandoned and broken-down marginal houses, with fallen masonry and drifted sand. The appearance is that of intentional construction, as may be seen in Pl. XXXIX.

The rarity of covered passageways in this village is noteworthy, and emphasizes the marked difference in the character of the Tusayan and Zuñi ground plans. The close crowding of rooms in the latter has made a feature of the covered way, which in the scattered plan of Oraibi is rarely called for. When found it does not seem an outgrowth of the same conditions that led to its adoption in Zuñi. A glance at the plans will show how different has been the effect of the immediate environment in the two cases. In Zuñi, built on a very slight knoll in the open plain, the absence of a defensive site has produced unusual development of the defensive features of the architecture, and the result is a remarkably dense clustering of the dwellings. At Tusayan, on the other hand, the largest village of the group does not differ in character from the smallest. Occupation of a defensive site has there in a measure taken the place of a special defensive arrangement, or close clustering of rooms. Oraibi is laid out quite as openly as any other of the group, and as additions to its size have from time to time been made the builders have, in the absence of the defensive motive for crowding the rows or groups into large clusters, simply followed the usual arrangement. The crowding that brought about the use of the covered way was due in Walpi to restricted site, as nearly all the available summit of its rocky promontory has been covered with buildings. In Zuñi, on the other hand, it was the necessity for defense that led to the close clustering of the dwellings and the consequent employment of the covered way.

A further contrast between the general plans of Oraibi and Zuñi is afforded in the different manner in which the roof openings have been employed in the two cases. The plan of Zuñi, Pl. LXXVI, shows great numbers of small openings, nearly all of which are intended exclusively for the admission of light, a few only being provided with ladders. In Oraibi, on the other hand, there are only seventeen roof openings above the first terrace, and of these not more than half are intended for the admission of light. The device is correspondingly rare in other villages of the group, particularly in those west of the first mesa. In Mashóngnavi the restricted use of the roof openings is particularly noticeable; they all are of the same type as those used for access to first terrace rooms. There is but one roof opening in a second story. An examination of the plan, Pl. XXX, will show that in Shupaúlovi but two such openings occur above the first terrace, and in the large village of Shumopavi, Pl. XXXIV, only about eight. None of the smaller villages can be fairly compared with Zuñi in the employment of this feature, but in Oraibi we should expect to find its use much more general, were it not for the fact that the defensive site has taken the place of the close clustering of rooms seen in the exposed village of Zuñi, and, in consequence, the devices for the admission of light still adhere to the more primitive arrangement (Pls. XL and XLI).

The highest type of pueblo construction, embodied in the large communal fortress houses of the valleys, could have developed only as the builders learned to rely for protection more upon their architecture and less upon the sites occupied. So long as the sites furnished a large proportion of the defensive efficiency of a village, the invention of the builders was not stimulated to substitute artificial for natural advantages. Change of location and consequent development must frequently have taken place owing to the extreme inconvenience of defensive sites to the sources of subsistence.

The builders of large valley pueblos must frequently have been forced to resort hastily to defensive sites on finding that the valley towns were unfitted to withstand attack. This seems to have been the case with the Tusayan; but that the Zuñi have adhered to their valley pueblo through great difficulties is clearly attested by the internal evidence of the architecture itself, even were other testimony altogether wanting.

### MOEN-KOPI.

About 50 miles west from Oraibi is a small settlement used by a few families from Oraibi during the farming season, known as Moen-kopi. (Pl. XLIII). The present village is comparatively recent, but, as is the case with many others, it has been built over the remains of an older settlement. It is said to have been founded within the memory of some of the Mormon pioneers at the neighboring town of Tuba City, named after an old Oraibi chief, recently deceased.

The site would probably have attracted a much larger number of settlers, had it not been so remote from the main pueblos of the province, as in many respects it far surpasses any of the present village sites. A large area of fertile soil can be conveniently irrigated from copious springs in the side of a small branch of the Moen-kopi wash. The village occupies a low, rounded knoll at the junction of this branch with the main wash, which on the opposite or southern side is quite precipitous. The gradual encroachments of the Mormons for the last twenty years have had some effect in keeping the Tusayan from more fully utilizing the advantages of this site (Pl. XLII).

Moen-kopi is built in two irregular rows of one-story houses. There are also two detached single rooms in the village—one of them built for a kiva, though apparently not in use at the time of our survey, and the other a small room with its principal door facing an adjoining row. The arrangement is about the same that prevails in the other villages, the rows having distinct back walls of rude masonry.

Rough stone work predominates also in the fronts of the houses, though it is occasionally brought to a fair degree of finish. Some adobe work is incorporated in the masonry, and at one point a new and still unroofed room was seen built of adobe bricks on a stone foundation about a foot high. There is but little adobe masonry, however, in Tusayan. Its use in this case is probably due to Mormon influence.

Moen-kopi was the headquarters of a large business enterprise of the Mormons a number of years ago. They attempted to concentrate the product of the Navajo wool trade at this point and to establish here a completely appointed woolen mill. Water was brought from a series of reservoirs built in a small valley several miles away, and was conducted to a point on the Moen-kopi knoll, near the end of the south row of houses, where the ditch terminated in a solidly constructed box of masonry. From this in turn the water was delivered through a large pipe to a turbine wheel, which furnished the motive power for the works. The ditch and masonry are shown on the ground plan of the village (Pl. XLIII). This mill was a large stone building, and no expense was spared in fitting it up with the most complete machinery. At the time of our visit the whole establishment had been abandoned for some years and was rapidly going to decay. The frames had been torn from the windows, and both the floor of the building and the ground in its vicinity were strewn with fragments of expensive machinery, broken cog-wheels, shafts, etc. This building is shown in Pl. XLV, and may serve as an illustration of the contrast between Tusayan masonry and modern stone-mason's work carried out with the same material. The comparison, however, is not entirely fair, as applied to the pueblo builders in general, as the Tusayan mason is unusually careless in his work. Many old examples are seen in which the finish of the walls compares very favorably with the American mason's work, though the result is attained in a wholly different manner, viz, by close and careful chinking with numberless small tablets of stone. This process brings the wall to a remarkably smooth and even surface, the joints almost disappearing in the mosaic-like effect of the wall mass. The masonry of Moen-kopi is more than ordinarily rough, as the small village was probably built hastily and used for temporary occupation as a farming center. In the winter the place is usually abandoned, the few families occupying it during the farming months returning to Oraibi for the season of festivities and ceremonials.

# CHAPTER III.

## RUINS AND INHABITED VILLAGES OF CIBOLA.

### PHYSICAL FEATURES OF THE PROVINCE.

Though the surroundings of the Cibolan pueblos and ruins exhibit the ordinary characteristics of plateau scenery, they have not the monotonous and forbidding aspect that characterizes the mesas and valleys of Tusayan. The dusty sage brush and the stunted cedar and piñon, as in Tusayan, form a conspicuous feature of the landscape, but the cliffs are often diversified in color, being in cases composed of alternating bands of light gray and dark red sandstone, which impart a considerable variety of tints to the landscape. The contrast is heightened by the proximity of the Zuñi Mountains, an extensive timber-bearing range that approaches within 12 miles of Zuñi, narrowing down the extent of the surrounding arid region.

Cibola has also been more generously treated by nature in the matter of water supply, as the province contains a perennial stream which has its sources near the village of Nutria, and, flowing past the pueblo of Zuñi, disappears a few miles below. During the rainy season the river empties into the Colorado Chiquito. The Cibolan pueblos are built on the foothills of mesas or in open valley sites, surrounded by broad fields, while the Tusayan villages are perched upon mesa promontories that overlook the valley lands used for cultivation.

### PLANS AND DESCRIPTIONS OF RUINS.

#### HAWIKUH.

The village of Hawikuh, situated about 15 miles to the south of Zuñi, consisted of irregular groups of densely clustered cells, occupying the point of a spur projecting from a low rounded hill. The houses are in such a ruined condition that few separate rooms can be traced, and these are much obscured by débris. This débris covers the entire area extending down the east slope of the hill to the site of the church. The large amount of débris and the comparative thinness of such walls as are found suggest that the dwellings had been densely clustered, and carried to the height of several stories. Much of the space between the village on the hill and the site of the Spanish church on the plain at its foot is covered with masonry débris, part of which has slid down from above (Pl. XLVI).

80

The arrangement suggests a large principal court of irregular form. The surrounding clusters are very irregularly disposed, the directions of the prevailing lines of walls greatly varying in different groups. There is a suggestion also of several smaller courts, as well as of alleyways leading to the principal one.

The church, built on the plain below at a distance of about 200 feet from the main village, seems to have been surrounded by several groups of rooms and inclosures of various sizes, differing somewhat in character from those within the village. These groups are scattered and open, and the small amount of débris leads to the conclusion that this portion of the village was not more than a single story in height. (Pl. XLVII.)

The destruction of the village has been so complete that no vestige of constructional details remains, with the exception of a row of posts in a building near the church. The governor of Zuñi stated that these posts were part of a projecting porch similar to those seen in connection with modern houses. (See Pls. LXXI, LXXV.) Suggestions of this feature are met with at other points on the plain, but they all occur within the newer portion of the village around the church. Some of the larger inclosures in this portion of the village were very lightly constructed, and cover large areas. They were probably used as corrals. Inclosures for this purpose occur at other pueblos traditionally ascribed to the same age.

The church in this village was constructed of adobe bricks, without the introduction of any stonework. The bricks appear to have been molded with an unusual degree of care. The massive angles of the northwest, or altar end of the structure, have survived the stonework of the adjoining village and stand to-day 13 feet high. (Pl. XLVIII.)

### KETCHIPAUAN.

The small village of Ketchipauan appears to have been arranged about two courts of unequal dimensions. It is difficult to determine, however, how much of the larger court, containing the stone church, is of later construction. (Pl. XLIX.)

All the northwest portion of the village is now one large inclosure or corral, whose walls have apparently been built of the fallen masonry from the surrounding houses, leaving the central space clear. This wall on the northeast side of the large inclosure apparently follows the jogs and angles of the original houses. This may have been the outer line of rooms, as traces of buildings occur for some distance within it. On the opposite side the wall is nearly continuous, the jogs being of slight projection. Here some traces of dwellings occur outside of the wall in places to a depth of three rooms. The same thing occurs also at the north corner. The continuation of these lines suggests a rectangular court of considerable size, bounded symmetrically by groups of compartments averaging three rooms deep. (Pl. L.)

Several much smaller inclosures made in the same way occur in the village, but they apparently do not conform to the original courts.

At the present time dwelling rooms are traceable over a portion of the area south and west of the church. As shown on the plan, upright posts occasionally occur. These appear to have been incorporated into the original walls, but the latter are so ruined that this can not be stated positively, as such posts have sometimes been incorporated in modern corral walls. In places they suggest the balcony-like feature seen in modern houses, as in Hawikuh, but in the east portion of the pueblo they are irregularly scattered about the rooms. A considerable area on the west side of the ruin is covered with loosely scattered stones, affording no suggestions of a ground plan. They do not seem sufficient in amount to be the remains of dwelling rooms.

The Spanish church in this pueblo was built of stone, but the walls were much more massive than those of the dwellings. The building is well preserved, most of the walls standing 8 or 10 feet high, and in places 14 feet. This church was apparently built by Indian labor, as the walls everywhere show the chinking with small stones characteristic of the native work. In this village also, the massive Spanish construction has survived the dwelling houses.

The ground plan of the church shows that the openings were splayed in the thickness of the walls, at an angle of about 45°. In the doorway, in the east end of the building, the greater width of the opening is on the inside, a rather unusual arrangement; in the window, on the north side, this arrangement is reversed, the splay being outward. On the south side are indications of a similar opening, but at the present time the wall is so broken out that no well defined jamb can be traced, and it is impossible to determine whether the splayed opening was used or not. The stones of the masonry are laid with extreme care at the angles and in the faces of these splays, producing a highly finished effect.

The position of the beam-holes on the inner face of the wall suggests that the floor of the church had been raised somewhat above the ground, and that there may have been a cellar-like space under it. No beams are now found, however, and no remains of wood are seen in the "altar" end of the church. At the present time there are low partitions dividing the inclosed area into six rooms or cells. The Indians state that these were built at a late date to convert the church into a defense against the hostile Apache from the south. These partitions apparently formed no part of the original design, yet it is difficult to see how they could have served as a defense, unless they were intended to be roofed over and thus converted into completely inclosed rooms. A stone of somewhat larger size than usual has been built into the south wall of the church. Upon its surface some native artist has engraved a rudely drawn mask.

About 150 yards southeast from the church, and on the edge of the low mesa upon which the ruin stands, has been constructed a reservoir of large size which furnished the pueblo with a reserve water supply. The ordinary supply was probably derived from the valley below, where water is found at no great distance from the pueblo. Springs may also have formerly existed near the village, but this reservoir, located where the drainage of a large area discharges, must have materially increased the water supply. The basin or depression is about 110 feet in diameter and its present depth in the center is about 4 feet; but it has undoubtedly been filled in by sediment since its abandonment. More than half of its circumference was originally walled in, but at the present time the old masonry is indicated only by an interrupted row of large foundation stones and fallen masonry. Some large stones, apparently undisturbed portions of the mesa edge, have been incorporated into the inclosing masonry. The Indians stated that originally the bottom of this basin was lined with stones, but these statements could not be verified. Without excavation on the upper side, the basin faded imperceptibly into the rising ground of the surrounding drainage. Other examples of these basin reservoirs are met with in this region.

## CHALOWE.

About 15° north of west from Hawikuh, and distant 1½ miles from it, begins the series of ruins called Chalowe. They are located on two low elevations or foothills extending in a southwestern direction from the group of hills, upon whose eastern extremity Hawikuh is built. The southernmost of the series covers a roughly circular area about 40 feet in diameter. Another cluster, measuring about 30 feet by 20, lies immediately north of it, with an intervening depression of a foot or so. About 475 feet northwest occurs a group of three rooms situated on a slight rise. A little east of north and a half a mile distant from the latter is a small hill, upon which is located a cluster of about the same form and dimensions as the one first described. Several more vaguely defined clusters are traceable near this last one, but they are all of small dimensions.

This widely scattered series of dwelling clusters, according to the traditional accounts, belonged to one tribe, which was known by the general name of Chalowe. It is said to have been inhabited at the time of the first arrival of the Spaniards. The general character and arrangement however, are so different from the prevailing type in this region that it seems hardly probable that it belonged to the same people and the same age as the other ruins.

No standing walls are found in any portion of the group, and the small amount of scattered masonry suggests that the rooms were only one story high. Yet the débris of masonry may have been largely covered up by drifting sand. Now it is hardly possible to trace the rooms, and over most of the area only scattered stones mark the positions of the groups of dwellings.

## HAMPASSAWAN.

Of the village of Hampassawan, which is said traditionally to have been one of the seven cities of Cibola visited by Coronado, nothing now remains but two detached rooms, both showing vestiges of an upper story. With this exception, the destruction of the village is complete and only a low rise in the plain marks its site. Owing to its exposed position, the fallen walls have been completely covered with drifting sand and earth, no vestige of the buildings showing through the dense growth of sagebrush that now covers it.

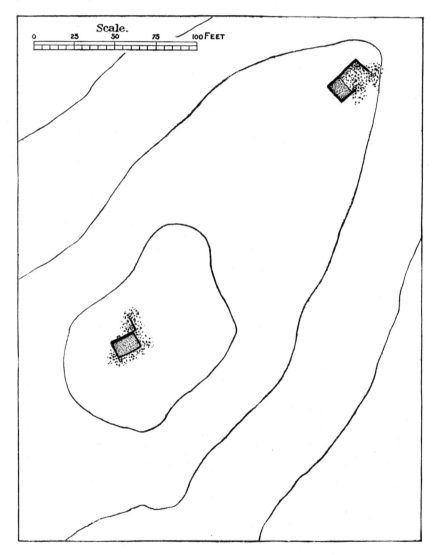

FIG. 15. Hampassawan, plan.

The two surviving rooms referred to appear to have been used from time to time, as outlooks over corn fields close by, and as a defense against the Navajo. Their final abandonment, and that of the cultivation of the adjoining fields, is said to have been due to the killing of a

Zuñi there, by the Navajo, within very recent times. These rooms have been several times repaired, the one on the west particularly. In the latter an additional wall has been built upon the northern side, as shown on the plan, Fig. 15. The old roof seems to have survived until recently, for, although at the present time the room is covered with a roof of rudely split cedar beams, the remains of the old, carefully built roof lie scattered about in the corners of the room, under the dirt and débris. The openings are very small and seem to have been modified since the original construction, but it is difficult to distinguish between the older original structure and the more recent additions.

## K'IAKIMA.

On the south side of the isolated mesa of Tâaaiyalana and occupying a high rounded spur of foothills, is the ruined village of K'iakima (Pl. LII). A long gulch on the west side of the spur contains, for 300 or 400 yards, a small stream which is fed from springs near the ruined village.

The entire surface of the hill is covered with scattered débris of fallen walls, which must at one time have formed a village of considerable size. Over most of this area the walls can not be traced; the few rooms which can be distinctly outlined, occurring in a group on the highest part of the hill. Standing walls are here seen, but they are apparently recent, one room showing traces of a chimney (Pl. LIV). Some of the more distinct inclosures, built from fallen masonry of the old village, seem to have been intended for corrals. This is the case also with the remains found on the cliffs to the north of the village, whose position is shown on the plan (Pl. LIII). Here nearly all the scattered stones of the original one-story buildings, have been utilized for these large inclosures. It is quite possible that these smaller structures on the ledge of the mesa were built and occupied at a much later date than the principal village. Pl. LIII illustrates a portion of the base of Tâaaiyalana where these inclosures appear.

A striking feature of this ruin is the occurrence in the northeast corner of the village of large upright slabs of stone. The largest of these is about 3 feet wide and stands 5½ feet out of the ground. One of the slabs is of such symmetrical form that it suggests skillful artificial treatment, but the stone was used just as it came from a seam in the cliff above. From the same seam many slabs of nearly equal size and symmetrical form have fallen out and now lie scattered about on the talus below. Some are remarkable for their perfectly rectangular form, while all are distinguished by a notable uniformity in thickness. Close by, and apparently forming part of the same group, are a number of stones imbedded in the ground with their upper edges exposed and placed at right angles to the faces of the vertical monuments. The taller slabs are said by the Indians to have been erected as a defense against the attacks of the Apache upon this pueblo, but only a portion of the group could, from their position, have been of any use for this purpose. The stones probably mark graves. Although thorough excavation of the hard soil could not be undertaken, digging to the depth of 18 inches revealed the same character of pottery fragments, ashes, etc., found in many of the pueblo graves. Mr. E. W. Nelson found identical remains in graves in the Rio San Francisco region which he excavated in collecting pottery. Comparatively little is known, however, of the burial practices of this region, so it would be difficult to decide whether this was an ordinary method of burial or not.

This pueblo has been identified by Mr. Cushing, through Zuñi tradition, as the scene of the death of Estevanico, the negro who accompanied the first Spanish expedition to Cibola.

MATSAKI.

Matsaki is situated on a foothill at the base of Tâaaiyalana, near its northwestern extremity. This pueblo is in about the same state of preservation as K'iakima, no complete rooms being traceable over most of the area. Traces of walls, where seen, are not uniform in direction, suggesting irregular grouping of the village. At two points on the plan rooms partially bounded by standing walls are found. These appear to owe their preservation to their occupation as outlooks over fields in the vicinity long after the destruction of the pueblo. One of the two rooms shows only a few feet of rather rude masonry. The walls of the other room, in one corner, stand the height of a full story above the surrounding débris, a low room under it having been partially filled up with fallen masonry and earth. The well preserved inner corner of the exposed room shows lumps of clay adhering here and there to the walls, the remnants of an interior corner chimney. No trace of the supports for a chimney hood, such as occur in the modern fireplaces, could be found. The form outlined against the wall by these slight remains indicates a rather rudely constructed feature which was added at a late date to the room and formed no part of its original construction. It was probably built while the room was used as a farming outlook. As shown on the ground plan (Pl. LV), a small cluster of houses once stood at some little distance to the southwest of the main pueblo and was connected with the latter by a series of rooms. The intervening space may have been a court. At the northern edge of the village a primitive shrine has been erected in recent times and is still in use. It is rudely constructed by simply piling up stones to a height of 2½ or 3 feet, in a rudely rectangular arrangement, with an opening on the east. This shrine, facing east, contains an upright slab of thin sandstone on which a rude sun-symbol has been engraved. The governor of Zuñi, in explaining the purpose of this shrine, compared its use to that of our own astronomical observatories, which he had seen.

PINAWA.

The ruins of the small pueblo of Pinawa occupy a slight rise on the south side of the Zuñi River, a short distance west of Zuñi. The road

from Zuñi to Ojo Caliente traverses the ruin. Over most of the area
rooms can not be traced. One complete room, however, has been preserved and appears to be still occupied during the cultivation of the
neighboring "milpas." It is roofed over and in good condition, though
the general character of the masonry resembles the older work. On
the plan (Fig. 16) it will be seen that the stones of the original masonry
have been collected and built into a number of large inclosures, which
have in turn been partly destroyed. The positions of the entrances to
these inclosures can be traced by the absence of stones on the surface.
The general outline of the corral-like inclosures appears to have followed comparatively well preserved portions of the original wall, as
was the case at Ketchipauan. (Pl. LVI.)

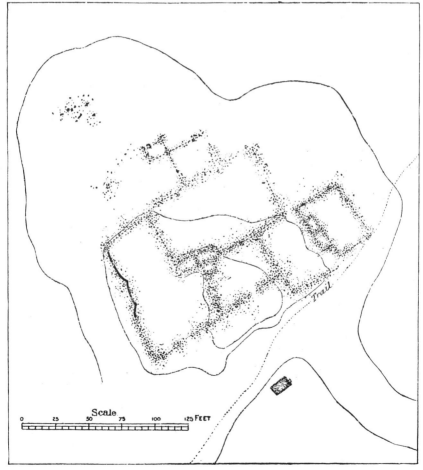

FIG. 16. Pinawa, plan.

On the southwest side of the pueblo, portions of the outer wall are
distinctly traceable, some of the stones being still in position. This

portion of the outline is distinguished by a curious series of curves, resembling portions of Nutria and Pescado, but intersecting in an unusual manner.

The Ojo Caliente road passes between the main ruin and the standing room above described. The remnants of the fallen masonry are so few and so promiscuously scattered over this area that the continuity of remains can not be fully traced.

HALONA.

An ancient pueblo called Halona is said to have belonged to the Cibolan group, and to have been inhabited at the time of the conquest. It occupied a portion of the site upon which the present pueblo of Zuñi stands. A part of this pueblo was built on the opposite side of the river, where the remains of walls were encountered at a slight depth below the surface of the ground in excavating for the foundations of Mr. Cushing's house. At that time only scattered remains of masonry were met with, and they furnished but little indication of details of plan or arrangement. Later—during the summer of 1888—Mr. Cushing made extensive additions to his house on the south side of the river, and in excavating for the foundations laid bare a number of small rooms. Excavation was continued until December of that year, when a large part of the ancient village had been exposed. Pl. LVII, from a photograph, illustrates a portion of these remains as seen from the southwest corner of Zuñi. The view was taken in the morning during a light fall of snow which, lightly covering the tops of the walls left standing in the excavations, sharply defined their outlines against the shadows of the rooms.

It seems impossible to restore the entire outline of the portion of Halona that has served as a nucleus for modern Zuñi from such data as can be procured. At several points of the present village, however, vestiges of the old pueblo can be identified. Doubtless if access could be obtained to all the innermost rooms of the pueblo some of them would show traces of ancient methods of construction sufficient, at least, to admit of a restoration of the general form of the ancient pueblo. At the time the village was surveyed such examination was not practicable. The portion of the old pueblo serving as a nucleus for later construction would probably be found under houses Nos. 1 and 4, forming practically one mass of rooms. Strangers and outsiders are not admitted to these innermost rooms. Outcrops in the small cluster No. 2 indicate by their position a continuous wall of the old pueblo, probably the external one. Portions of the ancient outer wall are probably incorporated into the west side of cluster No. 1. On the north side of cluster No. 2 (see Pl. LXXVI) may be seen a buttress-like projection whose construction of small tabular stones strongly contrasts with the character of the surrounding walls, and indicates that it is a fragment of the ancient pueblo. This projecting buttress answers no purpose whatever in its present position.

The above suggestions are confirmed by another feature in the same house-cluster. On continuing the line of this buttress through the governor's house we find a projecting fragment of second story wall, the character and finish of which is clearly shown in Pl. LVIII. Its general similarity to ancient masonry and contrast with the present careless methods of construction are very noticeable. The height of this fragment above the ground suggests that the original pueblo was in a very good state of preservation when it was first utilized as a nucleus for later additions. That portion under house No. 1 is probably equally well preserved. The frequent renovation of rooms by the application of a mud coating renders the task of determining the ancient portions of the cluster by the character of the masonry a very difficult one. Ceilings would probably longest retain the original appearance of the ancient rooms as they are not subjected to such renovation.

Mr. Cushing thought that the outer western wall of the ancient pueblo was curved in outline. It is more probable, however, that it regulated the lines of the present outer rooms, and is reflected in them, as the usual practice of these builders was to put one partition directly over another in adding to the height of a building. This would suggest a nearly rectangular form, perhaps with jogs and offsets, for the old builders could not incorporate a curved outer wall into a mass of rectangular cells, such as that seen in the present pueblo. On the other hand, the outer wall of the original pueblo may have been outside of rooms now occupied, for the village had been abandoned for some time before the colony returned to the site.

### TÂAAIYALANA.

On the abandonment of the pueblos known as the Seven Cities of Cibola, supposed to have occurred at the time of the general uprising of the pueblos in 1680, the inhabitants of all the Cibolan villages sought refuge on the summit of Tâaaiyalana, an isolated mesa, 3 miles southeast from Zuñi, and there built a number of pueblo clusters.

This mesa, otherwise known as "Thunder Mountain," rises to the height of 1,000 feet above the plain, and is almost inaccessible. There are two foot trails leading to the summit, each of which in places traverses abrupt slopes of sandstone where holes have been pecked into the rock to furnish foot and hand holds. From the northeast side the summit of the mesa can be reached by a rough and tortuous burro trail. All the rest of the mesa rim is too precipitous to be scaled. Its appearance as seen from Zuñi is shown in Pl. LIX.

On the southern portion of this impregnable site and grouped about a point where nearly the whole drainage of the mesa top collects, are found the village remains. The Zuñis stated that the houses were distributed in six groups or clusters, each taking the place of one of the abandoned towns. Mr. Frank H. Cushing[1] was also under the impres-

---

[1] See Millstone for April, 1884, Indianapolis, Indiana.

sion that these houses had been built as six distinct clusters of one village, and he has found that at the time of the Pueblo rebellion, but six
of the Cibolan villages were occupied.   An examination of the plan, however, will at once show that no such definite scheme of arrangement
governed the builders.   There are but three, or at most four groups that
could be defined as distinct clusters, and even in the case of these the disposition is so irregular and their boundaries so ill defined, through the
great number of outlying small groups scattered about, that they can
hardly be considered distinct.   There are really thirty-eight separate
buildings (Pl. LX) ranging in size from one of two rooms, near the southern
extremity to one of one hundred and three rooms, situated at the southwestern corner of the whole group and close to the western edge of the
mesa where the foot trails reach the summit.   There is also great diversity in the arrangement of rooms.   In some cases the clusters are quite
compact, and in others the rooms are distributed in narrow rows.   In
the large cluster at the northwestern extremity the houses are arranged
around a court; with this exception the clusters of rooms are scattered
about in an irregular manner, regardless of any defensive arrangement
of the buildings.   The builders evidently placed the greatest reliance
on their impregnable site, and freely adopted such arrangement as convenience dictated.

The masonry of these villages was roughly constructed, the walls being often less than a foot thick.   Very little adobe mortar seems to have
been used; some of the thickest and best preserved walls have apparently been laid nearly dry (Pl. LXI).   The few openings still preserved
also show evidence of hasty and careless construction.   Over most of
the area the débris of the fallen walls is verly clearly marked, and is but
little encumbered with earth or drifted sand.   This imparts an odd
effect of newness to these ruins, as though the walls had recently fallen.
The small amount of débris suggests that the majority of these buildings
never were more than one story high, though in four of the broadest
clusters (see plan, Pl. LX) a height of two, and possibly three, stories
may have been attained.   All the ruins are thickly covered by a very
luxurious growth of braided cactus, but little of which is found elsewhere in the neighborhood.   The extreme southeastern cluster, consisting of four large rooms, differs greatly in character from the rest of the
ruins.   Here the rooms or inclosures are defined only by a few stones
on the surface of the ground and partly embedded in the soil.   There is
no trace of the débris of fallen walls.   These outlined inclosures appear
never to have been walled to any considerable height.   Within one of
the rooms is a slab of stone, about which a few ceremonial plume sticks
have been set on end within recent times.

The motive that led to the occupation of this mesa was defense; the
cause that led to the selection of the particular site was facility for
procuring a water supply.   The trail on the west side passes a spring
half way down the mesa.   There was another spring close to the foot

trail on the south side; this, however, was lower, being almost at the foot of the talus.

In addition to these water sources, the builders collected and stored the drainage of the mesa summit near the southern gap or recess. At this point are still seen the remains of two reservoirs or dams built of heavy masonry. Only a few stones are now in place, but these indicate unusually massive construction. Another reservoir occurs farther along the mesa rim to the southeast, beyond the limits of the plan as given. As may be seen from the plan (Pl. LX) the two reservoirs at the gap are quite close together. These receptacles have been much filled up with sediment. Pl. LXII gives a view of the principal or western-most reservoir as seen from the northeast. On the left are the large stones once incorporated in the masonry of the dam. This masonry appears to have originally extended around three-fourths of the circum-ference of the reservoir. As at Ketchipauan, previously described, the upper portion of the basins merged insensibly into the general drainage and had no definite limit.

The Zuñi claim to have here practiced a curious method of water storage. They say that whenever there was snow on the ground the villagers would turn out in force and roll up huge snowballs, which were finally collected into these basins, the gradually melting snow furnishing a considerable quantity of water. The desert environment has taught these people to avail themselves of every expedient that could increase their supply of water.

It is proper to state that in the illustrated plan of the Tâaaiyalana ruins the mesa margin was sketched in without the aid of instrumental sights, and hence is not so accurately recorded as the plans and relative positions of the houses. It was all that could be done at the time, and will sufficiently illustrate the general relation of the buildings to the surrounding topography.

### KÍN-TIEL.

All the ruins above described bear close traditional and historic rela-tionship to Zuñi. This is not the case with the splendidly preserved ancient pueblo of Kin-tiel, but the absence of such close historic con-nection is compensated for by its architectural interest. Differing rad-ically in its general plan from the ruins already examined, it still sug-gests that some resemblance to the more ancient portions of Nutria and Pescado, as will be seen by comparing the ground plans (Pls. LXVII and LXIX). Its state of preservation is such that it throws light on details which have not survived the general destruction in the other pueblos. These features will be referred to in the discussion and com-parison of these architectural groups by constructional details in Chap-ter IV.

This pueblo, located nearly midway between Cibola and Tusayan, is given on some of the maps as Pueblo Grande. It is situated on a small arm of the Pueblo Colorado wash, 22 or 23 miles north of Navajo Springs, and about the same distance south from Pueblo Colorado (Ganado post-office). Geographically the ruins might belong to either Tusayan or Cibola, but Mr. Cushing has collected traditional references among the Zuñi as to the occupation of this pueblo by related peoples at a time not far removed from the first Spanish visit to this region.

The plan (Pl. LXIII) shows a marked contrast to the irregularity seen in the ruins previously described. The pueblo was clearly defined by a continuous and unbroken outer wall, which probably extended to the full height of the highest stories (Pl. LXIV). This symmetrical form is all the more remarkable in a pueblo of such large dimensions, as, with the exception of Pueblo Bonito of the Chaco group, it is the largest ancient pueblo examined by this Bureau. This village seems to belong to the same type as the Chaco examples, representing the highest development attained in building a large defensive pueblo practically as a single house. All the terraces faced upon one or more inclosed courts, through which access was gained to the rooms. The openings in this outer wall, especially near the ground, were few in number and very small in size, as shown in Pl. CIV. The pueblo was built in two wings of nearly equal size on the opposite slopes of a large sandy wash, traversing its center from east to west. This wash doubtless at one time furnished peculiar facilities for storage of water within or near the village, and this must have been one of the inducements for the selection of the site. At the time of our survey, however, not a drop of water was to be found about the ruin, nor could vestiges of any construction for gathering or storing water be traced. Such vestiges would not be likely to remain, as they must have been washed away by the violent summer torrents or buried under the accumulating sands. Two seasons subsequent to our work at this point it was learned that an American, digging in some rooms on the arroyo margin, discovered the remains of a well or reservoir, which he cleared of sand and débris and found to be in good condition, furnishing so steady a water supply that the discoverer settled on the spot. This was not seen by the writer. There is a small spring, perhaps a mile from the pueblo in a northeasterly direction, but this source would have been wholly insufficient for the needs of so large a village. It may have furnished a much more abundant supply, however, when it was in constant use, for at the time of our visit it seemed to be choked up. About a mile and a half west quite a lagoon forms from the collected drainage of several broad valleys, and contains water for a long time after the cessation of the rains. About 6 miles to the north, in a depression of a broad valley, an extensive lake is situated, and its supply seems to be constant throughout the year, except, perhaps, during an unusually dry season. These various bodies of water were undoubtedly utilized in the horticulture of the occupants of Kin-tiel; in fact, near the borders of the larger lake referred to is a small house of two rooms, much similar in workmanship to the main pueblo, evidently designed as an outlook over fields. This building is illustrated in Pl. LXVI.

The arrangement of the inner houses differs in the two halves of the ruin. It will be seen that in the north half the general arrangement is roughly parallel with the outer walls, with the exception of a small group near the east end of the arroyo. In the south half, on the other hand, the inner rows are nearly at right angles to the outer room clusters. An examination of the contours of the site will reveal the cause of this difference in the different configuration of the slopes in the two cases. In the south half the rows of rooms have been built on two long projecting ridges, and the diverging small cluster in the north half owes its direction to a similar cause. The line of outer wall being once fixed as a defensive bulwark, there seems to have been but little restriction in the adjustment of the inner buildings to conform to the irregularities of the site. (Pl. LXIII.)

Only three clearly defined means of access to the interior of the pueblo could be found in the outer walls, and of these only two were suitable for general use. One was at a reentering angle of the outer wall, just south of the east end of the arroyo, where the north wall, continued across the arroyo, overlaps the outer wall of the south half, and the other one was near the rounded northeastern corner of the pueblo. The third opening was a doorway of ordinary size in the thick north wall. It seems probable that other gateways once existed, especially in the south half. From its larger size and more compact arrangement this south half would seem to have greatly needed such facilities, but the preserved walls show no trace of them.

The ground plan furnishes indications, mostly in the north half, of several large rooms of circular form, but broken down remains of square rooms are so much like those of round ones in appearance, owing to the greater amount of débris that collects at the corners, that it could not be definitely determined that the ceremonial rooms here were of the circular form so common in the ancient pueblos. While only circular kivas have been found associated with ancient pueblos of this type, the kivas of all the Cibola ruins above described are said by the Zuñis to have been rectangular. The question can be decided for this pueblo only by excavation on a larger scale than the party was prepared to undertake. Slight excavation at a point where a round room was indicated on the surface, revealed portions of straight walls only.

The large size of the refuse heap on the south side of the village indicates that the site had been occupied for many generations. Notwithstanding this long period of occupation, no important structure of the village seems to have extended beyond the plan. On the north side, outside the main wall, are seen several rectangles faintly outlined by stones, but these do not appear to have been rooms. They resemble similar inclosures seen in connection with ruined pueblos farther south, which proved on excavation to contain graves.

The positions of the few excavations made are indicated on the plan (Pl. LXIII). Our facilities for such work were most meager, and whatever results were secured were reached at no great distance from the surface. One of these excavations, illustrated in Pl. C, will be described at greater length in Chapter IV.

## PLANS AND DESCRIPTIONS OF INHABITED VILLAGES.

### NUTRIA.

Nutria is the smallest of the three farming pueblos of Zuñi, and is located about 23 miles by trail northeast from Zuñi at the head of Nutria valley. The water supply at this point is abundant, and furnishes a running stream largely utilized in irrigating fields in the vicinity. Most of the village is compactly arranged, as may be seen from the plan (Pl. LXVII and Fig. 17), but a few small clusters of late construction, containing two or three rooms each, are situated toward the east at quite a distance from the principal group. It is now occupied solely as a farming pueblo during the planting and harvesting season.

The outline of this small pueblo differs greatly from those of most of the Cibolan villages. The village (Pl. LXVIII), particularly in its northernmost cluster, somewhat approximates the form of the ancient pueblo of Kin-tiel (Pl. LXIII), and has apparently been built on the remains of an older village of somewhat corresponding form, as indicated by its curved outer wall. Fragments of carefully constructed masonry of the ancient type, contrasting noticeably with the surrounding modern construction, afford additional evidence of this. The ancient village must have been provided originally with ceremonial rooms or kivas, but no traces of such rooms are now to be found.

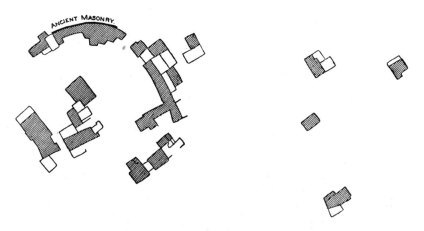

FIG. 17. Nutria, plan; small diagram, old wall.

At the close of the harvest, when the season of feasts and ceremonials begins, lasting through most of the winter, the occupants of these farming villages close up their houses and move back to the main pueblo leaving them untenanted until the succeeding spring.

The great number of abandoned and ruined rooms is very noticeable in the farming pueblos illustrated in this and two of the succeeding plans (Pls. LXIX and LXXIII). The families that farm in their vicinity seem to occupy scarcely more than half of the available rooms.

PESCADO.

This village, also a Zuñi farming pueblo, is situated in a large valley about 12 miles northeast from Zuñi. Although it is much larger than Nutria it is wholly comprised within the compact group illustrated. The tendency to. build small detached houses noticed at Nutria and at Ojo Caliente has not manifested itself here. The prevalence of abandoned and roofless houses is also noticeable.

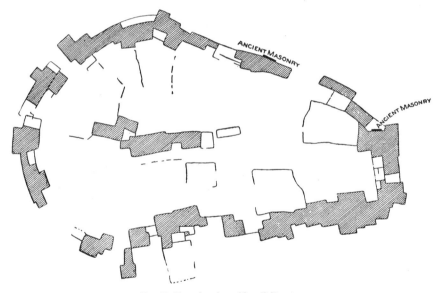

Fig. 18. Pescado, plan, old wall diagram.

The outlines of the original court inclosing pueblo (Pl. LXX) are very clearly marked, as the farming Zuñis in their use of this site have scarcely gone outside of the original limits of the ancient pueblo. The plan, Pl. LXIX and Fig. 18, shows a small irregular row built in the large inclosed court; this row, with the inclosures and corrals that surround it, probably formed no part of the original plan. The full curved outline is broken only at the west end of the village by small additions to the outer wall, and the north and east walls also closely follow the boundary of the original pueblo. In fact, at two points along the north wall fragments of carefully executed masonry, probably forming part of the external wall of the ancient pueblo, are still preserved (Pl. LXXII). This outer wall was probably once continuous to the full height of the pueblo, but the partial restorations of the buildings by the Zuñi farmers resemble more closely the modern arrangement. Small rooms have been added to the outside of the cluster and in some cases the terraces are reached by external stone steps, in contrast with the defensive arrangement prevailing generally in pueblos of this form. A number of dome-shaped ovens have been built outside the walls.

The principle of pueblo plan embodied in Kin-tiel, before referred to, is traceable in this village with particular clearness, distinguishing it from most of the Cibolan pueblos. No traces of kivas were met with in this village.

OJO CALIENTE.

The farming village of Ojo Caliente is located near the dry wash of the Zuñi River, and is about 15 miles distant from Zuñi, in a southerly direction. It is about midway between Hawikuh and Ketchipauan, two of the seven cities of Cibola above described. Though situated in fertile and well watered country and close to the remains of the ancient villages, it bears indications of having been built in comparatively recent times. There are no such evidences of connection with an older village as were found at Nutria and Pescado. The irregular and small clusters that form this village are widely scattered over a rather rough and broken site, as shown on the plan (Pl. LXXIII). Here again a large portion of the village is untenanted. The large cluster toward the eastern extremity of the group, and the adjoining houses situated on the low, level ground, compose the present inhabited village. The houses occupying the elevated rocky sites to the west (Pl. LXXIV) are in an advanced stage of decay, and have been for a long time abandoned.

This southern portion of the Cibola district seems to have been much exposed to the inroads of the Apache. One of the effects of this has already been noticed in the defensive arrangement in the Ketchipauan church. On account of such danger, the Zuñi were likely to have built the first house-clusters here on the highest points of the rocky promontory, notwithstanding the comparative inconvenience of such sites. Later, as the farmers gained confidence or as times became safer, they built houses down on the flat now occupied; but this apparently was not done all at once. The distribution of the houses over sites of varying degrees of inaccessibility, suggests a succession of approaches to the occupation of the open and unprotected valley.

Some of the masonry of this village is carelessly constructed, and, as in the other farming pueblos, there is much less adobe plastering and smoothing of outer walls than in the home pueblo.

At the time of the survey the occupation of this village throughout the year was proposed by several families, who wished to resort to the parent village only at stated ceremonials and important festivals. The comparative security of recent times is thus tending to the disintegration of the huge central pueblo. This result must be inevitable, as the dying out of the defensive motive brings about a realization of the great inconvenience of the present centralized system.

## ZUÑI.

The pueblo of Zuñi is built upon a small knoll on the north bank of the Zuñi River, about three miles west of the conspicuous mesa of Tâa-aiyalana. It is the successor of all the original "Seven Cities of Cibola" of the Spaniards, and is the largest of the modern pueblos. As before stated, the remains of Halona, one of the "seven cities," as identified by Mr. Cushing, have served as a nucleus for the construction of the modern pueblo, and have been incorporated into the most densely clustered portions, represented on the plan (Pl. LXXVI) by numbers 1 and 4.

Some of the Cibolan villages were valley pueblos, built at a distance from the rocky mesas and canyons that must have served as quarries for the stone used in building. The Halona site was of this type, the nearest supply of stone being 3 miles distant. At this point (Halona) the Zuñi River is perennial, and furnishes a plentiful supply of water at all seasons of the year. It disappears, however, a few miles west in a broad, sandy wash, to appear again 20 miles below the village, probably through the accession of small streams from springs farther down. The so-called river furnishes the sole water supply at Zuñi, with the exception of a single well or reservoir on the north side of the village.

Zuñi has been built at a point having no special advantages for defense; convenience to large areas of tillable soil has apparently led to the selection of the site. This has subjected it in part to the same influences that had at an earlier date produced the carefully walled fortress pueblos of the valleys, where the defensive efficiency was due to well planned and constructed buildings. The result is that Zuñi, while not comparable in symmetry to many of the ancient examples, displays a remarkably compact arrangement of dwellings in the portions of the pueblos first occupied, designated on the plan (Pl. LXXVI) as houses 1 and 4. Owing to this restriction of lateral expansion this portion of the pueblo has been carried to a great height.

Pl. LXXVIII gives a general view of these higher terraces of the village from the southeast. A height of five distinct terraces from the ground is attained on the south side of this cluster. The same point, however, owing to the irregularity of the site, is only three terraces above the ground on the north side. The summit of the knoll upon which the older portion of Zuñi has been built is so uneven, and the houses themselves vary so much in dimensions, that the greatest disparity prevails in the height of terraces. A three-terrace portion of a cluster may have but two terraces immediately alongside, and throughout the more closely built portions of the village the exposed height of terraces varies from 1 foot to 8 or 10 feet. Pl. LXXIX illustrates this feature.

The growth of the village has apparently been far beyond the original expectation of the builders, and the crowded additions seem to have been joined to the clusters wherever the demand for more space was most urgent, without following any definite plan in their arrangement. In such of the ancient pueblo ruins as afford evidence of having passed through a similar experience, the crowding of additional cells seems to have been made to conform to some extent to a predetermined plan. At Kin-tiel we have seen how such additions to the number of habitable rooms could readily be made within the open court without affecting the symmetry and defensive efficiency of the pueblo; but here the nucleus of the large clusters was small and compact, so that enlargement has taken place only by the addition of rooms on the outside, both on the ground and on upper terraces.

The highest point of Zuñi, now showing five terraces, is said to have had a height of seven terraces as late as the middle of the present century, but at the time of the survey of the village no traces were seen of such additional stories. The top of the present fifth terrace, however, is more than 50 feet long, and affords sufficient space for the addition of a sixth and seventh story.

The court or plaza in which the church (Pl. LXXX) stands is so much larger than such inclosures usually are when incorporated in a pueblo plan that it seems unlikely to have formed part of the original village. It probably resulted from locating the church prior to the construction of the eastern rows of the village. Certain features in the houses themselves indicate the later date of these rows.

The arrangement of dwellings about a court (Pl. LXXXII), characteristic of the ancient pueblos, is likely to have prevailed in the small pueblo of Halona, about which clustered the many irregular houses that constitute modern Zuñi. Occasional traces of such an arrangement are still met with in portions of Zuñi, although nearly all of the ancient pueblo has been covered with rooms of later date. In the arrangement of Zuñi houses a noticeable difference in the manner of clustering is found in different parts of the pueblo. That portion designated as house No. 1 on the plan, built over the remains of the original small pueblo, is unquestionably the oldest portion of the village. The clustering seems to have gone on around this center to an extraordinary and exceptional extent before any houses were built in other portions. House No. 4 is a portion of the same structure, for although a street or passageway intervenes it is covered with two or three terraces, indicating that such connection was established at an early date. The rows on the lower ground to the east (Pl. LXXXI), where the rooms are not so densely clustered, were built after the removal of the defensive motive that influenced the construction of the central pile. These portions, arranged approximately in rows, show a marked resemblance to pueblos of known recent date. That they were built subsequently to the main clusters is also indicated by the abundant use of oblique openings and roof holes, where there is very little necessity for such contrivances. This feature was originally devised to meet the exceptional conditions of lighting imposed by dense crowding of the living rooms. It will be referred to again in examining the details of openings, and its wide departure from the arrangement found to prevail generally in pueblo constructions will there be noted. The habit of making such provisions for lighting inner rooms became fixed and was applied generally to many clusters much smaller in size than those of other pueblos where this feature was not developed and where the necessity for it was not felt. These less crowded rooms of more recent construction form the eastern portion of the pueblo, and also include the governor's house on the south side.

The old ceremonial rooms or kivas, and the rooms for the meeting of the various orders or secret societies were, during the Spanish occupancy, crowded into the innermost recesses of this ancient portion of Zuñi under house No. 1. But the kivas, in all likelihood, occupied a more marginal position before such foreign influence was brought to bear on them, as do some of the kivas at the present time, and as is the general practice in other modern pueblos.

# CHAPTER IV.

## ARCHITECTURE OF TUSAYAN AND CÍBOLA COMPARED BY CONSTRUCTIONAL DETAILS.

### INTRODUCTION.

In the two preceding chapters the more general features of form and distribution in the ruined and inhabited pueblos of Tusayan and Cíbola have been described. In order to gain a full and definite idea of the architectural acquirements of the pueblo builders it will be necessary to examine closely the constructional details of their present houses, endeavoring, when practicable, to compare these details with the rather meager vestiges of similar features that have survived the destruction of the older villages, noting the extent to which these have departed from early types, and, where practicable, tracing the causes of such deviation. For convenience of comparison the various details of house-building for the two groups will be treated together.

The writer is indebted to Mr. A. M. Stephen, the collector of the traditionary data already given, for information concerning the rites connected with house building at Tusayan incorporated in the following pages, and also for the carefully collected and valuable nomenclature of architectural details appended hereto. Material of this class pertaining to the Cíbola group of pueblos unfortunately could not be procured.

### HOUSE BUILDING.

#### RITES AND METHODS.

The ceremonials connected with house building in Tusayan are quite meager, but the various steps in the ritual, described in their proper connection in the following paragraphs, are well defined and definitely assigned to those who participate in the construction of the buildings.

So far as could be ascertained there is no prearranged plan for an entire house of several stories, or for the arrangement of contiguous houses. Most of the ruins examined emphasize this absence of a clearly defined general plan governing the location of rooms added to the original cluster. Two notable exceptions to this want of definite plan occur among the ruins described. In Tusayan the Fire House (Fig. 7) is evidently the result of a clearly defined purpose to give a definite form to the entire cluster, just as, on a very much larger scale, does the ruin of Kin-tiel, belonging to the Cíbola group (Pl. LXIII). In both these cases the fixing of the outer wall on a definite line seems to have

100

been regarded as of more importance than the specific locations of individual rooms or dwellings within this outline. Throughout that part of Tusayan which has been examined, however, the single room seems now to be regarded as the pueblo unit, and is spoken of as a complete house. It is the construction of such a house unit that is here to be described.

A suitable site having been selected, the builder considers what the dimensions of the house should be, and these he measures by paces, placing a stone or other mark at each corner. He then goes to the woods and cuts a sufficient number of timbers for the roof of a length corresponding to the width of his house. Stones are also gathered and roughly dressed, and in all these operations he is assisted by his friends, usually of his own gens. These assistants receive no compensation except their food, but that of itself entails considerable expense on the builder, and causes him to build his house with as few helpers as possible.

The material having been accumulated, the builder goes to the village chief, who prepares for him four small eagle feathers. The chief ties a short cotton string to the stem of each, sprinkles them with votive meal, and breathes upon them his prayers for the welfare of the proposed house and its occupants. These feathers are called Nakwa kwoci, a term meaning a breathed prayer, and the prayers are addressed to Másauwu, the Sun, and to other deities concerned in house-life. These feathers are placed at the four corners of the house and a large stone is laid over each of them. The builder then decides where the door is to be located, and marks the place by setting some food on each side of it; he then passes around the site from right to left, sprinkling piki crumbs and other particles of food, mixed with native tobacco, along the lines to be occupied by the walls. As he sprinkles this offering he sings to the Sun his Kitdauwi, house song: "Si-ai, a-hai, si-ai, a-hai." The meaning of these words the people have now forgotten.

Mr. Stephen has been informed by the Indians that the man is a mason and the woman the plasterer, the house belonging to the woman when finished; but according to my own observation this is not the universal practice in modern Tusayan. In the case of the house in Oraibi, illustrated in Pl. XL from a photograph, much, if not all, of the masonry was laid, as well as finished and plastered, by the woman of the house and her female relatives. There was but one man present at this house-building, whose grudgingly performed duty consisted of lifting the larger roof beams and lintels into place and of giving occasional assistance in the heavier work. The ground about this house was strewn with quantities of broken stone for masonry, which seemed to be all prepared and brought to the spot before building began; but often the various divisions of the work are carried on by both men and women simultaneously. While the men were dressing the stones, the women brought earth and water and mixed a mud plaster. Then the walls were laid in irregular courses, using the mortar very sparingly.

The house is always built in the form of a parallelogram, the walls being from 7 to 8 feet high, and of irregular thickness, sometimes varying from 15 to 22 inches in different parts of the same wall.

Pine, piñon, juniper, cottonwood, willow, and indeed all the available trees of the region are used in house construction. The main beams for the roof are usually of pine or cottonwood, from which the bark has been stripped. The roof is always made nearly level, and the ends of the beams are placed across the side walls at intervals of about 2 feet. Above these are laid smaller poles parallel with the side walls, and not more than a foot apart. Across these again are laid reeds or small willows, as close together as they can be placed, and above this series is crossed a layer of grass or small twigs and weeds. Over this framework a layer of mud is spread, which, after drying, is covered with earth and firmly trodden down. The making of the roof is the work of the women. When it is finished the women proceed to spread a thick coating of mud for a floor. After this follows the application of plaster to the walls. Formerly a custom prevailed of leaving a small space on the wall unplastered, a belief then existing that a certain Katchina came and finished it, and although the space remained bare it was considered to be covered with an invisible plaster.

The house being thus far completed, the builder prepares four feathers similar to those prepared by the chief, and ties them to a short piece of willow, the end of which is inserted over one of the central roof beams. These feathers are renewed every year at the feast of Soyalyina, celebrated in December, when the sun begins to return northward. The builder also makes an offering to Másauwu (called "feeding the house") by placing fragments of food among the rafters, beseeching him not to hasten the departure of any of the family to the under world.

A hole is left in one corner of the roof, and under this the woman builds a fireplace and chimney. The former is usually but a small cavity about a foot square in the corner of the floor. Over this a chimney hood is constructed, its lower rim being about 3 feet above the floor.

As a rule the house has no eaves, the roof being finished with a stone coping laid flush with the wall and standing a few inches higher than the roof to preserve the earth covering from being blown or washed away. Roof-drains of various materials are also commonly inserted in the copings, as will be described later.

All the natives, as far as could be ascertained, regard this single-roomed house as being complete in itself, but they also consider it the nucleus of the larger structure. When more space is desired, as when the daughters of the house marry and require room for themselves, another house is built in front of and adjoining the first one, and a second story is often added to the original house. The same ceremony is observed in building the ground story in front, but there is no ceremony for the second and additional stories.

Anawita (war-chief of Sichumovi) describes the house in Walpi in which he was born as having had five rooms on the ground floor, and as being four stories high, but it was terraced both in front and rear, his sisters and their families occupying the rear portion. The fourth story consisted of a single room and had terraces on two opposite sides. This old house is now very dilapidated, and the greater portion of the walls have been carried away. There is no prescribed position for communicating doorways, but the outer doors are usually placed in the lee walls to avoid the prevailing southwest winds.

Formerly on the approach of cold weather, and to some extent the custom still exists, people withdrew from the upper stories to the kikoli rooms, where they huddled together to keep warm. Economy in the consumption of fuel also prompted this expedient; but these ground-floor rooms forming the first terrace, as a rule having no external doorways, and entered from without by means of a roof hatchway provided with a ladder, are ordinarily used only for purposes of storage. Even their roofs are largely utilized for the temporary storage of many household articles, and in the autumn, after the harvests have been gathered; the terraces and copings are often covered with drying peaches, and the peculiar long strips into which pumpkins and squashes have been cut to facilitate their desiccation for winter use. Among other things the household supply of wood is sometimes piled up at one end of this terrace, but more commonly the natives have so many other uses for this space that the sticks of fuel are piled up on a rude projecting skeleton of poles, supported on one side by two upright forked sticks set into the ground, and on the other resting upon the stone coping of the wall, as illustrated in Fig. 19. At other times poles are laid across a re-

FIG. 19. A Tusayan wood rack.

entering angle of a house and used as a wood rack, without any support from the ground. At the autumn season not only is the available space of the first terrace fully utilized, but every projecting beam or stick is covered with strings of drying meat or squashes, and many long poles are extended between convenient points to do temporary

Scale,

0    50    100    150 FEET.

K'IAKIMA.

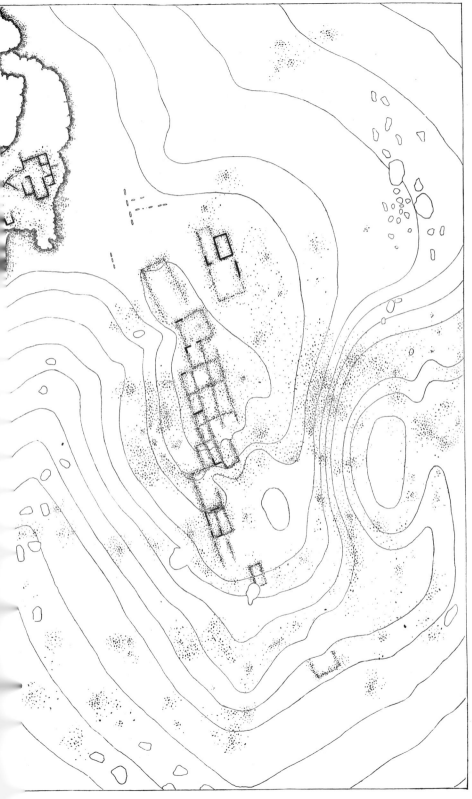

RECENT WALL AT KIAKIMA.

STANDING WALL AT PINAWA.

H.H.N.90.

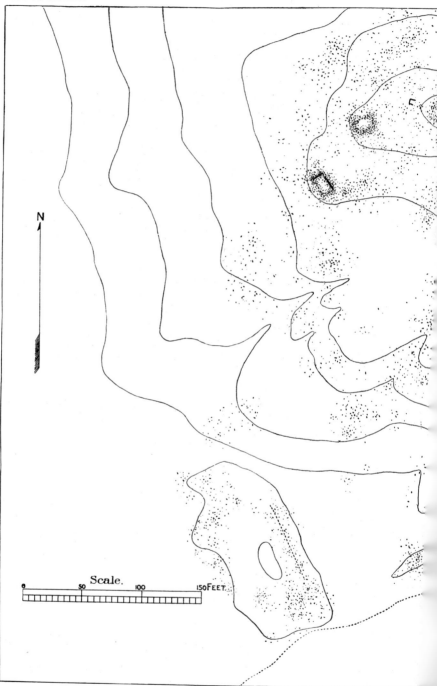

N

Scale.

MATSAKI.

HALONA EXCAVATIONS AS SEEN FROM ZUÑI.

FRAGMENTS OF HALONA WALL.

THE MESA OF TÁAAIYALANA FROM ZUÑI.

STANDING WALLS OF TÁAAIYALANA RUINS.

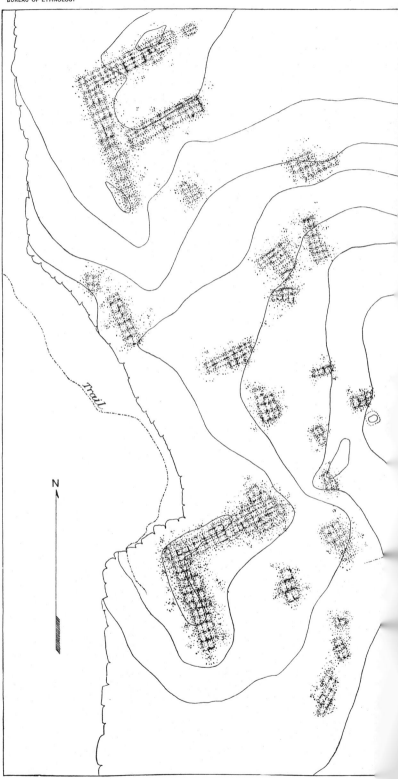

N

TÂAAIYALANA.

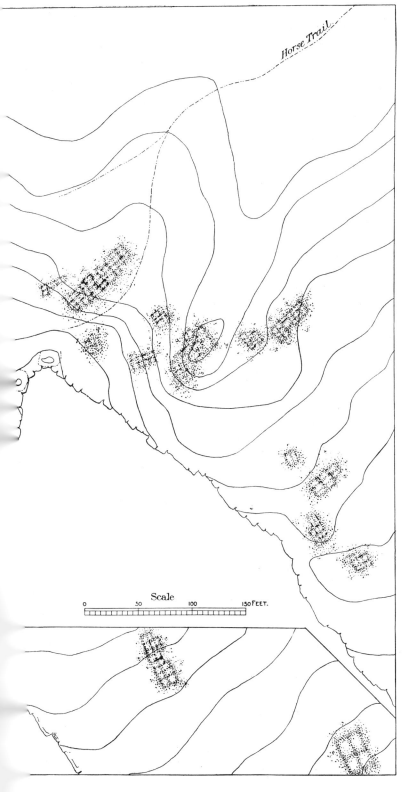

Horse Trail

Scale

0        50        100        150 FEET.

REMAINS OF A RESERVOIR ON TÂAAIYALANA.

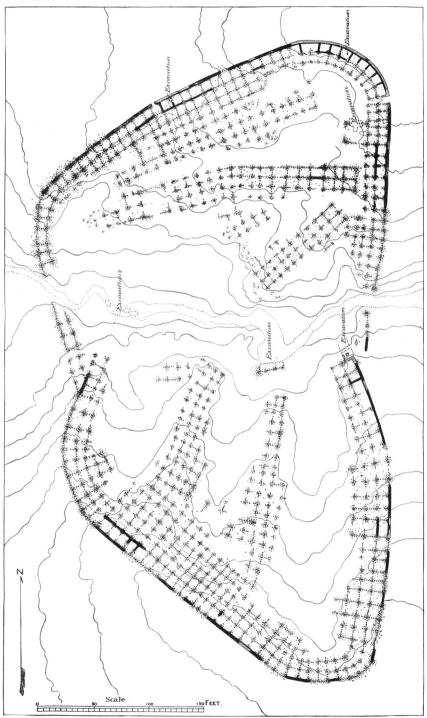

PLAN OF KIN-TIEL, ALSO SHOWING EXCAVATIONS.

NORTH WALL OF KIN-TIEL.

STANDING WALLS OF KIN-TIEL.

duty as additional drying racks. There was in all cases at least one fireplace on the inside in the upper stories, but the cooking was done on the terraces, usually at the end of the first or kikoli roof. This is still a general custom, and the end of the first terrace is usually walled up and roofed, and is called tupubi. Tuma is the name of the flat baking-stone used in the houses, but the flat stone used for baking at the kisi in the field is called tupubi.

Kikoli is the name of the ground story of the house, which has no opening in the outer wall.

The term for the terraced roofs is ihpobi, and is applied to all of them; but the tupatca ihpobi, or third terrace, is the place of general resort, and is regarded as a common loitering place, no one claiming distinct ownership. This is suggestive of an early communal dwelling, but nothing definite can now be ascertained on this point. In this connection it may also be noted that the eldest sister's house is regarded as their home by her younger brothers and her nieces and nephews.

Aside from the tupubi, there are numerous small rooms especially constructed for baking the thin, paper-like bread called piki. These are usually not more than from 5 to 7 feet high, with interior dimensions not larger than 7 feet by 10, and they are called tumcokobi, the place of the flat stone, tuma being the name of the stone itself, and tcok describing its flat position. Many of the ground-floor rooms in the dwelling houses are also devoted to this use.

The terms above are those more commonly used in referring to the houses and their leading features. A more exhaustive vocabulary of architectural terms, comprising those especially applied to the various constructional features of the kivas or ceremonial rooms, and to the "kisis," or temporary brush shelters for field use, will be found near the end of this paper.

The only trace of a traditional village plan, or arrangement of contiguous houses, is found in a meager mention in some of the traditions, that rows of houses were built to inclose the kiva, and to form an appropriate place for the public dances and processions of masked dancers. No definite ground plan, however, is ascribed to these traditional court-inclosing houses, although at one period in the evolution of this defensive type of architecture they must have partaken somewhat of the symmetrical grouping found on the Rio Chaco and elsewhere.

### LOCALIZATION OF GENTES.

In the older and more symmetrical examples there was doubtless some effort to distribute the various gentes, or at least the phratries, in definite quarters of the village, as stated traditionally. At the present day, however, there is but little trace of such localization. In the case of Oraibi, the largest of the Tusayan villages, Mr. Stephen has with great care and patience ascertained the distribution of the various gentes in the village, as recorded on the accompanying skeleton plan

(Pl. XXXVII). An examination of the diagram in connection with the appended list of the families occupying Oraibi will at once show that, however clearly defined may have been the quarters of various gentes in the traditional village, the greatest confusion prevails at the present time. The families numerically most important, such as the Reed, Coyote, Lizard, and Badger, are represented in all of the larger house clusters.

*Families occupying Oraibi.*

[See house plan—house numbers in blue.]

| | | | |
|---|---|---|---|
| 1. | Kokop | winwuh | Burrowing owl. |
| 2. | Pikyas | nyumuh | Young corn plant. |
| 3. | Bakab | winwuh | Reed (*Phragmites communis*). |
| 4. | Tuwa | winwuh | Sand. |
| 5. | Tdap | nyumuh | Jack rabbit. |
| 6. | Honan | winwuh | Badger. |
| 7. | Isn | winwuh | Coyote. |
| 8. | See 3 | | Reed. |
| 9. | Kukutc | winwuh | Lizard. |
| 10. | Honau | nyumuh | Bear. |
| 11. | Honau | | Bear. |
| 12. | See 3 | | Reed. |
| 13. | See 7 | | Coyote. |
| 14. | Tcuin | | Rattlesnake. |
| 15. | Awat | | Bow. |
| 16. | Kokuan | | Spider. |
| 17. | See 9 | | Lizard. |
| 18. | See 3 | | Reed. |
| 19. | See 1 | | Burrowing owl. |
| 20. | See 1 | | Burrowing owl. |
| 21. | See 5 | | Rabbit. |
| 22. | See 9 | | Lizard. |
| 23. | See 9 | | Lizard. |
| 23½. | See 9 | | Lizard. |
| 24. | See 2 | | Young corn. |
| 25. | Gyazro | nyumuh | Paroquet. |
| 26. | See 2 | | Young corn. |
| 27. | Kwah | nyumuh | Eagle. |
| 28. | See 7 | | Coyote. |
| 29. | See 27 | | Eagle. |
| 30. | See 9 | | Lizard. |
| 31. | See 9 | | Lizard. |
| 32. | See 7 | | Coyote. |
| 33. | See 7 | | Coyote. |
| 34. | See 2 | | Young corn. |
| 35. | See 6 | | Badger. |
| 36. | See 16 | | Spider. |
| 37. | Batun | winwuh | Squash. |
| 38. | See 15 | | Bow. |
| 39. | See 15 | | Bow. |
| 40. | See 1 | | Burrowing owl. |
| 41. | See 1 | | Burrowing owl. |
| 42. | See 6 | | Badger. |
| 43. | Tdawuh | winwuh | Sun. |

44. See 1............................................Burrowing owl.
45. See 25...........................................Paroquet.
46. See 1............................................Burrowing owl.
47. See 1............................................Burrowing owl.
48. See 3............................................Reed.
49. See 3............................................Reed.
50. See 3............................................Reed.
51. See 3............................................Reed.
52. See 27...........................................Eagle.
53. See 25...........................................Paroquet.
54. See 1............................................Burrowing owl.
55. See 5............................................Rabbit.
56. See 9............................................Lizard.
57. Pobol...............winwuh...................Moth.
58. See 6............................................Badger.
59. See 5............................................Rabbit.
60. See 5............................................Rabbit.
61. See 7............................................Coyote.
62. See 7............................................Coyote.
63. Atoko...............winwuh...................Crane.
64. See 3............................................Reed.
65. See 9............................................Lizard.
66. Keli ...............nyumuh...................Hawk.
67. See 7............................................Coyote.
68. See 43...........................................Sun.
69. Kwan...............nyumuh...................Mescal cake.
70. See 27...........................................Eagle.
71. See 27...........................................Eagle.
72. See 2............................................Corn.
73. See 6............................................Badger.
74. See 7............................................Coyote.
75. See 7............................................Coyote.
76. See 27...........................................Eagle.
77. See 3............................................Reed.
78. See 3............................................Reed.
79. See 3............................................Reed.
80. See 9............................................Lizard.
81. See 43...........................................Sun.
82. See 25...........................................Paroquet.
83. See 9............................................Lizard.
84. See 9............................................Lizard.
85. See 43...........................................Sun.
86. See 3............................................Reed.
87. See 3............................................Reed.
88. See 7............................................Coyote.
89. See 3............................................Reed.
90. Vacant.
91. See 2............................................Corn.
92. See 25...........................................Paroquet.
93. See 25...........................................Paroquet.
94. See 10...........................................Bear.
95. See 19...........................................Bear.
96. See 4............................................Sand.
97. See 4............................................Sand.
98. See 4............................................Sand.
99. See 3............................................Reed.

100. See 2............................................Corn.
101. See 2............................................Corn.
102. See 7............................................Coyote.
103. See 7............................................Coyote.
104. See 3............................................Reed.
105. See 3............................................Reed.
106. See 3............................................Reed.
107. See 5............................................Rabbit.
108. See 7............................................Coyote.
109. See 5............................................Rabbit.
110. See 5............................................Rabbit.
111. See 3............................................Reed.
112. See 5............................................Rabbit.
113. Vacant.
114. Vacant.
115. See 3............................................Reed.
116. See 6............................................Badger.
117. See 43...........................................Sun.
118. See 7............................................Coyote.
119. See 43...........................................Sun.
120. See 5............................................Rabbit.
121. See 43...........................................Sun.
122. See 3............................................Reed.
123. See 4............................................Sand.
124. See 4............................................Sand.
125. See 3............................................Reed.
126. See 3............................................Reed.
127. See 43...........................................Sun.
128. See 2............................................Corn.
129. See 9............................................Lizard.
130. See 4............................................Sand.
131. See 4............................................Sand.
132. See 7............................................Coyote.
133. See 9............................................Lizard.
134. See 25...........................................Paroquet.
135. See 25...........................................Paroquet.
136. See 6............................................Badger.
137. See 6............................................Badger.
138. Vacant.
139. See 10...........................................Bear.
140. See 3............................................Reed.
141. See 25...........................................Paroquet.
142. See 25...........................................Paroquet.
143. See 43...........................................Sun.
144. See 5............................................Rabbit.
145. See 15...........................................Bow.
146. Vacant.
147. See 6............................................Badger.
148. Katcin..............nyumuh....................Katcina.
149. See 7............................................Coyote.
150. See 6............................................Badger.
151. See 6............................................Badger.
152. See 6............................................Badger.
153. See 6............................................Badger.

Counting No. 23½, this makes 154 houses; 149 occupied, 5 vacant.

| | | | | | |
|---|---|---|---|---|---|
| Reed families | 25 | Paroquet families | 10 | Eagle families | 6 |
| Coyote families | 17 | Owl families | 9 | Bear families | 5 |
| Lizard families | 14 | Corn families | 9 | Bow families | 4 |
| Badger families | 13 | Sun families | 9 | Spider families | 2 |
| Rabbit families | 11 | Sand families | 8 | | |

Snake, Squash, Moth, Crane, Hawk, Mescal cake, Katcina, one each.

No tradition of gentile localization was discovered in Cibola. Notwithstanding the decided difference in the general arrangements of rooms in the eastern and western portions of the village, the architectural evidence does not indicate the construction of the various portions of the present Zuñi by distinct groups of people.

### INTERIOR ARRANGEMENT.

On account of the purpose for which much of the architectural data here given were originally obtained, viz, for the construction of large scale models of the pueblos, the material is much more abundant for the treatment of exterior than of interior details. Still, when the walls and roof, with all their attendant features, have been fully recorded, lit-

FIG. 20. Interior ground plan of a Tusayan room.

tle remains to be described about a pueblo house; for such of its interior details as do not connect with the external features are of the simplest character. At the time of the survey of these pueblos no exhaustive study of the interior of the houses was practicable, but the illustrations present typical dwelling rooms from both Tusayan and Zuñi. As a rule the rooms are smaller in Tusayan than at Zuñi.

The illustration, Fig. 20, shows the ground plan of a second-story room of Mashongnavi. This room measures 12 by 12½ feet, and is considerably below the average size of the rooms in these villages.   A projecting buttress or pier in the middle of the east wall divides that end of the room into two portions.   One side is provided with facilities for storage in the construction of a bench or ledge, used as a shelf, 3 feet high from the floor; and a small inclosed triangular bin, built directly on the floor, by fixing a thin slab of stone into the masonry.   The whole construction has been treated with the usual coating of mud, which has afterwards been whitewashed, with the exception of a 10-inch band that encircles the whole room at the floor line, occupying the position of a baseboard.   The other side of the dividing pier forms a recess, that is wholly given up to a series of metates or mealing stones; an indispensable feature of every pueblo household.   It is quite common to find a series of metates, as in the present instance, filling the entire available width of a recess or bay, and leaving only so much of its depth behind the stones as will afford floor space for the kneeling women who grind the corn.   In larger open apartments undivided by buttress or pier, the metates are usually built in or near one corner.   They are always so arranged that those who operate them face the middle of the room.   The floor is simply a smoothly plastered dressing of clay of the same character as the usual external roof covering.   It is, in fact, simply the roof of the room below smoothed and finished with special care. Such apartments, even in upper stories, are sometimes carefully paved over the entire surface with large flat slabs of stone.   It is often difficult to procure rectangular slabs of sufficient size for this purpose, but the irregularities of outline of the large flat stones are very skillfully interfitted, furnishing, when finished, a smoothly paved floor easily swept and kept clean.

On the right of the doorway as one enters this house are the fireplace and chimney, built in the corner of the room.   In this case the chimney hood is of semicircular form, as indicated on the plan.   The entire chimney is illustrated in Fig. 62, which represents the typical curved form of hood.   In the corner of the left as one enters are two ollas, or water jars, which are always kept filled.   On the floor near the water jars is indicated a jug or canteen, a form of vessel used for bringing in water from the springs and wells at the foot of the mesa.   At Zuñi water seems to be all brought directly in the ollas, or water jars, in which it is kept, this canteen form not being in use for the purpose.

The entrance doorway to this house, as indicated on the plan, is set back or stepped on one side, a type of opening which is quite common in Tusayan.   This form is illustrated in Fig. 84.

This room has three windows, all of very small size, but it has no interior communication with any other room.   In this respect it is exceptional.   Ordinarily rooms communicate with others of the cluster.

Pl. LXXXV shows another typical Tusayan interior in perspective.   It illustrates essentially the same arrangement as does the preceding example.   The room is much larger than the one above described, and it is divided midway of its length by a similar buttress. This buttress supports a heavy girder, thus admitting of the use of two tiers of floor beams to span the whole length of the room. The fireplace and chimney are similar to those described, as is also the single compartment for mealing stones. In this case, however, this portion of the room is quite large, and the row of mealing stones is built at right angles to its back wall and not parallel with it.

The right-hand portion of the room is provided with a long, straight pole suspended from the roof beams. This is a common feature in both Tusayan and Zuñi. The pole is used for the suspension of the household stock of blankets and other garments. The windows of this house are small, and two of them, in the right-hand division of the room, have been roughly sealed up with masonry.

Pl. LXXXVI illustrates a typical Zuñi interior. In this instance the example happens to be rather larger than the average room. It will be noticed that this apartment has many features in common with that at Tusayan last described. The pole upon which blankets are suspended is here incorporated into the original construction of the house, its two ends being deeply embedded in the masonry of the wall. The entire floor is paved with slabs of much more regular form than any used at Tusayan. The Zuñi have access to building stone which is of a much better grade than is available in Tusayan.

This room is furnished with long, raised benches of masonry along the sides, a feature much more common at Zuñi than at Tusayan. Usually such benches extend along the whole length of a wall, but here the projection is interrupted on one side by the fireplace and chimney, and on the left it terminates abruptly near the beginning of a tier of mealing stones, in order to afford floor space for the women who grind. The metates are arranged in the usual manner, three in a row, but there is an additional detached section placed at right angles to the main series. The sill of the doorway by which this room communicates with an adjoining one is raised about 18 inches above the floor, and is provided with a rudely mortised door in a single panel. Alongside is a small hole through which the occupant can prop the door on the inside of the communicating room. The subsequent sealing of the small hand-hole with mud effectually closes the house against intrusion. The unusual height of this door sill from the floor has necessitated the construction of a small step, which is built of masonry and covered with a single slab of stone. All the doors of Zuñi are more or less raised above the ground or floor, though seldom to the extent shown in the present example. This room has no external door and can be directly entered only by means of the hatchway and ladder shown in the drawing. At one time this room was probably bounded by outer walls and was provided with both door and windows, though now no evidence of the door remains, and the windows have become niches in the wall utilized for the reception of the small odds and ends of a Zuñi household. The chimney of this house will be noticed as differing materially, both in form and in its position in the room, from the Tusayan examples. This form is, however, the most common type of chimney used in Zuñi at the present time, although many examples of the curved type also occur. It is built about midway of the long wall of the room. The Tusayan chimneys seldom occupy such a position, but are nearly always built in corners. The use of a pier or buttress-projection for the support of a roof girder that is characteristic of Tusayan is not practiced at Zuñi to any extent. Deer horns have been built into the wall of the room to answer the purpose of pegs, upon which various household articles are suspended.

The various features, whose positions in the pueblo dwelling house have been briefly described above, will each be made the subject of more exhaustive study in tracing the various modifications of form through which they have passed. The above outline will furnish a general idea of the place that these details occupy in the house itself.

## KIVAS IN TUSAYAN.

*General use of kivas.*—Wherever the remains of pueblo architecture occur among the plateaus of the southwest there appears in every important village throughout all changes of form, due to variations of environment and other causes, the evidence of chambers of exceptional character. The chambers are distinguishable from the typical dwelling rooms by their size and position, and, generally, in ancient examples, by their circular form. This feature of pueblo architecture has survived to the present time, and is prominent in all modern pueblos that have come under the writer's notice, including the villages of Acoma and Jemez, belonging to the Rio Grande group, as well as in the pueblos under discussion. In all the pueblos that have been examined, both ancient and modern, with the exception of those of Tusayan, these special rooms, used for ceremonial purposes, occupy marginal or semi-detached positions in the house clusters. The latter are wholly detached from the houses, as may be seen from the ground plans.

*Origin of the name.*—Such ceremonial rooms are known usually by the Spanish term "estufa," meaning literally a stove, and here used in the sense of "sweat house," but the term is misleading, as it more properly describes the small sweat houses that are used ceremonially by lodge-building Indians, such as the Navajo. At the suggestion of Major Powell the Tusayan word for this everpresent feature of pueblo architecture has been adopted, as being much more appropriate. The word "kiva," then, will be understood to designate the ceremonial chamber of the pueblo building peoples, ancient and modern.

*Antiquity of the kiva.*—The widespread occurrence of this feature and its evident antiquity distinguish it as being especially worthy of exhaustive study, especially as embodied in its construction may be found survivals of early methods of arrangement that have long ago become extinct in the constantly improving art of housebuilding, but which are preserved through the well known tendency of the survival of ancient practice in matters pertaining to the religious observances of a primitive people. Unfortunately, in the past the Zuñi have been exposed to the repressive policy of the Spanish authorities, and this has probably seriously affected the purity of the kiva type. At one time, when the ceremonial observances of the Zuñi took place in secret for fear of incurring the wrath of the Spanish priests, the original kivas must have been wholly abandoned, and though at the present time some of the kivas of Zuñi occupy marginal positions in the cell clusters, just as in many ancient examples, it is doubtful whether these rooms faithfully represent the original type of kiva. There seems to be but little structural evidence to distinguish the present kivas from ordinary large Zuñi rooms beyond the special character of the fireplace and of the entrance trap door, features which will be fully described later. At Tusayan, on the other hand, we find a distinct and characteristic structural plan of the kiva, as well as many special constructive devices. Although the position of the ceremonial room is here exceptional in its entire separation from the dwelling, this is due to clearly traceable influences in the immediate orographic environment, and the wholly subterranean arrangement of most of the kivas in this group is also due to the same local causes.

*Excavation of the kiva.*—The tendency to depress or partly excavate the ceremonial chamber existed in Zuñi, as in all the ancient pueblo buildings which have been examined; but the solid rock of the mesa tops in Tusayan did not admit of the necessary excavation, and the persistence of this requirement, which, as I shall elsewhere show, has an important connection with the early types of pueblo building, compelled the occupants of these rocky sites to locate their kivas at points where depressions already existed. Such facilities were most abundant near the margins of the mesas, where in many places large blocks of sandstone have fallen out from the edge of the surface stratum, leaving nearly rectangular spaces at the summit of the cliff wall. The construction of their villages on these rocky promontories forced the Tusayan builders to sacrifice, to a large extent, the traditional and customary arrangement of the kivas within the house-inclosed courts of the pueblo, in order to obtain properly depressed sites. This accidental effect of the immediate environment resulted in giving unusual prominence to the sinking of the ceremonial room below the ground surface, but a certain amount of excavation is found as a constant accompaniment of this feature throughout the pueblo region in both ancient and modern villages. Even at Zuñi, where the kivas appear to retain but few of the specialized features that distinguish them at Tusayan, the floors are found to be below the general level of the ground. But at Tusayan the development of this single requirement has been carried to such an extent that many of the kivas are wholly subterranean. This is particularly the case with those that occupy marginal sites on the mesas, such as have been referred to above. In such instances the broken-out recesses in the upper rocks have been walled up on the outside, roughly lined with masonry within, and roofed over in the usual manner. In many cases the depth of these rock niches is such that the kiva roof when finished does not project above the general level of the mesa summit, and its earth covering is indistinguishable from the adjoining surface, except for the presence of the box-like projection of masonry that surrounds the entrance trap door and its ladder (see Pl. LXXXVII). Frequently in such cases the surface of the ground shows no evidence of the outlines or dimensions of the underlying room. Examples of such subterranean kivas may be seen in the foreground of the general view of a court in Oraibi (Pl. XXXVIII), and in the view of the dance rock at Walpi (Pl. XXIV). But such wholly subterranean arrangement of the ceremonial chamber is by no means universal even at Tusayan. Even when the kiva was placed within the village courts or close to the houses, in conformity to the traditional plan and ancient practice as evidenced in the ruins, naturally depressed sites were still sought; but such sites as the mesa margin affords were rarely available at any distance from the rocky rim. The result is that most of the court kivas are only partly depressed. This is particularly noticeable in a court kiva in Shumopavi, an illustration of which is given in Fig. 14.

The mungkiva or principal kiva of Shupaulovi, illustrated in Pl. XXXIII, is scarcely a foot above the ground level on the side towards the houses, but its rough walls are exposed to a height of several feet down on the declivity of the knoll. The view of the stone corrals of Mashongnavi, shown in Pl. CIX, also illustrates a kiva of the type described. This chamber is constructed on a sharp slope of the declivity where a natural depression favored the builders. On the upper side the roof is even with the ground, but on its outer or southern side the masonry is exposed to nearly the whole depth of the chamber. At the north end of Shumopavi, just outside the houses, are two kivas, one of which is of the semi-subterranean type. The other shows scarcely any masonry above the ground outside of the box-like entrance way. Pl. LXXXVIII illustrates these two kivas as seen from the northeast, and shows their relation to the adjacent houses. The following (Fig. 21) illustrates the same group from the opposite point of view.

*Access.*—The last described semi-subterranean kiva and the similar one in the court of the village, show a short flight of stone steps on their eastern side. Entrance to the ceremonial chamber is prevented when necessary by the removal of the ladder from the outside, or in some instances by the withdrawal of the rungs, which are loosely inserted into holes in the side pieces. There is no means of preventing access to the exposed trap doors, which are nearly on a level with the ground. As a matter of convenience and to facilitate the entrance into the kiva of costumed and masked dancers, often encumbered with clumsy paraphernalia, steps are permanently built into the outside wall of the kiva in direct contradiction to the ancient principles of construction; that is, in having no permanent or fixed means of access from the ground to the first roof. These are the only cases in which stone steps spring directly from the ground, although they are a very important feature in Tusayan house architecture above the first story, as may be seen in any of the general views of the villages. The justification of such an arrangement in connection with the indefensible kiva roof lies obviously in the different conditions here found as compared with the dwellings.

Fig. 21. North kivas of Shumopavi, seen from the southwest.

The subterranean kiva of the Shumopavi group, above illustrated, is exceptional as occurring at some distance from the mesa rim. Probably all such exceptions to the rule are located in natural fissures or crevices of the sandstone, or where there was some unusual facility for the excavation of the site to the required depth. The most noteworthy example of such inner kiva being located with reference to favorable rock fissures has been already described in discussing the ground plan of Walpi and its southern court-inclosed kiva (p. 65).

*Masonry.*—The exterior masonry of these chambers seems in all cases to be of ruder construction than that of the dwelling houses. This is particularly noticeable in the kivas of Walpi on the mesa edge, but is apparent even in some of the Zuñi examples. One of the kivas of house No. 1 in Zuñi, near the churchyard, has small openings in its wall that are rudely framed with stone slabs set in a stone wall of exceptional roughness. Apparently there has never been any attempt to smooth or reduce this wall to a finished surface with the usual coating of adobe mud.

In Tusayan also some of the kiva walls look as though they had been
built of the first material that came to hand, piled up nearly dry, and
with no attempt at the chinking of joints, that imparts some degree of
finish to the dwelling-house masonry.  The inside of these kivas, however, is usually plastered smoothly, but the interior plastering is applied
on a base of masonry even in the case of the kivas that are wholly
subterranean.  It seems to be the Tusayan practice to line all sides of
the kivas with stone masonry, regardless of the completeness and fitness
of the natural cavity.  It is impossible, therefore, to ascertain from the
interior of a kiva how much of the work of excavation is artificial and
how much has been done by nature.  The lining of masonry probably
holds the plastering of adobe mud much better than the naked surface
of the rock, but the Tusayan builders would hardly resort to so laborious a device to gain this small advantage.  The explanation of this
apparent waste of labor lies in the fact that kivas had been built of
masonry from time immemorial, and that the changed conditions of the
present Tusayan environment have not exerted their influence for a
sufficient length of time to overcome the traditional practice.  As will
be seen later, the building of a kiva is accompanied by certain rites and
ceremonies based on the use of masonry walls, additional testimony of
the comparatively recent date of the present subterranean types.

*Orientation.*—In questioning the Tusayan on this subject Mr. Stephen
was told that no attention to the cardinal points was observed in the
plan, although the walls are spoken of according to the direction to
which they most closely approximate.  An examination of the village
plans of the preceding chapters, however, will show a remarkable degree of uniformity in the directions of kivas which can scarcely be due
to accident in rooms built on such widely differing sites.  The intention
seems to have been to arrange these ceremonial chambers approximately on the north and south line, though none of the examples approach the meridian very closely.  Most of them face southeast, though
some, particularly in Walpi, face west of south.  In Walpi four of
the five kivas are planned on a southwest and northeast line, following
the general direction of the mesa edge, while the remaining one faces
southeast.  The difference in this last case may have been brought
about by exigencies of the site on the mesa edge and the form of the
cavity in which the kiva was built.  Again at Hano and Sichumovi
(Pls. XVI and XVIII) on the first mesa this uniformity of direction prevails, but, as the plans show, the kivas in these two villages are few in
number.  The two kivas of Shupaulovi will be seen (Pl. XXX) to have
the same direction, viz, facing southeast.  In Shumopavi (Pl. XXXIV)
there are four kivas all facing southeast.  In Mashongnavi, however
(Pl. XXVI), the same uniformity does not prevail.  Three of the kivas
face south of east, and two others built in the edge of the rocky bench
on the south side of the village face west of south.  In the large village

of Oraibi there is remarkable uniformity in the direction of the many kivas, there being a variation of only a few degrees in direction in the whole number of thirteen shown on the plan (Pl. XXXVI). But in the case of the large kiva partly above ground designated as the Coyote kiva, the direction from which it is entered is the reverse of that of the other kivas. No explanation is offered that will account for this curious single exception to the rule. The intention of the builders has evidently been to make the altar and its attendant structural features conform to a definite direction, fixed, perhaps, by certain requirements of the ceremonial, but the irregularity of the general village plan in many cases resulting from its adaptation to restricted sites, has given rise to the variations that are seen.

In Zuñi there was an evident purpose to preserve a certain uniformity of direction in the kiva entrances. In house No. 1 (Pls. LXXVI and LXXVII) there are two kivas, distinguishable on the plan by the large divided trap door. The entrance of these both face southeast, and it can readily be seen that this conformity has been provided intentionally, since the rooms themselves do not correspond in arrangement. The roof opening is in one case across the room and in the other it is placed longitudinally. As has been pointed out above, the general plan of arranging the kivas is not so readily distinguished in Zuñi as in Tusayan. Uniformity, so far as it is traceable, is all the more striking as occurring where there is so much more variation in the directions of the walls of the houses. Still another confirmation is furnished by the pueblo of Acoma, situated about 60 miles eastward from Zuñi. Here the kivas are six in number and the directions of all the examples are found to vary but a few degrees. These also face east of south.

There are reasons for believing that the use of rectangular kivas is of later origin in the pueblo system of building than the use of the circular form of ceremonial chamber that is of such frequent occurrence among the older ruins. Had strict orientation of the rectangular kiva prevailed for long periods of time it would undoubtedly have exerted a strong influence towards the orientation of the entire pueblo clusters in which the kivas were incorporated; but in the earlier circular form, the constructional ceremonial devices could occupy definite positions in relation to the cardinal points at any part of the inner curve of the wall without necessarily exerting any influence on the directions of adjoining dwellings.

*The ancient form of kiva.*—In none of the ruins examined in the province of Tusayan have distinct traces of ancient kivas been found, nor do any of them afford evidence as to the character of the ceremonial rooms. It is not likely, however, that the present custom of building these chambers wholly under ground prevailed generally among the earlier Tusayan villages, as some of the remains do not occupy sites that would suggest such arrangement. The typical circular kiva characteristic of most of the ancient pueblos has not been seen within the limits of Tusayan, although it occurs constantly in the ruins of Canyon de Chelly which are occasionally referred to in Tusayan tradition as having been occupied by related peoples.   Mr. Stephen, however, found vestiges of such ancient forms among the débris of fallen walls occupying two small knolls on the edge of the first mesa, at a point that overlooks the broken-down ruin of Sikyatki.   On the southeast shoulder of one of the knolls is a fragment of a circular wall which was originally 12 feet in diameter.   It is built of flat stones, from 2 to 4 inches thick, 6 to 8 inches wide, and a foot or more in length, nearly all of which have been pecked and dressed.   Mud mortar has been sparingly used, and the masonry shows considerable care and skill in execution; the curve of the wall is fairly true, and the interstices of the masonry are neatly filled in with smaller fragments, in the manner of some of the best work of the Canyon de Chelly ruins.

The knoll farther south shows similar traces, and on the southeast slope is the complete ground plan of a round structure 16½ feet in diameter.   At one point of the curved wall, which is about 22 inches thick, occurs the characteristic recessed katchinkihu (described later in discussing the interior of kivas) indicating the use of this chamber for ceremonial purposes.

Although these remains probably antedate any of the Tusayan ruins discussed above (Chapter II), they suggest a connection and relationship between the typical kiva of the older ruins and the radically different form in use at the present time.

*Native explanations of position.*—Notwithstanding the present practice in the location of kivas, illustrated in the plans, the ideal village plan is still acknowledged to have had its house-clusters so distributed as to form inclosed and protected courts, the kivas being located within these courts or occupying marginal positions in the house-clusters on the edge of the inclosed areas.   But the native explanations of the traditional plan are vague and contradictory.

In the floor of the typical kiva is a sacred cavity called the sipapuh, through which comes the beneficent influence of the deities or powers invoked.   According to the accounts of some of the old men the kiva was constructed to inclose this sacred object, and houses were built on every side to surround the kiva and form its outer wall.   In earlier times, too, so the priests relate, people were more devout, and the houses were planned with their terraces fronting upon the court, so that the women and children and all the people, could be close to the masked dancers (katchinas) as they issued from the kiva.   The spectators filled the terraces, and sitting there they watched the katchinas dance in the court, and the women sprinkled meal upon them, while they listened to their songs.   Other old men say the kiva was excavated in imitation of the original house in the interior of the earth, where the human family were created, and from which they climbed to the surface of the ground by means of a ladder, and through just such an opening as the hatch-way of the kiva. Another explanation commonly offered is that they are made underground because they are thus cooler in summer, and more easily warmed in winter.

All these factors may have had some influence in the design, but we have already seen that excavation to the extent here practiced is wholly exceptional in pueblo building and the unusual development of this requirement of kiva construction has been due to purely local causes. In the habitual practice of such an ancient and traditional device, the Indians have lost all record of the real causes of the perpetuation of this requirement. At Zuñi, too, a curious explanation is offered for the partial depression of the kiva floor below the general surrounding level. Here it is naively explained that the floor is excavated in order to attain a liberal height for the ceiling within the kiva, this being a room of great importance. Apparently it does not occur to the Zuñi archi-tect that the result could be achieved in a more direct and much less laborious manner by making the walls a foot or so higher at the time of building the kiva, after the manner in which the same problem is solved when it is encountered in their ordinary dwelling house con-struction. Such explanations, of course, originated long after the prac-tice became established.

### METHODS OF KIVA BUILDING AND RITES.

The external appearance of the kivas of Tusayan has been described and illustrated; it now remains to examine the general form and method of construction of these subterranean rooms, and to notice the at-tendant rites and ceremonies.

*Typical plans.*— All the Tusayan kivas are in the form of a paralello-gram, usually about 25 feet long and half as wide, the ceiling, which is from $5\frac{1}{2}$ to 8 feet high, being slightly higher in the middle than at either end. There is no prescribed rule for kiva dimensions, and seemingly the size of the chamber is determined according to the number who are to use it, and who assume the labor of its construction. A list of typi-cal measurements obtained by Mr. Stephen is appended (p. 136).

An excavation of the desired dimensions having been made, or an existing one having been discovered, the person who is to be chief of the kiva performs the same ceremony as that prescribed for the male head of a family when the building of a dwelling house is undertaken. He takes a handful of meal, mixed with piki crumbs, and a little of the crumbled herb they use as tobacco, and these he sprinkles upon the ground, beginning on the west side, passing southward, and so around, the sprinkled line he describes marking the position to be occupied by the walls. As he thus marks the compass of the kiva, he sings in a droning tone "Si-ai, a-hai, a-hai, si-ai, a-hai"—no other words but these. The meaning of these words seems to be unknown, but all the priests agree in saying that the archaic chant is addressed to the sun, and it is called Kitdauwi—the House Song.  The chief then selects four good-sized stones of hard texture for corner stones, and at each corner he lays a baho, previously prepared, sprinkles it with the mixture with which he has described the line of the walls, and then lays the corner stone upon it.  As he does this, he expresses his hope that the walls "will take good root hold," and stand firm and secure.

The men have already quarried or collected a sufficient quantity of stone, and a wall is built in tolerably regular courses along each side of the excavation.  The stones used are roughly dressed by fracture; they are irregular in shape, and of a size convenient for one man to handle.  They are laid with only a very little mud mortar, and carried up, if the ground be level, to within 18 inches of the surface.  If the kiva is built on the edge of the cliff, as at Walpi, the outside wall connects the sides of the gap, conforming to the line of the cliff.  If the surface is sloping, the level of the roof is obtained by building up one side of the kiva above the ground to the requisite height as illustrated in Fig. 21.  One end of the "Goat" kiva at Walpi is 5 feet above ground, the other end being level with the sloping surface.  When the ledge on the precipitous face of the mesa is uneven it is filled in with rough masonry to obtain a level for the floor, and thus the outside wall of some of·the Walpi kivas is more than 12 feet high, although in the interior the measurement from floor to ceiling is much less.

Both cottonwood and pine are used for the roof timbers; they are roughly dressed, and some of them show that an attempt has been made to hew them with four sides, but none are square.  In the roof of the "Goat" kiva, at Walpi, are four well hewn pine timbers, measuring exactly 6 by 10 inches, which are said to have been taken from the mission house built near Walpi by the Spanish priests some three centuries ago.  The ceiling plan of the mungkiva of Shupaulovi (Fig. 23) shows that four of these old Spanish squared beams have been utilized in its construction.  One of these is covered with a rude decoration of gouged grooves and bored holes, forming a curious line-and-dot ornament.  The other kiva of this village contains a single undecorated square Spanish roof beam.  This beam contrasts very noticeably with the rude round poles of the native work, one of which, in the case of the kiva last mentioned, is a forked trunk of a small tree.  Some of the Indians say that the timbers were brought by them from the Shumopavi spring, where the early Spanish priests had established a mission.  According to these accounts, the home mission was established at Walpi, with another chapel at Shumopavi, and a third and important one at Awatubi.

One man, Sikapiki by name, stated that the squared and carved beams were brought from the San Francisco Mountains, more than a hundred miles away, under the direction of the priests, and that they were carved and finished prior to transportation.  They were intended for the chapel and cloister, but the latter building was never finished.

The roof timbers were finally distributed among the people of Shumopavi and Shupaulovi. At Shumopavi one of the kivas, known as the Nuvwatikyuobi (The-high-place-of-snow — San Francisco Mountains) kiva, was built only 8 years ago. The main roof timbers are seven in number. Four of them are hewn with flat sides, 8 by 12 inches to 9 by 13 inches; the other three are round, the under sides slightly hewn, and they are 12 inches in diameter. These timbers were brought from the San Francisco Mountains while the Spaniards were here. The Shumopavi account states that the people were compelled to drag most of the timbers with ropes, although oxen were also used in some cases, and that the Spaniards used them to roof their mission buildings. After the destruction of the mission these timbers were used in the construction of a dwelling house, which, falling into ruin, was abandoned and pulled down. Subsequently they were utilized as described above. In the Tcosobi, Jay, the main timbers were taken out of it many years ago and used in another kiva. The timbers now in the roof are quite small and are laid in pairs, but they are old and much decayed. In the Gyarzobi, Paroquet, are six squared timbers from the Spanish mission buildings, measuring 9 by 13 inches, 8 by 12 inches, etc. These have the same curious grooved and dotted ornamentation that occurs on the square beam of Shupaulovi, above described. At the other end of the kiva are also two unusually perfect round timbers that may have come from the mission ruin. All of these show marks of fire, and are in places deeply charred.

In continuation of the kiva building process, the tops of the walls are brought to an approximate level. The main roof timbers are then laid parallel with the end walls, at irregular distances, but less than 3 feet apart, except near the middle, where a space of about 7 feet is left between two beams, as there the hatchway is to be built. The ends of the timbers rest upon the side walls, and as they are placed in position a small feather, to which a bit of cotton string is tied (nakwakwoci) is also placed under each. Stout poles, from which the bark has been stripped, are laid at right angles upon the timbers, with slight spaces between them. Near the center of the kiva two short timbers are laid across the two main beams about 5 feet apart; this is done to preserve a space of 5 by 7 feet for the hatchway, which is made with walls of stone laid in mud plaster, resting upon the two central beams and upon the two side pieces. This wall or combing is carried up so as to be at least 18 inches above the level of the finished roof. Across the poles, covering the rest of the roof, willows and straight twigs of any kind are laid close together, and over these is placed a layer of dry grass arranged in regular rows. Mud is then carefully spread over the grass to a depth of about 3 inches, and after it has nearly dried it is again gone over so as to fill up all the cracks. A layer of dry earth is then spread over all and firmly trodden down, to render the roof water-tight and bring its surface level with the surrounding ground, following the same method and order of construction that prevails in dwelling-house buildings.

Short timbers are placed across the top of the hatchway wall, one end of which is raised higher than the other, so as to form a slope, and upon these timbers stone slabs are closely laid for a cover. (See Pl. LXXXVII.) An open space, usually about 2 by 4½ feet, is preserved, and this is the only outlet in the structure, serving at once as doorway, window, and chimney.

The roof being finished, a floor of stone flags is laid; but this is never in a continuous level, for at one end it is raised as a platform some 10 or 12 inches high, extending for about a third of the length of the kiva and terminating in an abrupt step just before coming under the hatchway, as illustrated in the ground plan of the mungkiva of Shupaulovi (Fig. 22, and also in Figs. 25 and 27). On the edge of the platform rests the foot of a long ladder, which leans against the higher side of the hatchway, and its tapering ends project 10 or 12 feet in the air. Upon this platform the women and other visitors sit when admitted to witness any of the ceremonies observed in the kiva. The main floor in a few of the kivas is composed of roughly hewn planks, but this is a comparatively recent innovation, and is not generally deemed desirable, as the movement of the dancers on the wooden floor shakes the fetiches out of position.

On the lower or main floor a shallow pit of varying dimensions, but usually about a foot square, is made for a fireplace, and is located immediately under the opening in the hatchway. The intention in raising the hatchway above the level of the roof and in elevating the ceiling in the middle is to prevent the fire from igniting them. The ordinary fuel used in the kiva is greasewood, and there are always several bundles of the shrub in its green state suspended on pegs driven in the wall of the hatchway directly over the fire. This shrub, when green, smolders and emits a dense, pungent smoke, but when perfectly dry, burns with a bright, sparkling flame.

Across the end of the kiva on the main floor a ledge of masonry is built, usually about 2 feet high and 1 foot wide, which serves as a shelf for the display of fetiches and other paraphernalia during stated observances (see Fig. 22). A small, niche-like aperture is made in the middle of this ledge, and is called the katchin kihu (katchina house). During a festival certain masks are placed in it when not in use by the dancers. Some of the kivas have low ledges built along one or both sides for use as seats, and some have none, but all except two or three have the ledge at the end containing the katchina house.

In the main floor of the kiva there is a cavity about a foot deep and 8 or 10 inches across, which is usually covered with a short, thick slab of cottonwood, whose upper surface is level with the floor. Through the middle of this short plank and immediately over the cavity a hole of 2 or 2½ inches in diameter is bored. This hole is tapered, and is accurately fitted with a movable wooden plug, the top of which is flush with the surface of the plank. The plank and cavity usually occupy a position in the main floor near the end of the kiva.   This feature is the sipapuh, the place of the gods, and the most sacred portion of the ceremonial chamber.   Around this spot the fetiches are set during a festival; it typifies also the first world of the Tusayan genesis and the opening through which the people first emerged.   It is frequently so spoken of at the present time.

Other little apertures or niches are constructed in the side walls; they usually open over the main floor of the kiva near the edge of the dais that forms the second level, that upon which the foot of the ladder rests. These are now dedicated to any special purpose, but are used as receptacles for small tools and other ordinary articles.   In early days, however, these niches were used exclusively as receptacles for the sacred pipes and tobacco and other smaller paraphernalia.

In order to make clearer the relative positions of the various features of kiva construction that have been described several typical examples are here illustrated.   The three ground plans given are drawn to scale and represent kivas of average dimensions.   Mr. Stephen has made a series of typical kiva measurements, which is appended to this section, and comparison of these with the plans will show the relation of the examples selected to the usual dimensions of these rooms.   Fig. 22 is the ground plan of the mungkiva, or chief kiva, of Shupaulovi.

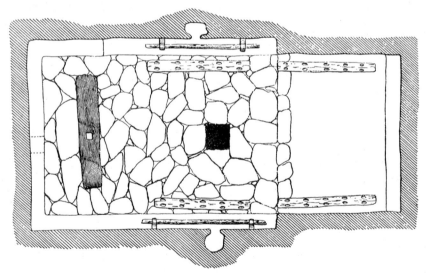

FIG. 22. Ground plan of the chief kiva of Shupaulovi.

It will be observed that the second level of the kiva floor, forming the dias before referred to, is about 15 inches narrower on each side than the main floor.   The narrowing of this portion of the kiva floor is not universal and does not seem to be regulated by any rule.   Sometimes the narrowing is carried out on one side only, as in the mungkiva of Mashongnavi (Fig. 27), sometimes on both, as in the present example,

and in other cases it is absent. In the second kiva of Shupaulovi, illustrated in Fig. 25, there is only one small jog that has been built midway along the wall of the upper level and it bears no relation to the
point at which the change of floor level occurs. The ledge, or dias, is
free for the use of spectators, the Indians say, just as the women stand
on the house terraces to witness a dance, and do not step into the court.
The ledge in this case is about a foot above the main floor. Benches of
masonry are built along each side, though, as the plan shows, they are
not of the same length. The bench on the eastern side is about 4 feet
shorter than the other, which is cut off by a continuation of the high
bench that contains the katchinkihu beyond the corner of the room.
These side benches are for the use of participants in the ceremonies.
When young men are initiated into the various societies during the
feasts in the fall of the year they occupy the floor of the sacred division of the kiva, while the old members of the order occupy the benches
along the wall. The higher bench at the end of the room is used as a
shelf for paraphernalia. The hole, or recess, in this bench, whose position is indicated by the dotted lines on the plan, is the sacred orifice
from which the katchina is said to come, and is called the katchinkihu.

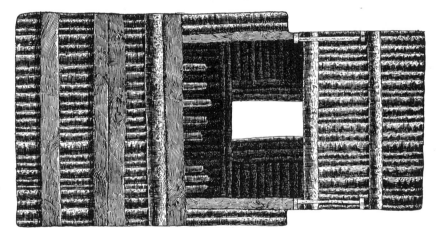

FIG. 23. Ceiling plan of the chief kiva of Shupaulovi.

In the floor of the kiva, near the katchinkihu, is the sipapuh, the cottonwood plug set into a cottonwood slab over a cavity in the floor. The
plan shows how this plank, about 18 inches wide and 6½ feet long, has
been incorporated into the paving of the main floor. The paving is
composed of some quite large slabs of sandstone whose irregular edges
have been skillfully fitted to form a smooth and well finished pavement.
The position of the niches that form pipe receptacles is shown on the
plan opposite the fireplace in each side wall. The position of the foot
of the ladder is indicated, the side poles resting upon the paved surface of the second level about 15 inches from the edge of the step. Fig.
23 gives a ceiling plan of the same kiva, illustrating the arrangement

of such of the roof beams and sticks as are visible from inside.  The plan shows the position of the four Spanish beams before referred to, the northernmost being the one that has the line and dot decoration. The next two beams, laid in contact, are also square and of Spanish make.  The fourth Spanish beam is on the northern edge of the hatchway dome and supports its wall.  The adjoining beam is round and of native workmanship.  The position and dimensions of the large hatchway projection are here indicated in plan, but the general appearance of this curious feature of the Tusayan kiva can be better seen from the interior view (Fig. 24).  Various uses are attributed to this domelike

FIG. 24. Interior view of a Tusayan kiva.

structure, aside from the explanation that it is built at a greater height in order to lessen the danger of ignition of the roof beams.  The old men say that formerly they smoked and preserved meat in it.  Others say it was used for drying bundles of wood by suspension over the fire preparatory to use in the fireplace.  It is also said to constitute an upper chamber to facilitate the egress of smoke, and doubtless it aids in the performance of this good office.

The mud plaster that has been applied directly to the stone work of the interior of this kiva is very much blackened by smoke.  From about half of the wall space the plaster has fallen or scaled off, and the exposed stonework is much blackened as though the kiva had long been used with the wall in this uncovered condition.

The fireplace is simply a shallow pit about 18 inches square that is placed directly under the opening of the combined hatchway and smoke hole. It is usually situated from 2 to 3 feet from the edge of the second level of the kiva floor. The paving stones are usually finished quite neatly and smoothly where their edges enframe the firepit.

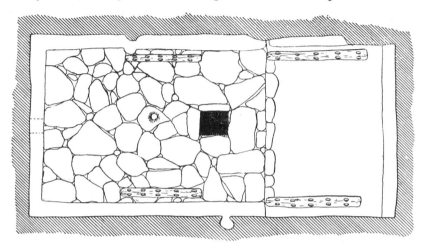

FIG. 25. Ground plan of a Shupaulovi kiva.

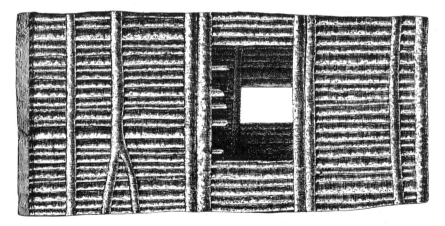

FIG. 26. Ceiling plan of a Shupaulovi kiva.

Figs. 25 and 26 illustrate the ground and ceiling plans of the second kiva of the same village. In all essential principles of arrangement it is identical with the preceding example, but minor modifications will be noticed in several of the features. The bench at the katchina, or "altar" end of the kiva, has not the height that was seen in the mung-kiva, but is on the same level as the benches of the sides. Here the

sipapuh is at much greater distance than usual from the katchina recess.   It is also quite exceptional in that the plug is let into an orifice
in one of the paving stones, as shown on the plan, instead of into a
cottonwood plank.   Some of the paving stones forming the floor of this
kiva are quite regular in shape and of unusual dimensions, one of them
being nearly 5 feet long and 2 feet wide.   The gray polish of long continued use imparts to these stones an appearance of great hardness.
The ceiling plan of this kiva (Fig. 26) shows a single specimen of Spanish beam at the extreme north end of the roof.   It also shows a forked
"viga" or ceiling beam, which is quite unusual.

This kiva is better plastered than the mungkiva and shows in places
evidences of many successive coats.   The general rule of applying the
interior plastering of the kiva on a base of masonry has been violated
in this example.   The north end and part of the adjoining sides have
been brought to an even face by filling in the inequalities of the excavation with reeds which are applied in a vertical position and are held
in place by long, slender, horizontal rods, forming a rude matting or

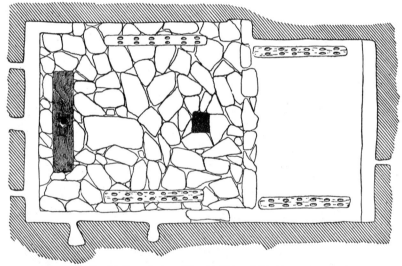

Fig. 27. Ground plan of the chief kiva of Mashóngnavi.

wattling.   The rods are fastened to the rocky wall at favorable points
by means of small prongs of some hard wood, and the whole of the
primitive lathing is then thickly plastered with adobe mud.   Mr.
Stephen found the Ponobi kiva of Oraibi treated in the same manner.
The walls are lined with a reed lathing over which mud is plastered.
The reed used is the Bakabi (*Phragmites communis*) whose stalks vary
from a quarter of an inch to three-quarters of an inch in diameter.   In
this instance the reeds are also laid vertically, but they are applied to
the ordinary mud-laid kiva wall and not directly to the sides of the
natural excavation.   The vertical laths are bound in place by horizontal reeds laid upon them 1 or 2 feet apart.   The horizontal reeds

are held in place by pegs of greasewood driven into the wall at intervals of 1 or 2 feet and are tied to the pegs with split yucca. These
specimens are very interesting examples of aboriginal lathing and plastering applied to stone work.

The ground plan of the mungkiva of Mashongnavi is illustrated in
Fig. 27. In this example the narrowing of the room at the second level
of the floor is on one side. The step by which the upper level is reached
from the main floor is 8 inches high at the east end, rising to 10 inches
at the west end. The south end of the kiva is provided with a small
opening like a loop-hole, furnishing an outlook to the south. The east
side of the main portion of the kiva is not provided with the usual
bench. The portion of the bench at the katchina end of the kiva is on
a level with the west bench and continuous for a couple of feet beyond
the northeast corner along the east wall. The small wall niches are on
the west side and nearer the north end than usual. The arrangement
of the katchinkihu is quite different from that described in the Shupaulovi kivas. The orifice occurs in the north wall at a height of $3\frac{1}{2}$ feet
above the floor, and 2 feet 3 inches above the top of the bench that extends across this end of the room. The firepit is somewhat smaller
than in the other examples illustrated. Fig. 28 illustrates the appear-

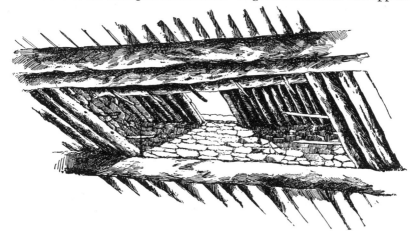

FIG. 28. Interior view of a kiva hatchway in Tusayan.

ance of the kiva hatchway from within as seen from the north end of
the kiva, but the ladder has been omitted from the drawing to avoid
confusion. The ladder rests against the edge of the coping that caps
the dwarf wall on the near side of the hatchway, its top leaning toward
the spectator. The small smoke-blackened sticks that are used for the
suspension of bundles of greasewood and other fuel in the hatchway
are clearly shown. At the far end of the trapdoor, on the outside, is
indicated the mat of reeds or rushes that is used for closing the openings when necessary. It is here shown rolled up at the foot of the
slope of the hatchway top, its customary position when not in use.

When this mat is used for closing the kiva opening it is usually held in place by several large stone slabs laid over it. Fig. 29 illustrates a specimen of the Tusayan kiva mat.

FIG. 29. Mat used in closing the entrance of Tusayan kivas.

The above kiva plans show that each of the illustrated examples is provided with four long narrow planks, set in the kiva floor close to the wall and provided with orifices for the attachment of looms. This feature is a common accompaniment of kiva construction and pertains to the use of the ceremonial room as a workshop by the male blanket weavers of Tusayan. It will be more fully described in the discussion of the various uses of the kiva.

The essential structural features of the kivas above described are remarkably similar, though the illustrations of types have been selected at random. Minor modifications are seen in the positions of many of the features, but a certain general relation between the various constructional requirements of the ceremonial room is found to prevail throughout all the villages.

*Work by women.*—After all the above described details have been provided for, following the completion of the roofs and floors, the women belonging to the people who are to occupy the kiva continue the labor of its construction. They go over the interior surface of the walls, breaking off projections and filling up the interstices with small stones, and then they smoothly plaster the walls and the inside of the hatchway with mud, and sometimes whitewash them with a gypsiferous clay found in the neighborhood. Once every year, at the feast of Powuma (the fructifying moon), the women give the kiva this same attention.

*Consecration.*—When all the work is finished the kiva chief prepares a baho and "feeds the house," as it is termed; that is, he thrusts a little meal, with piki crumbs, over one of the roof timbers, and in the same place inserts the end of the baho. As he does this he expresses his hope that the roof may never fall and that sickness and other evils may never enter the kiva.

It is difficult to elicit intelligent explanation of the theory of the baho and the prayer ceremonies in either kiva or house construction. The baho is a prayer token; the petitioner is not satisfied by merely speaking or singing his prayer, he must have some tangible thing upon which to transmit it. He regards his prayer as a mysterious, impalpable portion of his own substance, and hence he seeks to embody it in some object, which thus becomes consecrated. The baho, which is inserted in the roof of the kiva, is a piece of willow twig about six inches long, stripped of its bark and painted. From it hang four small feathers suspended by short cotton strings tied at equal distances along the twig. In order to obtain recognition from the powers especially addressed, different colored feathers and distinct methods of attaching them to bits of wood and string are resorted to. In the present case these are addressed to the "chiefs" who control the paths taken by the people after coming up from the interior of the earth. They are thus designated:

To the west: Siky'ak............oma'uwu ..........Yellow Cloud.
south: Sa'kwa............oma'uwu ..........Blue Cloud.
east: Pal'a..............oma'uwu ..........Red Cloud.
north: Kwetsh...........oma'uwu ..........White Cloud.

8 ETH——9

Two separate feathers are also attached to the roof. These are addressed to the zenith, héyap omáuwu—the invisible space of the above—and to the nadir, Myuingwa—god of the interior of the earth and maker of the germ of life. To the four first mentioned the bahos under the corner stones are also addressed. These feathers are prepared by the kiva chief in another kiva. He smokes devoutly over them, and as he exhales the smoke upon them he formulates the prayers to the chiefs or powers, who not only control the paths or lives of all the people, but also preside over the six regions of space whence come all the necessaries of life. The ancients also occupy his thoughts during these devotions; he desires that all the pleasures they enjoyed while here may come to his people, and he reciprocally wishes the ancients to partake of all the enjoyments of the living.

All the labor and ceremonies being completed the women prepare food for a feast. Friends are invited, and the men dance all night in the kiva to the accompaniment of their own songs and the beating of a primitive drum, rejoicing over their new home. The kiva chief then proclaims the name by which the kiva will be known. This is often merely a term of his choosing, often without reference to its appropriateness.

*Various uses of kivas.*—Allusions occur in some of the traditions, suggesting that in earlier times one class of kiva was devoted wholly to the purposes of a ceremonial chamber, and was constantly occupied by a priest. An altar and fetiches were permanently maintained, and appropriate groups of these fetiches were displayed from month to month, as the different priests of the sacred feasts succeeded each other, each new moon bringing its prescribed feast.

Many of the kivas were built by religious societies, which still hold their stated observances in them, and in Oraibi several still bear the names of the societies using them. A society always celebrates in a particular kiva, but none of these kivas are now preserved exclusively for religious purposes; they are all places of social resort for the men, especially during the winter, when they occupy themselves with the arts common among them. The same kiva thus serves as a temple during a sacred feast, at other times as a council house for the discussion of public affairs. It is also used as a workshop by the industrious and as a lounging place by the idle.

There are still traces of two classes of kiva, marked by the distinction that only certain ones contain the sipapuh, and in these the more important ceremonies are held. It is said that no sipapuh has been made recently. The prescribed operation is performed by the chief and the assistant priests or fetich keepers of the society owning the kiva. Some say the mystic lore pertaining to its preparation is lost and none can now be made. It is also said that a stone sipapuh was formerly used instead of the cottonwood plank now commonly seen. The use of stone for this purpose, however, is nearly obsolete, though the second kiva of Shupaulovi, illustrated in plan in Fig. 25, contains an example of this ancient form. In one of the newest kivas of Mashongnavi the plank of the sipapuh is pierced with a square hole, which is cut with a shoulder, the shoulder supporting the plug with which the orifice is closed (see Fig. 30). This is a decided innovation on the traditional form, as the orifice from which the people emerged, which is symbolized in the sipapuh, is described as being of circular form in all the versions of the Tusayan genesis myth. The presence of the sipapuh possibly at one time distinguished such kivas as were considered strictly consecrated

FIG. 30. Rectangular sipapuh in a Mashongnavi kiva.

to religious observances from those that were of more general use. At Tusayan, at the present time, certain societies do not meet in the ordinary kiva but in an apartment of a dwelling house, each society having its own exclusive place of meeting. The house so used is called the house of the "Sister of the eldest brother," meaning, probably, that she is the descendant of the founder of the society. This woman's house is also called the "house of grandmother," and in it is preserved the tiponi and other fetiches of the society. The tiponi is a ceremonial object about 18 inches long, consisting of feathers set upright around a small disk of silicified wood, which serves as its base when set upon the altar. This fetich is also called iso (grandmother), hence the name given to the house where it is kept. In the house, where the order of warriors (Kuleataka) meets, the eldest son of the woman who owns it is the chief of the order. The apartment in which they meet is a low room on the ground floor, and is entered only by a hatchway and ladder. There is no sipapuh in this chamber, for the warriors appeal directly to Cótukinungwa, the heart of the zenith, the sky god. Large figures of animal fetiches are painted in different colors upon the walls. On the west wall is the Mountain Lion; on the south, the Bear; on the east, the Wild Cat, surmounted with a shield inclosing a star; on the north, the White Wolf; and on the east side of this figure is painted a large disk, representing the sun. The walls of the chambers of the other societies are not decorated permanently. Here is, then, really another class of kiva, although it is not so called by the people on the Walpi mesa. The ordinary term for the ground story rooms is used, "kikoli," the house without any opening in its walls. But on the second mesa, and at Oraibi, although they sometimes use this term kikoli, they commonly apply the term "kiva" to the ground story of the dwelling house used as well as to the underground chambers.

It is probable that a class of kivas, not specially consecrated, has existed from a very early period. The rooms in the dwelling houses have always been small and dark, and in early times without chimneys.

Within such cramped limits it was inconvenient for the men to practice any of the arts they knew, especially weaving, which could have been carried on out of doors, as is done still occasionally, but subject to many interruptions. It is possible that a class of kivas was designed for such ordinary purposes, though now one type of room seems to answer all these various uses. In most of the existing kivas there are planks, in which stout loops are secured, fixed in the floor close to the wall, for attaching the lower beam of a primitive vertical loom, and projecting vigas or beams are inserted into the walls at the time of their construction as a provision for the attachment of the upper loom poles. The planks or logs to which is attached the lower part of the loom appear in some cases to be quite carefully worked. They are often partly buried in the ground and under the edges of adjacent paving stones in such a manner as to be held in place very securely against the strain of the tightly stretched warp while the blanket is being made. The holes pierced in the upper surface of these logs are very neatly executed in the manner illustrated in Fig. 31, which shows one of the orifices in

FIG. 31. Loom post in kiva at Tusayan.

section, together with the adjoining paving stones. The outward appearance of the device, as seen at short intervals along the length of the log, is also shown. Strips of buckskin or bits of rope are passed through these U-shaped cavities, and then over the lower pole of the loom at the bottom of the extended series of warp threads. The latter can thus be tightened preparatory to the operation of filling in with the woof. The kiva looms seem to be used mainly for weaving the dark-blue and black blankets of diagonal and diamond pattern, which form a staple article of trade with the Zuñi and the Rio Grande Pueblos. As an additional convenience for the practice of weaving, one of the kivas of Mashongnavi is provided with movable seats. These consist simply of single stones of suitable size and form. Usually they are 8 or 10 inches thick, a foot wide, and perhaps 15 or 18 inches long. Besides their use as seats, these stones are used in connection with the edges of the stone slabs that cap the permanent benches of the kiva to support temporarily the upper and lower poles of the blanket loom while the warp is gradually wound around them. The large stones that are incorporated into the side of the benches of some of the Mashongnavi kivas have occasionally round, cup-shaped cavities, of about an inch in diameter, drilled into them. These holes receive one end of a warp stick, the other end being supported in a corresponding hole of the heavy, movable stone seat. The other warp stick is supported in a similar manner, while the thread is passed around both in a horizontal direction preparatory to placing and stretching it in a vertical position for the final working of the blanket. A number of these cup-shaped pits are formed along the side of the stone bench, to provide for various lengths of warp that may be required. On the opposite side of this same kiva a number of similar holes or depressions are turned into the mud plastering of the wall. All these devices are of common occurrence at other of the Tusayan kivas, and indicate the antiquity of the practice of using the kivas for such industrial purposes. There is a suggestion of similar use of the ancient circular kivas in an example in Canyon de Chelly. At a small cluster of rooms, built partly on a rocky ledge and partly on adjoining loose earth and rocky débris, a land slide had carried away half of a circular kiva, exposing a well-defined section of its floor and the débris within the room. Here the writer found a number of partly finished sandals of yucca fiber, with the long, unwoven fiber carefully wrapped about the finished portion of the work, as though the sandals had been temporarily laid aside until the maker could again work on them. A number of coils of yucca fiber, similar to that used in the sandals, and several balls of brown fiber, formed from the inner bark of the cedar, were found on the floor of the room. The condition of the ruin and the débris that filled the kiva clearly suggested that these specimens were in use just where they were found at the time of the abandonment or destruction of the houses. No traces were seen, however, of any structural devices like those of Tusayan that would serve as aids to the weavers, though the weaving of the particular articles comprised in the collection from this spot would probably not require any cumbrous apparatus.

*Kiva ownership.*—The kiva is usually spoken of as being the home of the organization which maintains it. Different kivas are not used in common by all the inhabitants. Every man has a membership in some particular one and he frequents that one only. The same person is often a member of different societies, which takes him to different kivas, but that is only on set occasions. There is also much informal visiting among them, but a man presumes to make a loitering place only of the kiva in which he holds membership.

In each kiva there is a kiva mungwi (kiva chief), and he controls to a great extent all matters pertaining to the kiva and its membership. This office or trust is hereditary and passes from uncle to nephew through the female line—that is, on the death of a kiva chief the eldest son of his eldest sister succeeds him.

A kiva may belong either to a society, a group of gentes, or an individual. If belonging to a society or order, the kiva chief commonly has inherited his office in the manner indicated from the "eldest brother" of the society who assumed its construction. But the kiva chief is not necessarily chief of the society; in fact, usually he is but an ordinary member. A similar custom of inheritance prevails where the kiva belongs to a group of gentes, only in that case the kiva chief is usually chief of the gentile group.

As for those held by individuals, a couple of examples will illustrate the Tusayan practice. In Hano the chief kiva was originally built by a group of "Sun" gentes, but about 45 years ago, during an epidemic of smallpox, all the people who belonged to the kiva died except one man. The room fell into ruin, its roof timbers were carried off, and it became filled up with dust and rubbish. The title to it, however, rested with the old survivor, as all the more direct heirs had died, and he, when about to die, gave the kiva to Kotshve, a "Snake" man from Walpi, who married a Tewa (Hano) woman and still lives in Hano. This man repaired it and renamed it Tokónabi (said to be a Pah-Ute term, meaning black mountain, but it is the only name the Tusayan have for Navajo Mountain) because his people (the "Snake") came from that place. He in turn gave it to his eldest son, who is therefore kiva mungwi, but the son says his successor will be the eldest son of his eldest sister. The membership is composed of men from all the Hano gentes, but not all of any one gens. In fact, it is not now customary for all the members of a gens to be members of the same kiva.

Another somewhat similar instance occurs in Sichumovi. A kiva, abandoned for a long time after the smallpox plague, was taken possession of by an individual, who repaired it and renamed it Kevinyáp tshómo—Oak Mound. He made his friends its members, but he called the kiva his own. He also says that his eldest sister's son will succeed him as chief.

In each village one of the kivas, usually the largest one, is called (aside from its own special name) mungkiva—chief kiva. It is frequented by the kimungwi—house or village chief—and the tshaakmungwi—chief talker, councillor—and in it also the more elaborate ceremonies are observed.

No women frequent any of the kivas; in fact they never enter them except to plaster the walls at customary periods, or during the occasion of certain ceremonies. Yet one at least of the Oraibi kivas was built for the observances of a society of women, the Mamzrántiki. This and another female society—Lalénkobáki—exist in all the other villages, and on the occasion of their festivals the women are given the exclusive use of one of the kivas.

*Motives for building a kiva.*—Only two causes are mentioned for building a new kiva. Quarrels giving rise to serious dissensions among the occupants of a kiva are one cause. An instance of this occurred quite recently at Hano. The conduct of the kiva chief gave rise to dissensions, and the members opposed to him prepared to build a separate room of their own. They chose a gap on the side of the mesa cliff, close to Hano, collected stones for the walls, and brought the roof timbers from the distant wooded mesas; but when all was ready to lay the foundation their differences were adjusted and a complete reconciliation was effected.

The other cause assigned is the necessity for additional room when a gens has outgrown its kiva. When a gens has increased in numbers sufficiently to warrant its having a second kiva, the chief of the gen-

H.H.N. 90.

KINNA-ZINDE.

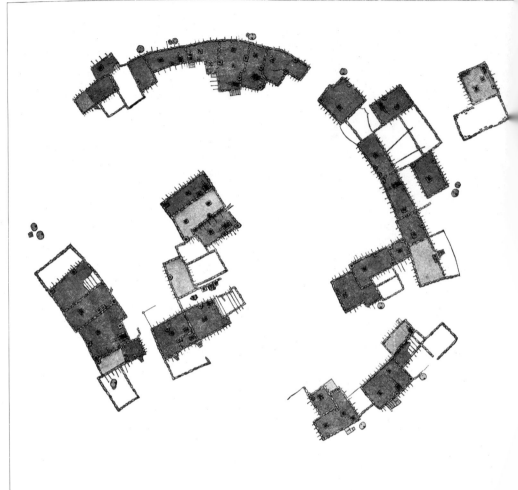

NUTRIA.

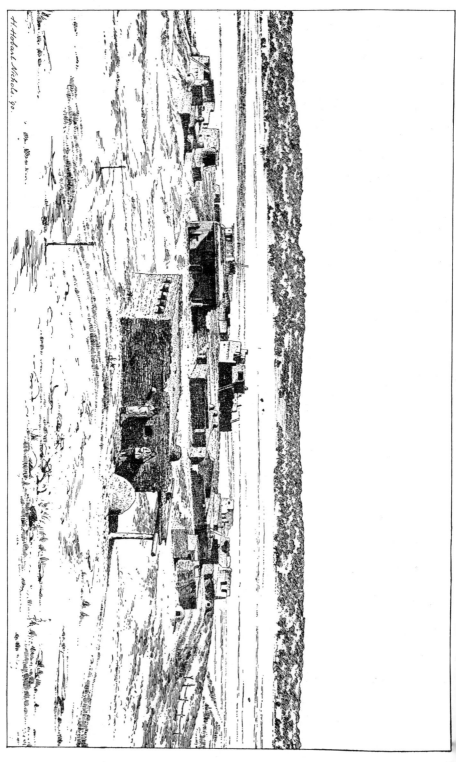

NUTRIA.

COURT VIEW OF PESCADO, SHOWING CORRALS.

PESCADO.

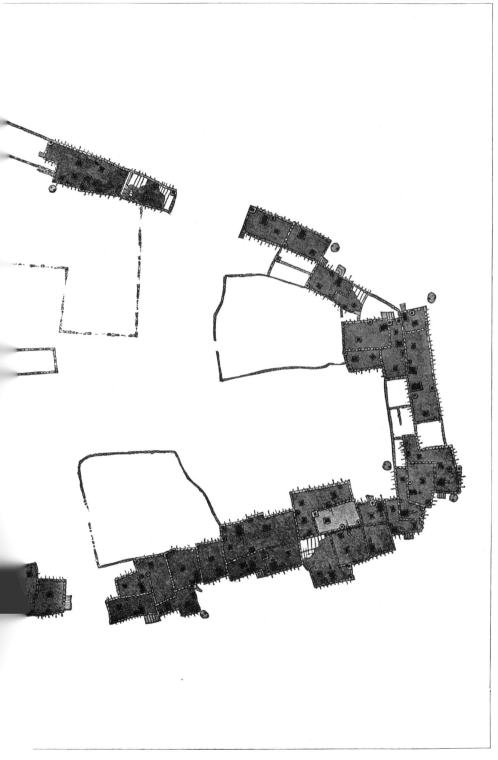

PESCADO HOUSES.

FRAGMENTS OF ANCIENT MASONRY IN PESCADO.

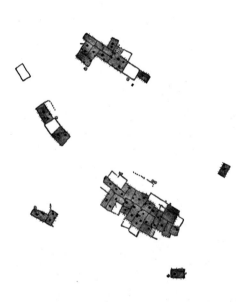

OJO CALIENTE.

GENERAL VIEW OF OJO CALIENTE.

HOUSE AT OJO CALIENTE.

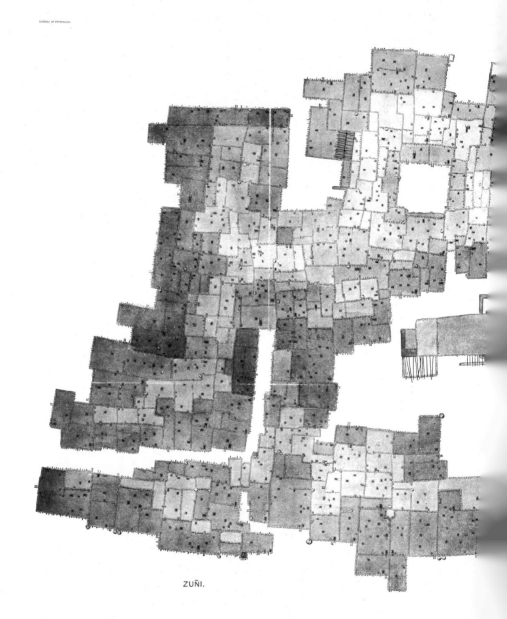

ZUÑI.

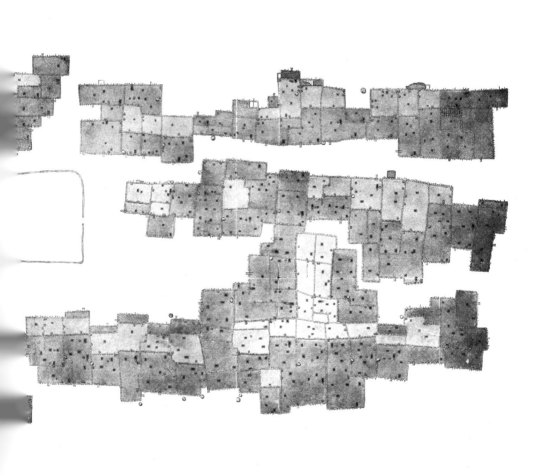

KEY TO ZUÑI PLAN.

Corral

tile group, who in this case is also chief of the order, proposes to his kin to build a separate kiva, and that being agreed to, he assumes the direction of the construction and all the dedicatory and other ceremonies connected with the undertaking.　An instance of this kind occurred within the last year or two at Oraibi, where the members of the "Katchina" gentes, who are also members of the religious order of Katchina, built a spacious kiva for themselves.

The construction of a new kiva is said to be of rare occurrence.　On the other hand, it is common to hear the kiva chief lament the decadence of its membership.　In the "Oak Mound" kiva at Sichumovi there are now but four members.　The young men have married and moved to their wives' houses in more thriving villages, and the older men have died.　The chief in this case also says that some 2 years ago the agent gave him a stove and pipe, which he set up in the room to add to its comfort.　He now has grave fears that the stove is an evil innovation, and has exercised a deleterious influence upon the fortune of his kiva and its members; but the stove is still retained.

*Significance of structural plan.*—The designation of the curious orifice of the sipapuh as "the place from which the people emerged" in connection with the peculiar arrangement of the kiva interior with its change of floor level, suggested to the author that these features might be regarded as typifying the four worlds of the genesis myth that has exercised such an influence on Tusayan customs; but no clear data on this subject were obtained by the writer, nor has Mr. Stephen, who is specially well equipped for such investigations, discovered that a definite conception exists concerning the significance of the structural plan of the kiva.　Still, from many suggestive allusions made by the various kiva chiefs and others, he also has been led to infer that it typifies the four "houses," or stages, described in their creation myths.　The sipapuh, with its cavity beneath the floor, is certainly regarded as indicating the place of beginning, the lowest house under the earth, the abode of Myuingwa, the Creator; the main or lower floor represents the second stage; and the elevated section of the floor is made to denote the third stage, where animals were created.　Mr. Stephen observed, at the New Year festivals, that animal fetiches were set in groups upon this platform.　It is also to be noted that the ladder leading to the surface is invariably made of pine, and always rests upon the platform, never upon the lower floor, and in their traditional genesis it is stated that the people climbed up from the third house (stage) by a ladder of pine, and through such an opening as the kiva hatchway; only most of the stories indicate that the opening was round.　The outer air is the fourth world, or that now occupied.

There are occasional references in the Tusayan traditions to circular kivas, but these are so confused with fantastic accounts of early mythic structures that their literal rendition would serve no useful purpose in the present discussion.

*Typical measurements.*—The following list is a record of a number of measurements of Tusayan kivas collected by Mr. Stephen. The wide difference between the end measurements of the same kiva are usually due to the interior offsets that have been noticed on the plans, but the differences in the lengths of the sides are due to irregularities of the site. The latter differences are not so marked as the former.

| Width at ends. | | Length of sides. | | Height at center. | Height at ends. | |
|---|---|---|---|---|---|---|
| 13 6 | ..... | 24 0 | ..... | 8 6 | ..... | ..... |
| 12 0 | ..... | 21 9 | ..... | 7 6 | 6 6 | ..... |
| 14 6 | 14 6 | 24 6 | 23 3 | 8 0 | 6 6 | 6 6 |
| 12 2 | 12 11 | 23 9 | 23 9 | 7 10 | 6 1 | 6 0 |
| 12 6 | 12 6 | 26 0 | 25 3 | 7 6 | 6 6 | 6 6 |
| 13 4 | 12 10 | 26 8 | 26 7 | 7 10 | 7 0 | 7 0 |
| 15 0 | 13 6 | 26 6 | 24 11 | 7 4 | 6 3 | 6 2 |
| 12 6 | 11 5 | 23 7 | 21 9 | 8 0 | 7 0 | 7 0 |
| 12 5 | 13 5 | 22 8 | 24 1 | 7 3 | 6 1 | 6 9 |
| 10 6 | 13 6 | 27 0 | 27 0 | 8 3 | 6 3 | 6 2 |
| 13 6 | 11 6 | 29 9 | 29 0 | 11 0 | 5 10 | ..... |
| 14 6 | ..... | 28 6 | 28 6 | 9 8 | 6 0 | ..... |
| 13 2 | 14 0 | 28 9 | 29 9 | 8 6 | 7 0 | 6 4 |
| 15 1 | 12 0 | 28 6 | ..... | 9 6 | 7 3 | 6 6 |
| 13 0 | 12 6 | 28 7 | 29 6 | ..... | 7 4 | 6 3 |

*List of Tusayan kivas.*—The following list gives the present names of all the kivas in use at Tusayan. The mungkiva or chief kiva of the village is in each case designated:

HANO.

1. Toko′nabi kiva.....................Navajo Mountain.
2. Hano sinte′ kiva ...................Place of the Hano.
　　Toko′nabi kiva is the mungkiva.

WALPI.

1. Djiva′to kiva ......................Goat.
2. Al kiva ............................A′la, Horn.
3. Naca′b kiva........................Na′cabi, half-way or central.
4. ⎰ Picku′ibi kiva....................Opening oak bud.[1]
　 ⎱ Wikwa′lobi kiva .................Place of the watchers.
5. Mung kiva.........................Mungwi chief.
　　No. 5 is the mungkiva.

SICHUMOVI.

1. Bave′ntcomo ......................Water mound.
2. Kwinzaptcomo.....................Oak mound.
　　Bave′ntcomo is the mungkiva.

MASHONGNAVI.

1. Tcavwu′na kiva....................A small coiled-ware jar.
2. Hona′n kiva ......................Honani, Badger, a gens.
3. Gy′arzobi kiva.....................Gy′arzo, Paroquet, a gens.
4. Kotcobi kiva......................High place.
5. Al kiva ...........................A′la, Horn.
　　Tcavwu′na kiva is the mungkiva.

---

[1] These two names are common to the kiva in which the Snake order meets and in which the indoor ceremonies pertaining to the Snake-dance are celebrated.

SHUPAULOVI.

1. A'tkabi kiva....................Place below.
2. Kokyangobi kiva .................Place of spider.
     A'tkabi kiva is the mungkiva.

SHUMOPAVI.

1. Nuvwa'tikyuobi ..................High place of snow, San Francisco
                                   Mountain.
2. Al kiva .........................A'la, Horn.
3. Gy'arzobi .......................Gy'arzo, Paroquet, a gens.
4. Tco'sobi ........................Blue Jay, a gens.
     Tco'sobi is the mungkiva.

ORAIBI.

1. Tdau kiva .......Tda'uollauwuh.The singers.
2. Ha'wiobi kiva....Ha'wi, stair ; High stair place.
                    obi, high place.
3. Ish kiva .........Isa'uwuh.......Coyote, a gens.
4. Kwang kiva .....Kwa'kwanti....Religious order.
5. Ma'zrau kiva ...Ma'mzrauti.....Female order.
6. Na'cabi kiva.....Half way or....Central place.
7. Sa'kwalen kiva ..Sa'kwa le'na ...Blue Flute, a religious order.
8. Po'ngobi kiva....Pongo, a circle .An order who decorate themselves
                                   with circular marks on the body.
9. Hano' kiva.......Ha'nomuh......A fashion of cutting the hair.
10. Motc kiva........Mo'mtci.-......The Warriors, an order.
11. Kwita'koli kiva..Kwita, ordure; Ordure heap.
                    ko'li, a heap.
12. Katcin kiva......Katcina .........A gens.
13. Tcu kiva.........Tcua, a snake ..Religious order.
     Tdau kiva is the mungkiva.

DETAILS OF TUSAYAN AND CIBOLA CONSTRUCTION.

WALLS.

The complete operation of building a wall has never been observed at Zuñi by the writer, but a close examination of numerous finished and some broken-down walls indicates that the methods of construction adopted are essentially the same as those employed in Tusayan, which have been repeatedly observed; with the possible difference, however, that in the former adobe mud mortar is more liberally used.   A singular feature of pueblo masonry as observed at Tusayan is the very sparing use of mud in the construction of the walls; in fact, in some instances when walls are built during the dry season, the larger stones are laid up in the walls without the use of mud at all, and are allowed to stand in this condition until the rains come; then the mud mortar is mixed, the interstices of the walls filled in with it and with chinking stones, and the inside walls are plastered.   But the usual practice is to complete the house at once, finishing it inside and out with the requisite mortar.   In some instances the outside walls are coated, completely covering the masonry, but this is not done in many of the houses, as may be seen by reference to the preceding illustrations of the Tusayan villages. At Zuñi, on the other hand, a liberal and frequently renewed coating of mud is applied to the walls. Only one piece of masonry was seen in the entire village that did not have traces of this coating of mud, viz, that portion of the second story wall of house No. 2 described as possibly belonging to the ancient nucleus pueblo of Halona and illustrated in Pl. LVIII. Even the rough masonry of the kivas is partly surfaced with this medium, though many jagged stones are still visible. As a result of this practice it is now in many cases impossible to determine from mere superficial inspection whether the underlying masonry has been constructed of stone or of adobe; a difficulty that may be realized from an examination of the views of Zuñi in Chapter III. Where the fall of water, such as the discharge from a roof-drain, has removed the outer coating of mud that covers stonework and adobe alike, a large proportion of these exposures reveal stone masonry, so that it is clearly apparent that Zuñi is essentially a stone village. The extensive use of sun-dried bricks of adobe has grown up within quite recent times. It is apparent, however, that the Zuñi builders preferred to use stone; and even at the present time they frequently eke out with stonework portions of a house when the supply of adobe has fallen short. An early instance of such supplementary use of stone masonry still survives in the church building, where the old Spanish adobe has been repaired and filled in with the typical tabular aboriginal masonry, consisting of small stones carefully laid, with very little intervening mortar showing on the face. Such reversion to aboriginal methods probably took place on every opportunity, though it is remarkable that the Indians should have been allowed to employ their own methods in this instance. Although this church building has for many generations furnished a conspicuous example of typical adobe construction to the Zuñi, he has never taken the lesson sufficiently to heart to closely imitate the Spanish methods either in the preparation of the material or in the manner of its use. The adobe bricks of the church are of large and uniform size, and the mud from which they were made had a liberal admixture of straw. This binding material does not appear in Zuñi in any other example of adobe that has been examined, nor does it seem to have been utilized in any of the native pueblo work either at this place or at Tusayan. Where molded adobe bricks have been used by the Zuñi in housebuilding they have been made from the raw material just as it was taken from the fields. As a result these bricks have little of the durability of the Spanish work. Pl. XCVI illustrates an adobe wall of Zuñi, part of an unroofed house. The old adobe church at Hawikuh (Pl. XLVIII), abandoned for two centuries, has withstood the wear of time and weather better than any of the stonework of the surrounding houses. On the right-hand side of the street that shows in the foreground of Pl. LXXVIII is an illustration of the construction of a wall with adobe bricks. This example is very recent, as it has not yet been roofed over. The top of the wall, however, is temporarily protected by the usual series of thin sandstone slabs used in the finishing of wall copings. The very rapid disintegration of native-made adobe

walls has brought about the use in Zuñi of many protective devices, some of which will be noticed in connection with the discussion of roof drains and wall copings. Figs. 32 and 33 illustrate a curious employment of pottery fragments on a mud-plastered wall and on the base of a chimney to protect the adobe coating against rapid erosion by the rains. These pieces, usually fragments from large vessels, are embedded in the adobe

FIG. 32. A Zuñi chimney, showing pottery fragments embedded in its adobe base.

with the convex side out, forming an armor of pottery scales well adapted to resist disintegration by the elements.

FIG. 33. A Zuñi oven with pottery scales embedded in its surface.

The introduction of the use of adobe in Zuñi should probably be attributed to foreign influence, but the position of the village in the open plain at a distance of several miles from the nearest outcrop of suitable building stone naturally led the builders to use stone more sparingly when an available substitute was found close at hand. The thin slabs of stone, which had to be brought from a great distance, came to be used only for the more exposed portions of buildings, such as copings on walls and borders around roof openings. Still, the pueblo builders never attained to a full appreciation of the advantages and requirements of this medium as compared with stone. The adobe walls are built only as thick as is absolutely necessary, few of them being more than a foot in thickness. The walls are thus, in proportion to height and weight, sustained, thinner than the crude brick construction of other peoples, and require protection and constant repairs to insure durability. As to thickness, they are evidently modeled directly after the walls of stone masonry, which had already, in both Tusayan and Cíbola, been pushed to the limit of thinness. In fact, since the date of the survey of Zuñi, on which the published plan is based, the walls of several rooms over the court passageway in the house, illustrated in Pl. LXXXII, have entirely fallen in, demonstrating the insufficiency of the thin walls to sustain the weight of several stories.

The climate of the pueblo region is not wholly suited to the employment of adobe construction, as it is there practiced. For several months in the year (the rainy season) scarcely a day passes without violent storms which play havoc with the earth-covered houses, necessitating constant vigilance and frequent repairs on the part of the occupants.

Though the practice of mud-coating all walls has in Cibola undoubtedly led to greater carelessness and a less rigid adherence to ancient methods of construction, the stone masonry may still be seen to retain some of the peculiarities that characterize ancient examples. Features of this class are still more apparent at Tusayan, and notwithstanding the rudeness of much of the modern stone masonry of this province, the fact that the builders are familiar with the superior methods of the ancient builders, is clearly shown in the masonry of the present villages.

Perhaps the most noteworthy characteristic of pueblo masonry, and one which is more or less present in both ancient and modern examples, is the use of small chinking stones for bringing the masonry to an even face after the larger stones forming the body of the wall have been laid in place. This method of construction has, in the case of some of the best built ancient pueblos, such as those on the Chaco in New Mexico, resulted in the production of marvelously finished stone walls, in which the mosaic-like bits are so closely laid as to show none but the finest joints on the face of the wall with but little trace of mortar. The chinking wedges necessarily varied greatly in dimensions to suit the sizes of the interstices between the larger stones of the wall. The use of stone in this manner no doubt suggested the banded walls that form so striking a feature in some of the Chaco houses. This arrangement was likely to be brought about by the occurrence in the cliffs of seams of stone of two degrees of thickness, suggesting to the builders the use of stones of similar thickness in continuous bands. The ornamental effect of this device was originally an accidental result of adopting the most convenient method of using the material at hand. Though the masonry of the modern pueblos does not afford examples of distinct bands, the

introduction of the small chinking spalls often follows horizontal lines
of considerable length.    Even in mud-plastered Zuñi, many outcrops
of these thin, tabular wedges protrude from the partly eroded mud-
coating of a wall and indicate the presence of this kind of stone
masonry.    An example is illustrated in Fig. 34, a tower-like projection
at the northeast corner of house No. 2.

FIG. 34. Stone wedges of Zuñi masonry exposed in rain-washed wall.

In the Tusayan house illustrated in Pl. LXXXIV, the construction of
which was observed at Oraibi, the interstices between the large stones
that formed the body of the wall, containing but small quantities of

mud mortar, were filled in or plugged with small fragments of stone, which, after being partly embedded in the mud of the joint, were driven in with unhafted stone hammers, producing a fairly even face of masonry, afterward gone over with mud plastering of the consistency of modeling clay, applied a handful at a time. Piled up on the ground near the new house at convenient points for the builders may be seen examples of the larger wall stones, indicating the marked tabular character of the pueblo masons' material. The narrow edges of similar stones are visible in the unplastered portions of the house wall, which also illustrates the relative proportion of chinking stones. This latter, however, is a variable feature. Pl. xv affords a clear illustration of the proportion of these small stones in the old masonry of Payupki; while in Pl. xi, illustrating a portion of the outer wall of the Fire House, the tablets are fewer in number and thinner, their use predominating in the horizontal joints, as in the best of the old examples, but not to the same extent. Fig. 35 illustrates the inner face of an unplastered wall of a

FIG. 35. An unplastered house wall in Ojo Caliente.

small house at Ojo Caliente, in which the modern method of using the chinking stones is shown. This example bears a strong resemblance to the Payupki masonry illustrated in Pl. xv in the irregularity with which the chinking stones are distributed in the joints of the wall. The same room affords an illustration of a cellar-like feature having the appearance of an intentional excavation to attain a depth for this room corresponding to the adjoining floor level, but this effect is due simply to a clever adaptation of the house wall to an existing ledge of sandstone. The latter has had scarcely any artificial treatment beyond the partial smoothing of the rock in a few places and the cutting out of a small niche from the rocky wall. This niche occupies about the same position in this room that it does in the ordinary pueblo house. It is remarkable that the pueblo builders did not to a greater extent utilize their skill in working stone in the preparation of some of the irregular rocky sites that they have at times occupied for the more convenient reception of their wall foundations; but in nearly all such cases the buildings have been modified to suit the ground. An example of this practice is illustrated in Pl. XXIII, from the west side of Walpi. In some of the ancient examples the labor required to so prepare the sites would not have exceeded that expended on the massive masonry composed of numberless small stones. Many of the older works testify to the remarkable patience and industry of the builders in amassing and carefully adjusting vast quantities of building materials, and the modern Indians of Tusayan and Cibola have inherited much of this ancient spirit; yet this industry was rarely diverted to the excavation of room or village sites, except in the case of the kivas, in which special motives led to the practice. In some of the Chaco pueblos, as now seen, the floors of outer marginal rooms seem to be depressed below the general level of the surrounding soil; but it is now difficult to determine whether such was the original arrangement, as much sand and soil have drifted against the outer walls, raising the surface. In none of the pueblos within the limits of the provinces under discussion has there been found any evidence of the existence of underground cellars; the rooms that answer such purpose are built on the level of the ground. At Tusayan the ancient practice of using the ground-floor rooms for storage still prevails. In these are kept the dried fruit, vegetables, and meats that constitute the principal winter food of the Tusayan. Throughout Tusayan the walls of the first terrace rooms are not finished with as much care as those above that face the open courts. A quite smoothly finished coat of adobe is often seen in the upper stories, but is much more rarely applied to the rough masonry of the ground-floor rooms. At Zuñi no such difference of treatment is to be seen, a result of the recent departure from their original defensive use. At the present day most of the rooms that are built on the ground have external doors, often of large size, and are regarded by the Zuñi as preferable to the upper terraces as homes. This indicates that the idea of convenience has already largely overcome the traditional defensive requirements of pueblo arrangement. The general finish and quality of the masonry, too, does not vary noticeably in different portions of the village. An occasional wall may be seen in which underlying stones may be traced through the thin adobe covering, as in one of the walls of the court illustrated in Pl. LXXXII, but most of the walls have a fairly smooth finish. The occasional examples of rougher masonry do not seem to be confined to any particular portion of the village. At Tusayan, on the other hand, there is a noticeable difference in the extent to which the finishing coat of adobe has been used in the masonry. The villages of the first mesa, whose occupants have come in frequent contact with the eastern pueblo Indians and with outsiders generally, show the effect in the adoption of several devices still unknown to their western neighbors, as is shown in the discussion of the distribution of roof openings in these villages, pp. 201–208. The builders of the first mesa seem also to have imitated their eastern brethren in the free use of the adobe coating over their masonry, while at the villages of the middle mesa, and particularly at Oraibi, the practice has been comparatively rare, imparting an appearance of ruggedness and antiquity to the architecture.

The stonework of this village, perhaps approaches the ancient types more closely than that of the others, some of the walls being noticeable for the frequent use of long bond stones. The execution of the masonry at the corners of some of the houses enforces this resemblance and indicates a knowledge of the principles of good construction in the proper alternation of the long stones. A comparison with the Kin-tiel masonry (Pl. LXXXIX) will show this resemblance. As a rule in pueblo masonry an upper house wall was supported along its whole length by a wall of a lower story, but occasional exceptions occur in both ancient and modern work, where the builders have dared to trust the weight of upper walls to wooden beams or girders, supported along part of their length by buttresses from the walls at their ends or by large, clumsy pieces of masonry, as was seen in the house of Sichumovi. In an upper story of Walpi also, partitions occur that are not built immediately over the lower walls, but on large beams supported on masonry piers. In the much higher terraces of Zuñi, the strength of many of the inner ground walls must be seriously taxed to withstand the superincumbent weight, as such walls are doubtless of only the average thickness and strength of ground walls. The dense clustering of this village has certainly in some instances thrown the weight of two, three, or even four additional stories upon walls in which no provision was made for the unusual strain. The few supporting walls that were accessible to inspection did not indicate any provision in their thickness for the support of additional weight; in fact, the builders of the original walls could have no knowledge of their future requirements in this respect. In the pueblos of the Chaco upper partition walls were, in a few instances, supported directly on double girders, two posts of 12 or 14 inches in diameter placed side by side, without reinforcement by stone piers or buttresses, the room below being left wholly unobstructed. This construction was practicable for the careful builders of the Chaco, but an attempt by the Tusayan to achieve the same result would probably end in disaster. It was quite common among the ancient builders to divide the ground or storage floor into smaller rooms than the floor above, still preserving the vertical alignment of the walls.

The finish of pueblo masonry rarely went far beyond the two leading forms, to which attention has been called, the free use of adobe on the one hand and the banded arrangement of ancient masonry on the other. These types appear to present development along divergent lines. The banded feature doubtless reached such a point of development in the Chaco pueblos that its decorative value began to be appreciated, for it is apparent that its elaboration has extended far beyond the requirements of mere utility. This point would never have been reached had the practice prevailed of covering the walls with a coating of mud. The cruder examples of banded construction, however—those that still kept well within constructional expediency—were doubtless covered with a coating of plaster where they occurred inside of the rooms. At Tusayan and Cíbola, on the other hand, the tendency has been rather to elaborate the plastic element of the masonry. The nearly universal use of adobe is undoubtedly largely responsible for the more slovenly methods of building now in vogue, as it effectually conceals careless construction. It is not to be expected that walls would be carefully constructed of banded stonework when they were to be subsequently covered with mud. The elaboration of the use of adobe and its employment as a periodical coating for the dwellings, probably developed gradually into the use of a whitewash for the house walls, resulting finally in crude attempts at wall decoration.

Many of the interiors in Zuñi are washed with a coating of white, clayey gypsum, used in the form of a solution made by dissolving in hot water the lumps of the raw material, found in many localities. The mixture is applied to the walls while hot, and is spread by means of a rude glove-like sack, made of sheep or goat skin, with the hair side out. With this primitive brush the Zuñi housewives succeed in laying on a smooth and uniform coating over the plaster. An example of this class of work was observed in a room of house No. 2. It is difficult to determine to what extent this idea is aboriginal; as now employed it has doubtless been affected by the methods of the neighboring Spanish population, among whom the practice of white-coating the adobe houses inside and out is quite common. Several traces of whitewashing have been found among the cliff-dwellings of Canyon de Chelly, notably at the ruin known as Casa Blanca, but as some of these ruins contained evidences of post-Spanish occupation, the occurrence there of the whitewash does not necessarily imply any great antiquity for the practice.

External use of this material is much rarer, particularly in Zuñi, where only a few walls of upper stories are whitened. Where it is not protected from the rains by an overhanging coping or other feature, the finish is not durable. Occasionally where a doorway or other opening has been repaired the evidences of patchwork are obliterated by a surrounding band of fresh plastering, varying in width from 4 inches to a foot or more. Usually this band is laid on as a thick wash of adobe, but in some instances a decorative effect is attained by using white. It is curious to find that at Tusayan the decorative treatment of the finishing wash has been carried farther than at Zuñi. The use of a darker band of color about the base of a whitewashed room has already been noticed in the description of a Tusayan interior. On many of the outer walls of upper stories the whitewash has been stopped within a foot of the coping, the unwhitened portion of the walls at the top having the effect of a frieze. In a second story house of Mashongnavi, that had been carefully whitewashed, additional decorative effect was produced by tinting a broad band about the base of the wall with an application of bright pinkish clay, which was also carried around the doorway as an enframing band, as in the case of the Zuñi door above described. The angles on each side, at the junction of the broad base band with the narrower doorway border, were filled in with a design of alternating pink and white squares. This doorway is illustrated in Fig. 36. Farther north, on the same terrace, the jamb of a whitewashed

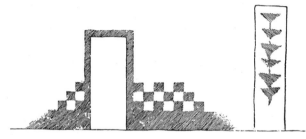

FIG. 36. Wall decorations in Mashongnavi executed in pink on a white ground.

doorway was decorated with the design shown on the right hand side of Fig. 36, executed also in pink clay. This design closely resembles a pattern that is commonly embroidered upon the large white " kachina," or ceremonial blankets. It is not known whether the device is here regarded as having any special significance. The pink clay in which these designs have been executed has in Sichumovi been used for the coating of an entire house front.

In addition to the above-mentioned uses of stone and earth in the masonry of house walls, the pueblo builders have employed both these materials in a more primitive manner in building the walls of corrals and gardens, and for other purposes. The small terraced gardens of Zuñi, located on the borders of the village on the southwest and southeast sides, close to the river bank, are each surrounded by walls 2½ or 3 feet high, of very light construction, the average thickness not exceeding 6 or 8 inches. These rude walls are built of small, irregularly rounded lumps of adobe, formed by hand, and coarsely plastered with mud. When the crops are gathered in the fall the walls are broken down in places to facilitate access to the inclosures, so that they require repairing at each planting season. Aside from this they are so frail as to require frequent repairs throughout the period of their use. This method of building walls was adopted because it was the readiest and least laborious means of inclosing the required space. The character of these garden walls is illustrated in Pl. xc, and their construction with rough lumps of crude adobe shows also the contrast between the weak appearance of this work and the more substantial effect of the masonry of the adjoining unfinished house. At the Cibolan farming pueblos inclosing walls were usually made of stone, as were also those of Tusayan. Pl. lxx indicates the manner in which the material has been used in the corrals of Pescado, located within the village. The stone walls are used in combination with stakes, such as are employed at the main pueblo.

Small inclosed gardens, like those of Zuñi, occur at several points in Tusayan. The thin walls are made of dry masonry, quite as rude in character as those inclosing the Zuñi gardens. The smaller clusters are usually located in the midst of large areas of broken stone that has fallen from the mesa above. In the foreground of Pl. xxii may be seen a number of examples of such work. Pl. xci illustrates a group of corrals at Oraibi whose walls are laid up without the use of mud mortar.

Where exceptionally large blocks of stone are available they have been utilized in an upright position, and occur at greater or less intervals along the thin walls of dry masonry. An example of this use was seen in a garden wall on the west side of Walpi, where the stones had been set on end in the yielding surface of a sandy slope among the foothills. A similar arrangement, occurring close to the houses at Ojo Caliente, is illustrated in Pl. xcii. Large, upright slabs of stone have been used by the pueblo builders in many ways, sometimes incorporated into the architecture of the houses, and again in detached positions at some distance from the villages. Pls. xciii and xciv, drawn from the photographs of Mr. W. H. Jackson, afford illustrations of this usage in the ancient ruins of Montezuma Canyon. In the first of these cases the stones were utilized, apparently, in house masonry. Among the ruins in the valley of the San Juan and its tributaries, as described by Messrs. W. H. Holmes and W. H. Jackson, varied arrangements of upright slabs of stone are of frequent occurrence. The rows of stones are sometimes arranged in squares, sometimes in circles, and occasionally are incorporated into the walls of ordinary masonry, as in the example illustrated. Isolated slabs are also met with among the ruins. At K'iakima, at a point near the margin of the ruin, occurs a series of very large, upright slabs, which occupy the positions of headstones to a number of small inclosures, thought to be mortuary, outlined upon the ground. These have been already described in connection with the ground plan of this village.

The employment of upright slabs of stone to mark graves probably prevailed to some extent in ancient practice, but other uses suggest themselves. Occupying a conspicuous point in the village of Kin-tiel (Pl. lxiii) is an upright slab of sandstone which seems to stand in its original position undisturbed, though the walls of the adjoining rooms are in ruins. A similar feature was seen at Peñasco Blanco, on the east side of the village and a short distance without the inclosing wall. Both these rude pillars are, in character and in position, very similar to an upright stone of known use at Zuñi. A hundred and fifty feet from this pueblo is a large upright block of sandstone, which is said to be used as a datum point in the observations of the sun made by a priest of Zuñi for the regulation of the time for planting and harvesting, for determining the new year, and for fixing the dates of certain other ceremonial observances. By the aid of such devices as the native priests have at their command they are enabled to fix the date of the winter solstice with a fair degree of accuracy. Such rude determination of time was probably an aboriginal invention, and may have furnished the motive in other cases for placing stone pillars in such unusual positions. The explanation of the governor of Zuñi for a sun symbol seen on an upright stone at Matsaki has been given in the description of that place. Single slabs are also used, as seen in the easternmost room group of Tâaaiyalana, and in the southwestern cluster on the same mesa, in the building of shrines for the deposit of plume sticks and other ceremonial objects.

An unusual employment of small stones in an upright position occurs at Zuñi. The inclosing wall of the church yard, still used as a burial place, is provided at intervals along its top with upright pieces of stone set into the joints of a regular coping course that caps the wall. This feature may have some connection with the idea of vertical grave stones, noted at K'iakima. It is difficult to surmise what practical purpose could have been subserved by these small upright stones.

Notwithstanding the use of large stones for special purposes the pueblo builders rarely appreciated the advantages that might be obtained by the proper use of such material. Pueblo masonry is essentially made up of small, often minute, constructional units. This restriction doubtless resulted in a higher degree of mural finish than would otherwise have been attained, but it also imposes certain limitations upon their architectural achievement. Some of these are noted in the discussion of openings and of other details of construction.

Pl. XLV, an illustration of a Mormon mill building at Moen-kopi, already referred to in the description of that village, is introduced for the purpose of comparing the methods adopted by the natives and by the whites in the treatment of the same class of material. Perhaps the most noteworthy contrast is seen in the sills and lintels of the openings.

### ROOFS AND FLOORS.

In the pueblo system of building, roof and floor is one; for all the floors, except such as are formed immediately on the surface of the ground, are at the same time the roofs and ceilings of lower rooms. The pueblo plan of to-day readily admits of additions at any time and almost at any point of the basal construction. The addition of rooms above converts a roof into the floor of the new room, so that there can be no distinction in method of construction between floors and roofs, except the floors are occasionally covered with a complete paving of thin stone slabs, a device that in external roofs is confined to the copings that cap the walls and enframe openings.

The methods of roofing their houses practiced by the pueblo builders varied but little, and followed the general order of construction that has been outlined in describing Tusayan house building. The diagram shown in Fig. 37, an isometric projection illustrating roof

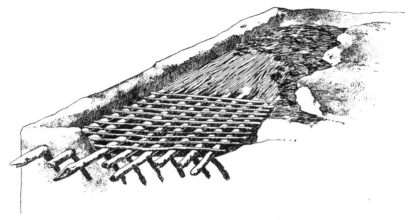

Fig. 37. Diagram of Zuñi roof construction.

construction, is taken from a Zuñi example, the building of which was observed by the writer. The roof is built by first a series of principal beams or rafters. These are usually straight, round poles of 6 or 8 inches in diameter, with all bark and projecting knots removed. Squared beams are of very rare occurrence; the only ones seen were those of the Tusayan kivas, of Spanish manufacture. In recently constructed houses the principal beams are often of large size and are very neatly squared off at the ends. Similar square ended beams of large size are met with in the ancient work of the Chaco pueblos, but there the enormous labor involved in producing the result with only the aid of stone implements is in keeping with the highly finished character of the masonry and the general massiveness of the construction. The same treatment was adopted in Kin-tiel, as may be seen in Pl. xcv, which illustrates a beam resting upon a ledge or offset of the inner walls. The recent introduction of improved mechanical aids has exerted a strong influence on the character of the construction in greatly facilitating execution. The use of the American ax made it a much easier task to cut large timbers, and the introduction of the "burro" and ox greatly facilitated their transportation. In the case of the modern pueblos, such as Zuñi, the dwelling rooms that were built by families so poor as not to have these aids would to some extent indicate the fact by their more primitive construction, and particularly by their small size, in this respect more closely resembling the rooms of the ancient pueblos. As a result the poorer classes would be more likely to perpetuate primitive devices, through the necessity for practicing methods that to the wealthier members of the tribe were becoming a matter of tradition only. In such a sedentary tribe as the present Zuñi, these differences of wealth and station are more marked than one would expect to find among a people practicing a style of architecture so evidently influenced by the communal principle, and the architecture of to-day shows the effect of such distinctions. In the house of the governor of Zuñi a new room has been recently built, in which the second series of the roof, that applied over the principal beams, consisted of pine shakes or shingles, and these supported the final earth covering without any intervening material. In the typical arrangement, however, illustrated in the figure, the first series, or principal beams, are covered by another series of small poles, about an inch and a half or two inches in diameter, at right angles to the first, and usually laid quite close together. The ends of these small poles are partially embedded in the masonry of the walls. In an example of the more careful and laborious work of the ancient builders seen at Peñasco Blanco, on the Chaco, the principal beams were covered with narrow boards, from 2 to 4 inches wide and about 1 inch thick, over which was put the usual covering of earth. The boards had the appearance of having been split out with wedges, the edges and faces having the characteristic fibrous appearance of torn or split wood. At Zuñi an instance occurs where split poles have been used for the second series of a roof extending through the whole thickness of the wall and projecting outside, as is commonly the case with the first series. A similar arrangement was seen in a ruined tower in the vicinity of Fort Wingate, New Mexico. In the typical roof construction illustrated the second series is covered with small twigs or brush, laid in close contact and at right angles to the underlying series, or parallel with the main beams. Pl. xcvi, illustrating an unroofed adobe house in Zuñi, shows several bundles of this material on an adjoining roof. This series is in turn covered with a layer of grass and small brush, again at right angles, which prepares the frame for the reception of the final earth covering, this latter being the fifth application to the roof. In the example illustrated the entire earth covering of the roof was finished in a single application of the material. It has been seen that at Tusayan a layer of moistened earth is applied, followed by a thicker layer of the dry soil.

In ancient construction, the method of arranging the material varied somewhat. In some cases series 3 was very carefully constructed of straight willow wands laid side by side in contact. This gave a very neat appearance to the ceiling within the room. Examples were seen in Canyon de Chelly, at Mummy Cave, and at Hungo Pavie and Pueblo Bonito on the Chaco.

Again examples occur where series 2 is composed of 2-inch poles in contact and the joints are chinked on the upper side with small stones to prevent the earth from sifting through. This arrangement was seen in a small cluster on the canyon bottom on the de Chelly.

The small size of available roofing rafters has at Tusayan brought about a construction of clumsy piers of masonry in a few of the larger rooms, which support the ends of two sets of main girders, and these in turn carry series 1, or the main ceiling beams of the roof. The girders are generally double, an arrangement that has been often employed in ancient times, as many examples occur among the ruins. The purpose of such arrangement may have been to admit of the abutment of the ends of series 1, when the members of the latter were laid in contact.

In the absence of squared beams, which seem never to have been used in the old work, this abutment could only be securely accomplished by the use of double girders, as suggested in the following diagram, Fig. 38.

FIG. 38. Showing abutment of smaller roof beams over round girders.

The final roof covering, composed of clay, is usually laid on very carefully and firmly, and, when the surface is unbroken, answers fairly well as a watershed. A slight slope or fall is given to the roof. This roof subserves every purpose of a front yard to the rooms that open upon it, and seems to be used exactly like the ground itself. Sheepskins are stretched and pegged out upon it for tanning or drying, and the characteristic Zuñi dome-shaped oven is frequently built upon it. In Zuñi generally upper rooms are provided only with a mud floor, although occasionally the method of paving with large thin slabs of stone is adopted. These are often somewhat irregular in form, the object being to have them as large as possible, so that considerable ingenuity is often displayed in selecting the pieces and in joining the irregular edges. This arrangement, similar to that of the kiva floors of Tusayan, is occasionally met with in the kivas.

In making excavations at Kin-tiel, the floor of the ground room in which the circular door illustrated in Pl. C, was found was paved with large, irregular fragments of stone, the thickness of which did not average more than an inch. Its floor, whose paving was all in place, was strewn with broken, irregular fragments similar in character, which must have been used as the flooring of an upper chamber.

### WALL COPINGS AND ROOF DRAINS.

In the construction of the typical pueblo house the walls are carried up to the height of the roof surface, and are then capped with a continuous protecting coping of thin flat stones, laid in close contact, their outer edges flush with the face of the wall. This arrangement is still the prevailing one at Tusayan, though there is an occasional example of the projecting coping that practically forms a cornice. This latter is the more usual form at Zuñi, though in the farming pueblos of Cibola it does not occur with any greater frequency than at Tusayan. The flush coping is in Tusayan made of the thinnest and most uniform specimens of building stone available, but these are not nearly so well adapted to the purpose as those found in the vicinity of Zuñi.

Here the projecting stones are of singularly regular and symmetrical form, and receive very little artificial treatment. Their extreme thinness makes it easy to trim off the projecting corners and angles, reducing them to such a form that they can be laid in close contact. Thus laid they furnish an admirable protection against the destructive action of the violent rains. The stones are usually trimmed to a width corresponding to the thickness of the walls. Of course where a projecting cornice is built, it can be made, to some extent, to conform to the width of available coping stones. These can usually be procured, however, of nearly uniform width. In the case of the overhanging cornices the necessary projection is attained by continuing either the main roof beams, or sometimes the smaller poles of the second series, according to the position of the required cornice, for a foot or more beyond the outer face of the wall. Over these poles the roofing is continued as in ordinary roof construction with the exception that the edge of the earth covering is built of masonry, an additional precaution against its destruction by the rains. In many places the adobe plastering originally applied to the faces of these cornices, as well as to the walls, has been washed away, exposing the whole construction. In some of these instances the face of the cornice furnishes a complete section of the roof, in which all the series of its construction can be readily identified. The protective agency of these coping stones is well illustrated in Pl. XCVII, which shows the destructive effect of rain at a point where an open joint has admitted enough water to bare the masonry of the cornice face, eating through its coating of adobe, while at the firmly closed joint toward the left there has been no erosive action. The much larger proportion of projecting copings or cornices in Zuñi, as compared with Tusayan, is undoubtedly attributable to the universal smoothing of the walls with adobe, and to the more general use of this perishable medium in this village, and the consequent necessity for protecting the walls. The efficiency of this means of protecting the wall against the wear of weather is seen in the preservation of external whitewashing for several feet below such a cornice on the face of the walls. At the pueblo of Acoma a similar extensive use of projecting cornices is met with, particularly on the third story walls. Here again it is due to the use of adobe, which has been more frequently employed in the finish of the higher and newer portions of the village than in the lower terraces. As a rule these overhanging copings occur pricipally on the southern exposures of the buildings and on the terraced sides of house rows. When walls rise to the height of several stories directly from the ground, such as the back walls of house rows, they are not usually provided with this feature but are capped with flush copings.

The rapid and destructive erosion of the earthen roof covering must have early stimulated the pueblo architect to devise means for promptly distributing where it would do the least harm the water which came upon his house. This necessity must have led to the early use of roof drains, for in no other way could the ancient builders have provided for the effectual removal of the water from the roofs and at the same time have preserved intact the masonry of the walls. Unfortunately we have no examples of such features in the ruined pueblos, for in the destruction or decay of the houses they are among the first details to be lost. The roof drain in the modern architecture becomes a very prominent feature, particularly at Zuñi.

These drains are formed by piercing an opening through the thickness of the coping wall, at a point where the drainage from the roof would collect, the opening being made with a decided pitch and furnished with a spout or device of some kind to insure the discharge of the water beyond the face of the wall. These spouts assume a variety of forms. Perhaps the most common is that of a single long, narrow slab of stone, set at a suitable angle and of sufficient projection to throw the discharge clear of the wall. Fig. 39 illustrates drains of this type, No.

FIG. 39. Single stone roof drains.

1 being a Tusayan example and No. 2 from Zuñi. It will be noted that the surrounding masonry of the former, as well as the stone itself, are much ruder than the Zuñi example. Another type of drain, not differ-

FIG. 40. Trough roof drains of stone.

ing greatly from the preceding, is illustrated in Fig. 40. This form is a slight improvement on the single stone drain, as it is provided with side pieces which convert the device into a trough-like spout, and more effectually direct the discharge. No. 1 is a Tusayan spout and No. 2 a Zuñi example. Wooden spouts are also commonly used for this purpose. Fig. 41 illustrates an example from each province of this form of

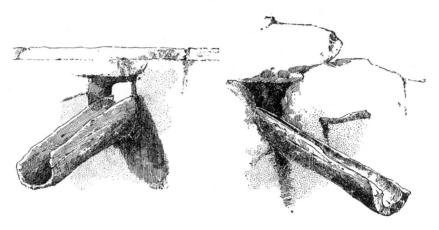

FIG. 41. Wooden roof drains.

drain. These are usually made from small tree trunks, not exceeding 3 or 4 inches in diameter, and are gouged out from one side. No tubular specimens of wooden spouts were seen. At Tusayan the builders have utilized stone of a concretionary formation for roof drains. The workers in stone could not wish for material more suitably fashioned for the purpose than these specimens. Two of these curious stone channels are illustrated in Fig. 42. Two more examples of Tusayan roof

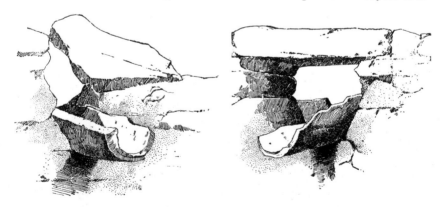

FIG. 42. Curved roof drains of stone in Tusayan.

drains are illustrated in Fig. 43. The first of the latter shows the use of a discarded metate, or mealing stone, and the second of a gourd that has been walled into the coping.

It is said that tubes of clay were used at Awatubi in olden times for roof drains, but there remains no positive evidence of this. Three forms of this device are attributed to the people of that village. Some are

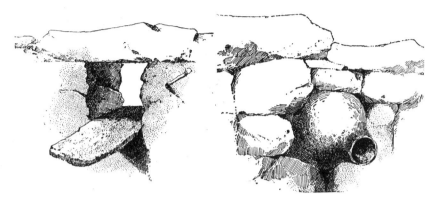

FIG. 43. Tusayan roof drains; a discarded metate and a gourd.

said to have been made of wood, others of stone, and some again of sun-dried clay. The native explanation of the use in this connection of sun-dried clay, instead of the more durable baked product, was that the application of fire to any object that water passes through would be likely to dry up the rains. It was stated in this connection that at the present day the cobs of the corn used for planting are not burned until rain has fallen on the crop. If the clay spout described really existed among the people at Awatubi, it was likely to have been an innovation introduced by the Spanish missionaries. Among the potsherds picked up at this ruin was a small piece of coarsely made clay tube, which seemed to be too large and too roughly modeled to have been the handle of a ladle, which it roughly resembled, or to have belonged to any other known form of domestic pottery. As a roof drain its use would not accord with the restrictions referred to in the native account, as the piece had been burnt.

In some cases in Zuñi where drains discharge from the roofs of upper terraces directly upon those below, the lower roofs and also the adjoining vertical walls are protected by thin tablets of stone, as shown in Fig. 44. It will be seen that one of these is placed upon the lower roof in such a position that the drainage falls directly upon it. Where the adobe roof covering is left unprotected its destruction by the rain is very rapid, as the showers of the rainy season in these regions, though usually of short duration, are often extremely violent. The force of the torrents is illustrated in the neighboring country. Here small ruts in the surface of the ground are rapidly converted into large arroyos. Frequently ordinary wagon tracks along a bit of valley slope serve as an initial channel to the rapidly accumulating waters and are eaten away in a few weeks so that the road becomes wholly impassable, and must be abandoned for a new one alongside.

FIG. 44. Zuñi roof drain, with splash stones on roof below.

The shiftlessness of the native builders in the use of the more convenient material brings its own penalty during this season in a necessity for constant watchfulness and frequent repairs to keep the houses habitable. One can often see in Zuñi where an inefficient drain or a broken coping has given the water free access to the face of a plastered wall, carrying away all its covering and exposing in a vertical space the jagged stones of the underlying masonry. It is noticeable that much more attention has been paid to protective devices at Zuñi than at Tusayan. This is undoubtedly due to the prevalent use of adobe in the former. This friable material must be protected at all vulnerable points with slabs of stone in order quickly to divert the water and preserve the roofs and walls from destruction.

### LADDERS AND STEPS.

In the inclosed court of the old fortress pueblos the first terrace was reached only by means of ladders, but the terraces or rooms above this were reached both by ladders and steps. The removal of the lower tier of ladders thus gave security against intrusion and attack. The builders of Tusayan have preserved this primitive arrangement in much greater purity than those of Cibola.

In Zuñi numerous ladders are seen on every terrace, but the purpose of these, on the highest terraces, is not to provide access to the rooms of the upper story, which always have external doors opening on the terraces, but to facilitate repairs of the roofs. At Tusayan, on the other hand, ladders are of rare occurrence above the first terrace, their place being supplied by flights of stone steps. The relative scarcity of stone at Zuñi, suitable for building material, and its great abundance at Tusayan, undoubtedly account for this difference of usage, especially as the proximity of the timber supply of the Zuñi mountains to the former facilitates the substitution of wood for steps of masonry.

FIG. 45. A modern notched ladder in Oraibi.

FIG. 46. Tusayan notched ladders from Mashongnavi.

The earliest form of ladder among the pueblos was probably a notched log, a form still occasionally used. Figures 45 and 46 illustrate examples of this type of ladder from Tusayan.

A notched ladder from Oraibi, made with a modern axe, is shown. This specimen has a squareness of outline and an evenness of surface not observed in the ancient examples.   The ladder from Mashongnavi, illustrated on the left of Fig. 46, closely resembles the Oraibi specimen, though the workmanship is somewhat ruder.   The example illustrated on the right of the same figure is from Oraibi.   This ladder is very old, and its present rough and weatherbeaten surface affords but little evidence of the character of the implement used in making it.

The ladder having two poles connected by cross rungs is undoubtedly a native invention, and was probably developed through a series of improvements on the primitive notched type.   It is described in detail in the earliest Spanish accounts.   Fig. 47 illustrates on the left the notched

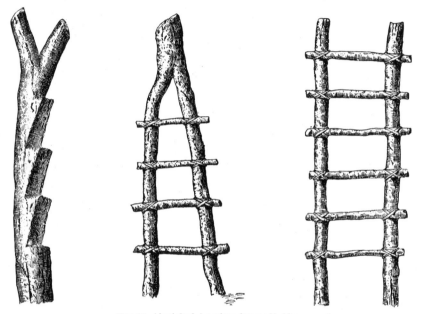

FIG. 47. Aboriginal American forms of ladder.

ladder, and on the right a typical two-pole ladder in its most primitive form.   In this case the rungs are simply lashed to the uprights.   The center ladder of the diagram is a Mandan device illustrated by Mr. Lewis H. Morgan.[1]   As used by the Mandans this ladder is placed with its forked end on the ground, the reverse of the Pueblo practice. It will readily be seen, on comparing these examples, that an elongation of the fork which occurs as a constant accompaniment of the notched ladder might eventually suggest a construction similar to that of the Mandan ladder reversed.   The function of the fork on the notched ladder in steadying it when placed against the wall would be more effectually performed by enlarging this feature.

---

[1] Cont. to N. A. Ethn., vol. 4, Houses and House Life, pp. 129–131.

At one stage in the development of the form of ladder in common use to-day the rungs were laid in depressions or notches of the vertical poles, resembling the larger notches of the single ladder, and then lashed on with thongs of rawhide or with other materials. Later, when the use of iron became known, holes were burned through the side poles. This is the nearly universal practice to-day, though some of the more skillful pueblo carpenters manage to chisel out rectangular holes. The piercing of the side poles, particulary prevalent in Zuñi, has brought about a curious departure from the ancient practice of removing the ladder in times of threatened danger. Long rungs are loosely slipped into the holes in the side pieces, and the security formerly gained by taking up the entire ladder is now obtained, partially at least, by the removal of the rungs. The boring of the side pieces and the employment of loose rungs seriously interferes with the stability of the structure, as means must be provided to prevent the spreading apart of the side pieces. The Zuñi architect has met this difficulty by prolonging the poles of the ladder and attaching a cross piece near their upper ends to hold them together. As a rule this cross piece is provided with a hole near each end into which the tapering extremities of the poles are inserted. From their high position near the extremities of the ladders, seen in silhouette against the sky, they form peculiarly striking features of Zuñi. They are frequently decorated with rude carvings of terraced notches. Examples of this device may be seen in the views of Zuñi, and several typical specimens are illustrated in detail in Pl. XCVIII. The use of cross pieces on ladders emerging from roof openings is not so common as on external ones, as there is not the same necessity for holding together the poles, the sides of the opening performing that office.

There are two places in Zuñi, portions of the densest house cluster, where the needs of unusual traffic have been met by the employment of double ladders, made of three vertical poles, which accommodate two tiers of rungs. The sticks forming the rungs are inserted in continuous lengths through all three poles, and the cross pieces at the top are also continuous, being formed of a single flat piece of wood perforated by three holes for the reception of the tips of the poles. In additional to the usual cross pieces pierced for the reception of the side poles and rudely carved into ornamental forms, many temporary cross pieces are added during the harvest season in the early autumn to support the strips of meat and melons, strings of red peppers, and other articles dried in the open air prior to storage for winter use. At this season every device that will serve this purpose is employed. Occasionally poles are seen extending across the reentering angles of a house or are supported on the coping and rafters. The projecting roof beams also are similarly utilized at this season.

Zuñi ladders are usually provided with about eight rungs, but a few have as many as twelve. The women ascend these ladders carrying ollas of water on their heads, children play upon them, and a few of the most expert of the numerous dogs that infest the village can clumsily make their way up and down them. As described in a previous section all houses built during the year are consecrated at a certain season, and among other details of the ceremonial, certain rites, intended to prevent accidents to children, etc., are performed at the foot of the ladders.

In Tusayan, where stone is abundant, the ladder has not reached the elaborate development seen in Zuñi. The perforated cross piece is rarely seen, as there is little necessity for its adoption. The side poles are held together by the top and bottom rungs, which pass entirely through the side pieces and are securely fixed, while the ends of the others are only partly embedded in the side pieces. In other cases (Pl. XXXII) the poles are rigidly held in place by ropes or rawhide lashings.

Short ladders whose side poles are but little prolonged beyond the top rung are of common occurrence, particularly in Oraibi. Three such ladders are shown in Pl. LXXXIV. A similar example may be seen in Pl. CVII, in connection with a large opening closed with rough masonry. In these cases the rungs are made to occupy slight notches or depressions in the upright poles and are then firmly lashed with rawhide, forming a fairly rigid structure. This type of ladder is probably a survival of the earliest form of the pueblo ladder.

In addition to the high cross piece whose function is to retain in place the vertical poles, the kiva ladders are usually provided, both in Zuñi and Tusayan, with a cross piece consisting of a round stick tied to the uprights and placed at a uniform height above the kiva roof. This stick affords a handhold for the masked dancers who are often encumbered with ceremonial paraphernalia as they enter the kiva. In the case of the Oraibi kiva occupying the foreground of Pl. XXXVIII, it may be seen that this handhold cross piece is inserted into holes in the side poles, an exception to the general practice. In Pl. LXXXVII, illustrating kivas, the position of this feature will be seen.

The exceptional mode of access to Tusayan kiva hatchways by means of short flights of stone steps has already been noticed. In several instances the top steps of these short flights cover the thickness of the wall. The remains of a similar stairway were observed in Pueblo Bonito, where it evidently reached directly from the ground to an external doorway. Access by such means, however, is a departure from the original defensive idea.

Modern practice in Zuñi has departed more widely from the primitive system than at Tusayan. In the former pueblo short flights of stone steps giving access to doors raised but a short distance above the ground are very commonly seen. Even in the small farming pueblo of Pescado two examples of this arrangement are met with. Pl. XCIX illustrates one of these found on the north outside wall. In the general views of the Tusayan villages the closer adherence to primitive methods is

clearly indicated, although the modern compare very unfavorably with
the ancient examples in precision of execution.  Pl. XXXII illustrates

FIG. 48. Stone steps at Oraibi, with platform at corner.

two flights of stone steps of Shupaulovi.  In many cases the workmanship of these stone steps does not surpass that seen in the Walpi
trail, illustrated in Pl. XXV.

FIG. 49. Stone steps, with platform at chimney, in Oraibi.

Perhaps in no one detail of pueblo construction are the careless and shiftless modern methods so conspicuous as in the stone steps of the upper terraces of Tusayan. Here are seen many awkward makeshifts by means of which the builders have tried to compensate for their lack of foresight in planning. The absence of a definite plan for a house cluster of many rooms, already noted in the discussion of dwelling-house construction, is rendered conspicuous by the manner in which the stone stairways are used. Figs. 48 and 49 illustrate stone steps on upper terraces in Oraibi. In both cases the steps have been added long after the rooms against which they abut were built. In order to conform to the fixed requirement of placing such means of access at the corners of the upper rooms, the builders constructed a clumsy platform to afford passage around the previously built chimney. Fig. 50 shows the result of a similar lack of foresight. The upper portion of

FIG. 50. Stone steps in Shumopavi.

the flight, consisting of three steps, has been abruptly turned at right angles to the main flight, and is supported upon rude poles and beams. The restriction of this feature to the corners of upper rooms where they were most likely to conflict with chimneys is undoubtedly a survival of ancient practice, and due to the necessary vertical alignment of walls and masonry in this primitive construction.

### COOKING PITS AND OVENS.

Most of the cooking of the ancient Pueblos was probably done out of doors, as among the ruins vestiges of cooking pits, almost identical in character with those still found in Tusayan, are frequently seen. In Cibola the large dome-shaped ovens, common to the Pueblos of the Rio Grande and to their Mexican neighbors are in general use. In Tusayan a few examples of this form of oven occur upon the roofs of the terraces, while the cooking pit in a variety of forms is still extensively used.

The distribution of the dome-shaped ovens in Cibola and in Tusayan may be seen on the ground plans in Chapters III and IV. The simplest form of cooking pit, still commonly used in Tusayan, consists of a depression in the ground, lined with a coating of mud. The pit is usually of small size and is commonly placed at some little distance from the house; in a few cases it is located in a sheltered corner of the building. Fig. 51 illustrates a series of three such primitive ovens built against a house wall, in a low bench or ledge of masonry raised 6 inches above the ground; the holes measure about a foot across and are

FIG. 51. A series of cooking pits in Mashongnavi.

about 18 or 20 inches deep. Many similar pits occur in the Tusayan villages; some of them are walled in with upright stone slabs, whose rough edges project 6 or 8 inches above the ground, the result closely resembling the ancient form of in-door fireplace, such as that seen in a room of Kin-tiel. (Pl. C.)

FIG. 52. Pi-gummi ovens of Mashongnavi.

In its perfected form the cooking pit in Tusayan takes the place of the more elaborate oven used in Zuñi. Figs. 52 and 53 show two speci-

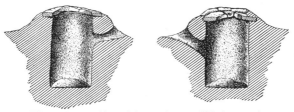

Fig. 53. Cross sections of pi-gummi ovens of Mashongnavi.

mens of pits used for the preparation of pi-gummi, a kind of baked mush.

These occur on the east side of Mashongnavi. They project 6 or 8 inches above the ground, and have a depth of from 18 to 24 inches. The débris scattered about the pits indicates the manner in which they are covered with slabs of stone and sealed with mud when in use. In all the oven devices of the pueblos the interior is first thoroughly heated by a long continued fire within the structure. When the temperature is sufficiently high the ashes and dirt are cleaned out, the articles to be cooked inserted, and the orifices sealed. The food is often left in these heated receptacles for 12 hours or more, and on removal it is generally found to be very nicely cooked. Each of the pi-gummi ovens illustrated above is provided with a tube-like orifice 3 or 4 inches in diameter, descending obliquely from the ground level into the cavity. Through this opening the fire is arranged and kept in order, and in this respect it seems to be the counterpart of the smaller hole of the Zuñi dome-shaped ovens. When the principal opening, by which the vessel containing the pi-gummi or other articles is introduced, has been covered with a slab of stone and sealed with mud, the effect is similar to that of the dome-shaped oven when the ground-opening or doorway is hermetically closed.

No example of the dome-shaped oven of pre-Columbian origin has been found among the pueblo ruins, although its prototype probably existed in ancient times, possibly in the form of a kiln for baking a fine quality of pottery formerly manufactured. However, the cooking pit alone, developed to the point of the pi-gummi oven of Tusayan, may have been the stem upon which the foreign idea was engrafted. Instances of the complete adoption by these conservative people of a wholly foreign idea or feature of construction are not likely to be found, as improvements are almost universally confined to the mere modification of existing devices. In the few instances in which more radical changes are attempted the resulting forms bear evidence of the fact.

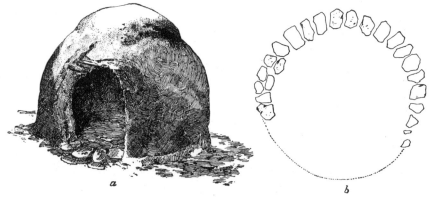

a                                                                    b

Fig. 54. Diagram showing foundation stones of a Zuñi oven.

In Cibola the construction of a dome-shaped oven is begun by laying out roughly a circle of flat stones as a foundation. Upon these the upper structure is rudely built of stones laid in the mud and approximately in the courses, though often during construction one side will be carried considerably higher than another. The walls curve inward to an apparently unsafe degree, but the mud mortar is often allowed to partly dry before carrying the overhanging portion so far as to endanger the structure, and accidents rarely happen. The oven illustrated in Pl. XCVII shows near its broken doorway the arrangement of foundation stones referred to. Typical examples of the dome oven occur in the foreground of the general view of Zuñi shown in Pl. LXXVIII.

The dome ovens of Cibola are generally smoothly plastered, inside and out, but a few examples are seen in which the stones of the masonry are exposed. In Pl. XCIX may be seen two ovens differing in size, one of which shows the manner in which the opening is blocked up with stone to keep out stray dogs during periods of disuse. Fig. 55 illustrates a mud-plastered oven at Pescado, which is elevated about a foot above the ground on a base or plinth of masonry. The opening of this oven is on the side toward the houses. This form is quite exceptional in Cibola,

FIG. 55. Dome-shaped oven on a plinth of masonry.

though of frequent occurrence among the Rio Grande pueblos. A very large and carefully finished example was examined at Jemez.

Figs. 56 and 57 illustrate two specimens of rough masonry ovens seen at Pescado. In one of these a decided horizontal arrangement of the stones

FIG. 56. Oven in Pescado exposing stones of masonry.

in the masonry prevails. The specimen at the right is small and rudely constructed, showing but little care in the use of the building material. The few specimens of dome ovens seen in Tusayan are characterized by the same rudeness of construction noticed in their house masonry. The rarity of this oven at Tusayan, where so many of the constructions have

FIG. 57. Oven in Pescado exposing stones of masonry.

retained a degree of primitiveness not seen elsewhere, is perhaps an additional evidence of its foreign origin.

In Tusayan, there are other structures, of rude dome-shape, likely to be mistaken for some form of cooking device. Fig. 58 illustrates two specimens of shrines that occur in courts of Mashongnavi. These are

FIG. 58. Shrines in Mashongnavi.

receptacles for plume sticks (bahos) and other votive offerings used at certain festivals, which, after being so used, are sealed up with stone slabs and adobe. These shrines occur at several of the villages, as noted in the discussion of the plans in Chapter III. In the foreground of Pl. XXXVIII may be seen an Oraibi specimen somewhat resembling those seen at Mashongnavi.

FIG. 59. A poultry house in Sichumovi resembling an oven.

Fig. 59 illustrates a very rude structure of stones in Sichumovi, resembling in form a dome oven, which is used as a poultry house. Several of these are seen in the Tusayan villages.

FIREPLACES AND CHIMNEYS.

The original fireplace of the ancient pueblo builders was probably the simple cooking pit transferred to a position within the dwelling room, and employed for the lighter cooking of the family as well as for warm-

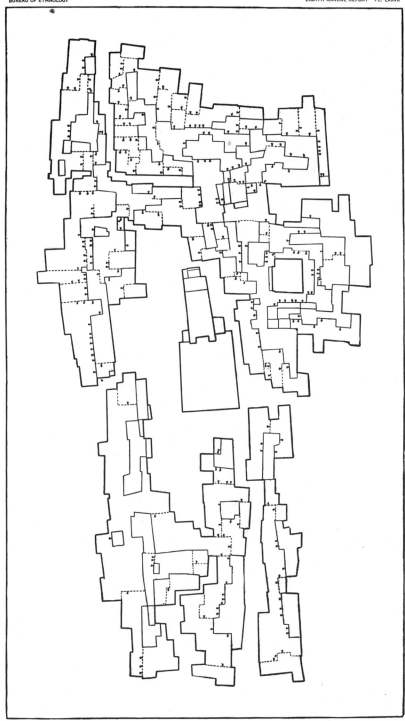

OUTLINE PLAN OF ZUÑI, SHOWING DISTRIBUTION OF OBLIQUE OPENINGS.

GENERAL INSIDE VIEW OF ZUÑI, LOOKING WEST.

EIGHTH ANNUAL REPORT    PL. LXXIX

OLD ADOBE CHURCH OF ZUÑI.

EASTERN ROWS OF ZUÑI.

A ZUÑI COURT.

A ZUÑI SMALL HOUSE.

A HOUSE BUILDING AT ORAIBI.

A TUSAYAN INTERIOR.

A ZUÑI INTERIOR.

A KIVA HATCHWAY OF TUSAYAN.

NORTH KIVAS OF SHUMOPAVI, FROM THE NORTHEAST.

MASONRY IN THE NORTH WING OF KIN-TIEL

ADOBE GARDEN WALLS NEAR ZUÑI.

A GROUP OF STONE CORRALS NEAR ORAIBI.

AN INCLOSING WALL OF UPRIGHT STONES AT OJO CALIENTE.

ing the dwelling. It was placed in the center of the floor in order that the occupants of the house might conveniently gather around it. One of the first improvements made in this shallow indoor cooking pit must have consisted in surrounding it with a wall of sufficient height to protect the fire against drafts, as seen in the outdoor pits of Tusayan. In excavating a room in the ancient pueblo of Kin-tiel, a completely preserved fireplace, about a foot deep, and walled in with thin slabs of stone set on edge, was brought to light. The depression had been hollowed out of the solid rock.

This fireplace, together with the room in which it was found, is illustrated in Pl. c and Fig. 60. It is of rectangular form, but other ex-

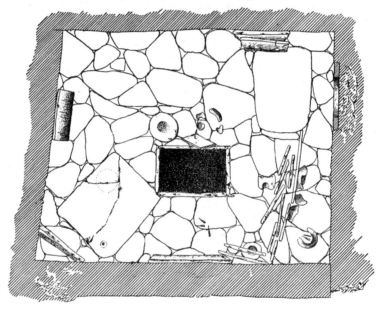

FIG. 60. Ground plan of an excavated room in Kin-tiel.

amples have been found which are circular. Mr. W. H. Jackson describes a fireplace in a cliff dwelling in "Echo Cave" that consisted of a circular, basin-like depression 30 inches across and 10 inches deep. Rooms furnishing evidence that fires were made in the corners against the walls are found in many cliff dwellings; the smoke escaped overhead, and the blackened walls afford no trace of a chimney or flue of any kind.

The pueblo chimney is undoubtedly a post-Spanish feature, and the best forms in use at the present time are probably of very recent origin, though they are still associated with fireplaces that have departed little from the aboriginal form seen at Kin-tiel and elsewhere. It is interesting to note, in this connection, that the ceremony consecrating the house is performed in Tusayan before the chimney is added, suggesting that the latter feature did not form a part of the aboriginal dwelling.

In Cibola a few distinct forms of chimney are used at the present time, but in the more remote Tusayan the chimney seems to be still in the experimental stage. Numbers of awkward constructions, varying from the ordinary cooking pit to the more elaborate hooded structures, testify to the chaotic condition of the chimney-building art in the latter province.

Before the invention of a chimney hood, and while the primitive fireplace occupied a central position in the floor of the room, the smoke probably escaped through the door and window openings. Later a hole in the roof provided an exit, as in the kivas of to-day, where ceremonial use has perpetuated an arrangement long since superseded in dwelling-house construction. The comfort of a dwelling room provided with this feature is sufficiently attested by the popularity of the modern kivas as a resort for the men. The idea of a rude hood or flue to facilitate the egress of the smoke would not be suggested until the fireplace was transferred from the center of a room to a corner, and in the first adoption of this device the builders would rely upon the adjacent walls for the needed support of the constructional members. Practically all of the chimneys of Tusayan are placed in corners at the present time, though the Zuñi builders have developed sufficient skill to construct a rigid hood and flue in the center of a side wall, as may be seen in the view of a Zuñi interior, Pl. LXXXVI.

Although the pueblo chimney owes its existence to foreign suggestion it has evidently reached its present form through a series of timid experiments, and the proper principles of its construction seem to have been but feebly apprehended by the native builders, particularly in Tusayan. The early form of hood, shown in Fig. 66, was made by placing a short supporting pole across the corner of a room at a sufficient distance from the floor and upon it arranging sticks to form the frame work of a contracting hood or flue. The whole construction was finally covered with a thick coating of mud. This primitive wooden construction has probably been in use for a long time, although it was modified in special cases so as to extend across the entire width of narrow rooms to accommodate "piki" stones or other cumbersome cooking devices. It embodies the principle of roof construction that must have been employed in the primitive house from which the pueblo was developed, and practically constitutes a miniature conical roof suspended over the fireplace and depending upon the walls of the room for support. On account of the careful and economical use of fuel by these people the light and inflammable material of which the chimney is constructed does not involve the danger of combustion that would be expected. The perfect feasibility of such use of wood is well illustrated in some of the old log-cabin chimneys in the Southern States, where, however, the arrangement of the pieces is horizontal, not vertical. These latter curiously exemplify also the use of a miniature section of house construction to form a conduit for the smoke, placed at a sufficient height to admit of access to the fire.

A further improvement in the chimney was the construction of a corner hood support by means of two short poles instead of a single

piece, thus forming a rectangular smoke hood of enlarged capacity. This latter is the most common form in use at the present time in both provinces, but its arrangement in Tusayan, where it represents the highest achievement of the natives in chimney construction, is much more varied than in Cibola. In the latter province the same form is occasionally executed in stone. Fig. 61 illustrates a corner hood, in which the crossed ends of the supporting poles are exposed to view. The outer end of the lower pole is supported from the roof beams by a cord or rope, the latter being embedded in the mud

FIG. 61. A corner chimney hood with two supporting poles (Tusayan).

plastering with which the hood is finished. The vertically ridged character of the surface reveals the underlying construction, in which

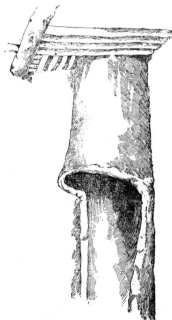

light sticks have been used as a base for the plaster. The Tusayans say that large sunflower stalks are preferred for this purpose on account of their lightness. Figs. 63 and 64 show another Tusayan hood of the type described, and in Fig. 69 a large hood of the same general form, suspended over a piki-stone, is noticeable for the frank treatment of the suspending cords, which are clearly exposed to view for nearly their entire length.

In a chimney in a Mashongnavi house, illustrated in Fig. 62, a simple, sharply curved piece of wood has been used for the lower rim of this hood, thus obtaining all the capacity of the two-poled form. The vertical sticks in this example are barely discernible through the plastering, which has been applied with more than the usual degree of care.

FIG. 62. A curved chimney hood of Mashongnavi.

A curious example illustrating a rudimentary form of two-poled hood is shown in Fig. 63. A straight pole of unusual length is built into the

Fig. 63. A Mashongnavi chimney hood and walled up fireplace.

walls across the corner of a room, and its insertion into the wall is much farther from the corner on one side than the other. From the longer stretch of inclosed wall protrudes a short pole that joins the principal one and serves as a support for one side of the chimney-hood. In this case the builder appears to have been too timid to venture on the bolder construction required in the perfected two-poled hood. This example probably represents a stage in the development of the higher form.

In some instances the rectangular corner hood is not suspended from the ceiling, but is supported from beneath by a stone slab or a piece of wood. Such a chimney hood seen in a house of Shupaulovi measures nearly 4 by 5 feet. The short side is supported by two stone slabs built into the wall and extending from the hood to the floor. Upon the upper stone rests one end of the wooden lintel supporting the long side, while the other end, near the corner of the room, is held in position by a light crotch of wood. Fig. 64 illustrates this hood; the plan indicating the relation of the stones and the forked stick to the corner of the room. Fig. 71, illustrating a terrace fireplace and chimney of Shumopavi, shows the employment of similar supports.

Corner chimney hoods in Zuñi do not differ essentially from the more symmetrical of the Tusayan specimens, but they are distinguished by better finish and by less exposure of the framework, having been, like the ordinary masonry, subjected to an unusually free application of adobe.

Fig. 64. A chimney hood of Shupaulovi.

The builders of Tusayan appear to have been afraid to add the necessary weight of mud mortar to produce this finished effect, the hoods

usually showing a vertically ridged or crenated surface, caused by the sticks of the framework showing through the thin mud coat. Stone also is often employed in their construction, and its use has developed a large, square-headed type of chimney unknown at Tusayan. This is illustrated in Fig. 65. This form of hood, projecting some distance beyond its flue, affords space that may be used as a mantel-shelf, an advantage gained only to a very small degree by the forms discussed above. This chimney, as before stated, is built against one of the walls of a room, and near the middle.

Fig. 65. A semi-detached square chimney hood of Zuñi.

All the joints of these hoods, and even the material used, are generally concealed from view by a carefully applied coating of plaster, supplemented by a gypsum wash, and usually there is no visible evidence of the manner in which they are built, but the construction is little superior to that of the simple corner hoods. The method of framing the various types of hoods is illustrated in Fig. 66. The example on the left shows an unplastered wooden hood skeleton. The arrangement of the parts in projecting rectangular stone hoods is illustrated in the right-hand diagram of the figure. In constructing such a chimney a thin buttress is first built against the wall of sufficient width and height to support one side of the hood.   The opposite side of the hood is supported by a flat stone, firmly set on edge into the masonry of the

FIG. 66.  Unplastered Zuñi chimney hoods, illustrating construction.

wall.   The front of the hood is supported by a second flat stone which rests at one end on a rude shoulder in the projecting slab, and at the other end upon the front edge of the buttress.   It would be quite practicable for the pueblo builders to form a notch in the lower corner of the supported stone to rest firmly upon a projection of the supporting stone, but in the few cases in which the construction could be observed no such treatment was seen, for they depended mainly on the interlocking of the ragged ends of the stones.   This structure serves to support the body of the flue, usually with an intervening stone-covered space forming a shelf.   At the present period the flue is usually built of thin sandstone slabs, rudely adjusted to afford mutual support.   The whole structure is bound together and smoothed over with mud plastering, and is finally finished with the gypsum wash, applied also to the rest of the room.   Mr. A. F. Bandelier describes "a regular chimney, with mantel and shelf, built of stone slabs," which he found "in the caves of the Rito de los Frijoles, as well as in the cliff dwellings of the regular detached family house type,"[1] which, from the description, must have closely resembled the Zuñi chimney described above.   Houses containing such devices may be quite old, but if so they were certainly reoccupied in post-Spanish times.   Such dwellings are likely to have been used as places of refuge in times of danger up to a comparatively recent date.

Among the many forms of chimneys and fireplaces seen in Tusayan a curious approach to our own arrangement of fireplace and mantel was noticed in a house in Sichumovi.   In addition to the principal mantel ledge, a light wooden shelf was arranged against the wall on one side of the flue, one of its ends being supported by an upright piece of wood with a cap, and the other resting on a peg driven into the wall. This fireplace and mantel is illustrated in Fig. 67.

Aside from the peculiar " guyave" or " piki" baking oven, there is but little variation in the form of indoor fireplaces in Cibola, while in Tusayan it appears to have been subjected to about the same mutations

already noted in the outdoor cooking pits.   A serious problem was encountered by the Tusayan builder when he was called upon to construct cooking-pit fireplaces, a foot or more deep, in a room of an upper

FIG. 67.  A fireplace and mantel in Sichumovi.

terrace.   As it was impracticable to sink the pit into the floor, the necessary depth was obtained by walling up the sides, as is shown in Fig.

FIG. 68.  A second-story fireplace in Mashongnavi.

68, which illustrates a second-story fireplace in Mashongnavi.   Other examples may be seen in the outdoor chimneys shown in Figs. 72 and 73.

A modification of the interior fireplace designed for cooking the thin, paper-like bread, known to the Spanish-speaking peoples of this region as "guyave," and by the Tusayan as "piki," is common to both Cibola and Tusayan, though in the former province the contrivance is more carefully constructed than in the latter, and the surface of the baking stone itself is more highly finished. In the guyave oven a tablet of carefully prepared sandstone is supported in a horizontal position by two slabs set on edge and firmly imbedded in the floor. A horizontal flue is thus formed in which the fire is built. The upper stone, whose surface is to receive the thin guyave batter, undergoes during its original preparation a certain treatment with fire and piñon gum, and perhaps other ingredients, which imparts to it a highly polished black finish. This operation is usually performed away from the pueblo, near a point where suitable stone is found, and is accompanied by a ceremonial, which is intended to prevent the stone from breaking on exposure to the fire when first used. During one stage of these rites the strictest silence is enjoined, as, according to the native account, a single word spoken at such a time would crack the tablet.

When the long guyave stone is in position upon the edges of the back and front stones the fire must be so applied as to maintain the stone at a uniform temperature. This is done by frequent feeding with small bits of sage brush or other fuel. The necessity for such economy in the use of fuel has to a certain extent affected the forms of all the heating and cooking devices. Fig. 69 illustrates a Sichumovi piki

FIG. 69. Piki stone and chimney hood in Sichumovi.

stone, and Fig. 70 shows the use of the oven in connection with a cooking fireplace, a combination that is not uncommon. The latter ex-

ample is from Shumopavi.   The illustration shows an interesting feature
in the use of a primitive andiron or boss to support the cooking pot in

FIG. 70. Piki stone and primitive andiron in Shumopavi.

position above the fire.   This boss is modeled from the same clay as
the fireplace floor and is attached to it and forms a part of it.   Mr.
Stephen has collected free specimens of these primitive props which
had never been attached to the floor.   These were of the rudely conical form illustrated in the figure, and were made of a coarsely mixed
clay thoroughly baked to a stony hardness.

Chimneys and fireplaces are often found in Tusayan in the small, recessed, balcony-like rooms of the second terrace.   When a deep cooking-
pit is required in such a position, it is obtained by building up the sides,
as in the indoor fireplaces of upper rooms.   Such a fireplace is illustrated
in Fig. 71.   A roofed recess which usually occurs at one end of the first
terrace, called "tupubi," takes its name from the flat piki oven, the
variety of fireplace generally built in these alcoves.   The transfer of the
fireplace from the second-story room to the corner of such a roofed-ter-
race alcove was easily accomplished, and probably led to the occasional
use of the cooking-pit, with protecting chimney hood on the open and
unsheltered roof.   Fig. 72 illustrates a deep cooking-pit on an upper

terrace of Walpi. In this instance the cooking pit is very massively built, and in the absence of a sheltering "tupubi" corner is effectually

Fig. 71. A terrace fireplace and chimney of Shumopavi.

protected on three sides by mud-plastered stone work, the whole being capped with the usual chimney pot. The contrivance is placed conveniently near the roof hatchway of a dwelling room.

Fig. 72. A terrace cooking-pit and chimney of Walpi.

The outdoor use of the above-described fireplaces on upper terraces has apparently suggested the improvement of the ground cooking pit

8 ETH——12

in a similar manner. Several specimens were seen in which the cooking pit of the ordinary depressed type, excavated near an inner corner of a house wall, was provided with sheltering masonry and a chimney cap; but such an arrangement is by no means of frequent occurrence. Fig. 73 illustrates an example that was seen on the east side of Shumopavi. It will be noticed that in the use of this arrangement on the ground—an

Fig. 73. A ground cooking-pit of Shumopavi covered with a chimney.

arrangement that evidently originated on the terraces—the builders have reverted to the earlier form of excavated pit. In other respects the example illustrated is not distinguishable from the terrace forms above described.

In the discussion of the details of kiva arrangement in Tusayan (p. 121) it was shown that the chimney is not used in any form in these ceremonial chambers; but the simple roof-opening forming the hatchway serves as a smoke vent, without the addition of either an internal hood or an external shaft. In the Zuñi kivas the smoke also finds vent through the opening that gives access to the chamber, but in the framing of the roof, as is shown elsewhere, some distinction between door and chimney is observed. The roof-hole is made double, one portion accommodating the ingress ladder and the other intended to serve for the egress of the smoke.

The external chimney of the pueblos is a simple structure, and exhibits but few variations from the type. The original form was undoubtedly a mere hole in the roof; its use is perpetuated in the kivas. This primitive form was gradually improved by raising its sides above the roof, forming a rudimentary shaft. The earlier forms are likely to have been rectangular, the round following and developing later short masonry shafts which were finally given height by the addition of chimney pots. In Zuñi the chimney has occasionally developed into a rather tall shaft, projecting sometimes to a height of 4 or 5 feet above the roof. This is particularly noticeable on the lower terraces of Zuñi, the chimneys of the higher rooms being more frequently of the short types prevalent in the farming pueblos of Cibola and in Tusayan. The tall chimneys found in Zuñi proper, and consisting often of four or five chimney pots on a substructure of masonry, are undoubtedly due to the same conditions that have so much influenced other constructional details; that is, the exceptional height of the clusters and crowding of the rooms. As a result of this the chimney is a more conspicuous feature in Zuñi than elsewhere, as will be shown by a comparison of the views of the villages given in Chapters III and IV.

In Tusayan many of the chimneys are quite low, a single pot surmounting a masonry substructure not more than 6 inches high being quite common. As a rule, however, the builders preferred to use a series of pots. Two typical Tusayan chimneys are illustrated in Fig. 74. Most of the substructures for chimneys in this province are rudely

Fig. 74. Tusayan chimneys.

rectangular in form, and clearly expose the rough stonework of the masonry, while in Zuñi the use of adobe generally obliterates all traces of construction. In both provinces chimneys are seen without the chimney pot. These usually occur in clusters, simply because the builder of a room or group of rooms preferred that form of chimney. Pl. CI illustrates a portion of the upper terraces of Zuñi where a number of masonry chimneys are grouped together. Those on the highest roof are principally of the rectangular form, being probably a direct development from the square roof hole. The latter is still sometimes seen with a rim rising several inches above the roof surface and formed of slabs set on edge or of ordinary masonry. These upper chimneys are often closed or covered with thin slabs of sandstone laid over them in the same manner as the roof holes that they resemble. The fireplaces to which some of them belong appear to be used for heating the rooms rather than for cooking, as they are often disused for long periods during the summer season.

Pl. CI also illustrates chimneys in which pots have been used in connection with masonry bases, and also a round masonry chimney. The latter is immediately behind the single pot chimney seen in the foreground. On the extreme left of the figure is shown a chimney into which fire pots have been incorporated, the lower ones being almost concealed from view by the coating of adobe. A similar effect may be seen in the small chimney on the highest roof shown in Pl. LVIII. Pl. LXXXII shows various methods of using the chimney pots. In one case the chimney is capped with a reversed large-mouthed jar, the broken bottom serving as an outlet for the smoke. The vessel usually employed for this purpose is an ordinary black cooking pot, the bottom being burned out, or otherwise rendered unfit for household use. Other vessels are occasionally used. Pl. LXXXIII shows the use, as the crowning member of the chimney, of an ordinary water jar, with dark decorations on a white ground. A vessel very badly broken is often made to serve in chimney building by skillful use of mud and mortar. To facilitate smoke exit the upper pot is made to overlap the neck of the one below by breaking out the bottom sufficiently. The joining is not often visible, as it is usually coated with adobe. The lower pots of a series are in many cases entirely embedded in the adobe.

The pueblo builder has never been able to construct a detached chimney a full story in height, either with or without the aid of chimney pots; where it is necessary to build such shafts to obtain the proper draft he is compelled to rely on the support of adjoining walls, and usually seeks a corner. Pl. CI shows a chimney of this kind that has been built of masonry to the full height of a story. A similar example is shown in the foreground of Pl. LXXVIII. In Pl. XXII may be seen a chimney of the full height of the adjoining story, but in this instance it is constructed wholly of pots. Pl. LXXXV illustrates a similar case indoors.

The external chimney probably developed gradually from the simple roof opening, as previously noted. The raised combing about trap-doors or roof holes afforded the first suggestion in this direction. From this developed the square chimney, and finally the tall round shaft, crowned with a series of pots. The whole chimney, both internal and external, excluding only the primitive fireplace, is probably of comparatively recent origin, and based on the foreign (Spanish) suggestion.

### GATEWAYS AND COVERED PASSAGES.

Gateways, arranged for defense, occur in many of the more compactly-built ancient pueblos. Some of the passageways in the modern villages of Tusayan and Cibola resemble these older examples, but most of the narrow passages, giving access to the inner courts of the inhabited villages, are not the result of the defensive idea, but are formed by the crowding together of the dwellings. They occur, as a rule, within the pueblo and not upon its periphery. Many of the terraces now face outward and are reached from the outside of the pueblo, being in marked contrast to the early arrangement, in which narrow passages to inclose courts were exclusively used for access. In the ground plans of several villages occupied within historic times, but now ruined, vestiges of openings arranged on the original defensive plan may be traced. About midway on the northeast side of Awatubi fragments of a standing wall were seen, apparently the two sides of a passageway to the inclosed court of the pueblo. The masonry is much broken down, however, and no indication is afforded of the treatment adopted, nor do the remains indicate whether this entrance was originally covered or not. It is illustrated in Pl. CII.

Other examples of this feature may be seen in the ground plans of Tebugkihu, Chukubi, and Payupki (Fig. 7, and Pls. XII and XIII). In the first of these the deep jambs of the opening are clearly defined, but in the other two only low mounds of débris suggest the gateway. In the ancient Cibolan pueblos, including those on the mesa of Tâaaiyalana, no remains of external gateways have been found; the plans suggest that the disposition of the various clusters approximated somewhat the irregular arrangement of the present day. There are only occasional traces, as of a continuous defensive outer wall, such as those seen at Nutria and Pescado. In the pueblos of the Cibola group, ancient and modern, access to the inner portion of the pueblo was usually afforded at a number of points. In the pueblo of Kin-tiel, however, occurs an excellent example of the defensive gateway. The jambs and corners of the opening are finished with great neatness, as may be seen in the illustration (Pl. CIII). This gateway or passage was roofed over, and the rectangular depressions for the reception of cross-beams still contain short stumps, protected from destruction by the masonry. The masonry over the passageway in falling carried away part of the masonry above the jamb corner, thus indicating continuity of bond. The ground plan of this ruin (Pl. LXIII) indicates clearly the various points at which access to the inner courts was obtained. On the east side a noticeable feature is the overlapping of the boundary wall of the south wing, forming an indirect entranceway. The remains do not indicate that this passage, like the one just described, was roofed over. In some cases the modern passageways, as they follow the jogs and angles of adjoining rows of houses, display similar changes of direction. In Shupaulovi, which preserves most distinctly in its plan the idea of the inclosed court, the passageway at the south end of the village changes its direction at a right angle before emerging into the court (Pl. XXX). This arrangement was undoubtedly determined by the position of the terraces long before the passageway was roofed over and built upon. Pl. XXII shows the south passageway of Walpi; the entrances are made narrower than the rest of the passage by building buttresses of masonry at the sides. This was probably done to secure the necessary support for the north and south walls of the upper story. One of the walls, as may be seen in the illustration, rests directly upon a cross beam, strengthened in this manner.

One of the smaller inclosed courts of Zuñi, illustrated in Pl. LXXXII, is reached by means of two covered passages, bearing some general resemblance to the ancient defensive entrances, but these houses, reached from within the court, have also terraces without. The low passage shown in the figure has gradually been surmounted by rooms, reaching in some cases a height of three terraces above the openings; but the accumulated weight finally proved too much for the beams and sustaining walls—probably never intended by the builders to withstand the severe test afterwards put upon them—and following an unusually protracted period of wet weather, the entire section of rooms above fell to the ground. This occurred since the surveying and photographing. It is rather remarkable that the frail adobe walls withstood so long the unusual strain, or even that they sustained the addition of a top story at all.

In the preceding examples the passageway was covered throughout its length by rooms, but cases occur in both Tusayan and Cibola in which only portions of the roof form the floor of superstructures. Pl. CIV shows a passage roofed over beyond the two-story portion of the building for a sufficient distance to form a small terrace, upon which a ladder stands. Pl. XXIII illustrates a similar arrangement on the west side of Walpi. The outer edges of these terraces are covered with coping stones and treated in the same manner as outer walls of lower rooms. In Zuñi an example of this form of passage roof occurs between two of the eastern house rows, where the rooms have not been subjected to the close crowding characteristic of the western clusters of the pueblo.

### DOORS.

In Zuñi many rooms of the ground story, which in early times must have been used largely for storage, have been converted into well-lighted, habitable apartments by the addition of external doors. In Tusayan this modification has not taken place to an equal extent, the distinctly defensive character of the first terrace reached by removable ladders being still preserved. In this province a doorway on the ground is always provided in building a house, but originally this space was not designed to be permanent; it was left merely for convenience of passing in and out during the construction, and was built up before the walls were completed. Of late years, however, such doorways are often preserved, and additional small openings are constructed for windows.

In ancient times the larger doorways of the upper terraces were probably never closed, except by means of blankets or rabbit-skin robes hung over them in cold weather. Examples have been seen that seem to have been constructed with this object in view, for a slight pole, of the same kind as those used in the lintels, is built into the masonry of the jambs a few inches below the lintel proper. Openings imperfectly closed against the cold and wind were naturally placed in the lee walls to avoid the prevailing southwest winds, and the ground plans of the exposed mesa villages were undoubtedly influenced by this circumstance, the tendency being to change them from the early inclosed court type and to place the houses in longitudinal rows facing eastward. This is noticeable in the plans given in Chapter II.

Doorways closed with masonry are seen in many ruins. Possibly these are an indication of the temporary absence of the owner, as in the harvest season, or at the time of the destruction or abandonment of the village; but they may have been closed for the purpose of economizing warmth and fuel during the winter season. No provision was made for closing them with movable doors. The practice of fastening up the doors during the harvesting season prevails at the present time among the Zuñi, but the result is attained without great difficulty by means of rude cross bars, now that they have framed wooden doors. One of these is illustrated in Fig. 75. These doors are usually opened by a latch-string, which, when not hung outside, is reached by means of a small round hole through the wall at the side of the door. Through this hole the owner of the house, on leaving it, secures the door by props and braces on the inside of the room, the hole being sealed up and plastered in the same manner that other openings are treated.

This curious arrangement affords another illustration of the survival of ancient methods in modified forms. It is not employed, however, in closing the doors of the first terrace; these are fastened by barring from the inside, the exit being made by means of internal ladders to the ter race above, the upper doors only being fastened in the manner illus-

FIG. 75. A barred Zuñi door.

trated. In Pl. LXXIX may be seen good examples of the side hole. Fig. 75 shows a barred door. The plastering or sealing of the small side hole instead of the entire opening was brought about by the introduction of the wooden door, which in its present paneled form is of foreign introduction, but in this, as in so many other cases, some analogous feature which facilitated the adoption of the idea probably already existed. Tradition points to the early use of a small door, made of a single slab of wood, that closed the small rectangular wall niches, in which valuables, such as turquoise, shell, etc., were kept. This slab, it is said, was reduced and smoothed by rubbing with a piece of sandstone. A number of beams, rafters, and roofing planks, seen in the Chaco pueblos, were probably squared and finished in this way. The latter examples show a degree of familiarity with this treatment of wood that would enable the builders to construct such doors with ease. As yet, however, no examples of wooden doors have been seen in any of the pre-Columbian ruins.

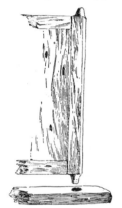

The pueblo type of paneled door is much more frequently seen in Cibola than in Tusayan, and in the latter province it does not assume the variety of treatment seen in Zuñi, nor is the work so neatly executed. The views of the modern pueblos, given in Chapters III and IV, will indicate the extent to which this feature occurs in the two groups. In the construction of a paneled door the vertical stile on one side is prolonged at the top and bottom into a rounded pivot, which works into cup-like sockets in the lintel and sill, as illustrated in Fig. 76. The hinge is thus produced in the wood itself without the aid of any external appliances.

Fig. 76. Wooden pivot hinges of a Zuñi door.

It is difficult to trace the origin of this device among the pueblos. It closely resembles the pivot hinges sometimes used in mediæval Europe in connection with massive gates for closing masonry passages; in such cases the prolonged pivots worked in cavities of stone sills and lintels. The Indians claim to have employed it in very early times, but no evidence on this point has been found. It is quite possible that the idea was borrowed from some of the earlier Mormon settlers who came into the country, as these people use a number of primitive devices which are undoubtedly survivals of methods of construction once common in the countries from which they came. Vestiges of the use of a pivotal hinge, constructed on a much more massive scale than any of the pueblo examples, were seen at an old fortress-like, stone storehouse of the Mormons, built near the site of Moen-kopi by the first Mormon settlers.

The paneled door now in use among the pueblos is rudely made, and consists of a frame inclosing a single panel. This panel, when of large size, is occasionally made of two or more pieces. These doors vary greatly in size. A few reach the height of 5 feet, but the usual height is from 3½ to 4 feet.   As doors are commonly elevated a foot or more above the ground or floor, the use of such openings does not entail the full degree of discomfort that the small size suggests.   Doors of larger size, with sills raised but an inch or two above the floor or ground, have recently been introduced in some of the ground stories in Zuñi; but these are very recent, and the idea has been adopted only by the most progressive people.

Fig. 77. Paneled wooden doors in Hano.

Pl. xli shows a small paneled door, not more than a foot square, used as a blind to close a back window of a dwelling.   The smallest examples of paneled doors are those employed for closing the small, square open-

ings in the back walls of house rows, which still retain the defensive
arrangement so marked in many of the ancient pueblos. In some
instances doors occur in the second stories of unterraced walls, their
sills being 5 or 6 feet above the ground. In such cases the doors are
reached by ladders whose upper ends rest upon the sills. Elevated
openings of this kind are closed in the usual manner with a rude, single-
paneled door, which is often whitened with a coating of clayey gypsum.

Carefully worked paneled doors are much more common in Zuñi than
in Tusayan, and within the latter province the villages of the first mesa
make more extended use of this type of door, as they have come into
more intimate contact with their eastern brethren than other villages of
the group. Fig. 77 illustrates a portion of a Hano house in which two
wooden doors occur. These specimens indicate the rudeness of Tusayan
workmanship. It will be seen that the workman who framed the upper
one of these doors met with considerable difficulty in properly joining
the two boards of the panel and in connecting these with the frame.
The figure shows that at several points the door has been reenforced
and strengthened by buckskin and rawhide thongs. The same device
has been employed in the lower door, both in fastening together the two
pieces of the panel and in attaching the latter to the framing. These
doors also illustrate the customary manner of barring the door during
the absence of the occupant of the house.

The doorway is usually framed at the time the house is built. The
sill is generally elevated above the ground outside and the floor inside,

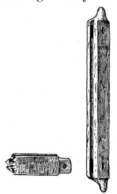

and the door openings, with a few exceptions,
are thus practically only large windows. In this
respect they follow the arrangement characteristic of the ancient pueblos, in which all the larger
openings are window-like doorways. These are
sometimes seen on the court margin of house
rows, and frequently occur between communicating rooms within the cluster. They are usually
raised about a foot and a half above the floor,
and in some cases are provided with one or two
steps. In Zuñi, doorways between communicating rooms, though now framed in wood, preserve
the same arrangement, as may be seen in Pl.
LXXXVI.

FIG. 78. Framing of a Zuñi
door-panel.

The side pieces of a paneled pueblo door are mortised, an achievement far beyond the aboriginal art of these people. Fig. 78 illustrates
the manner in which the framing is done. All the necessary grooving,
and the preparation of the projecting tenons is laboriously executed
with the most primitive tools, in many cases the whole frame, with all
its joints, being cut out with a small knife.

Doors are usually fastened by a simple wooden latch, the bar of which
turns upon a wooden pin. They are opened from without by lifting the

latch from its wooden catch by means of a string passed through a small hole in the door, and hanging outside. Some few doors are, however, provided with a cumbersome wooden lock, operated by means of a square, notched stick that serves as a key. These locks are usually fastened to the inner side of the door by thongs of buckskin or rawhide, passed through small holes bored or drilled through the edge of the lock, and through the stile and panel of the door at corresponding points. The entire mechanism consists of wood and strings joined together in the rudest manner. Primitive as this device is, however, its conception is far in advance of the aboriginal culture of the pueblos, and both it and the string latch must have come from without. The lock was probably a contrivance of the early Mormons, as it is evidently roughly modeled after a metallic lock.

Many doors having no permanent means of closure are still in use. These are very common in Tusayan, and occur also in Cibola, particularly in the farming pueblos. The open front of the "tupubi" or balcony-like recess, seen so frequently at the ends of first-terrace roofs in Tusayan, is often constructed with a transom-like arrangement in connection with the girder supporting the edge of the roof, in the same manner in which doorways proper are treated. Pl. XXXII illustrates a balcony in which one bounding side is formed by a flight of stone steps, producing a notched or terraced effect. The supporting girder in this instance is embedded in the wall and coated over with adobe, obscuring the construction. Fig. 79 shows a rude transom over the supporting beam of a balcony roof in the principal house of Hano. The upper doorway shown in this house has been partly walled in, reducing its size somewhat. It is also provided with a small horizontal opening over the main lintel, which, like the doorway, has been partly filled with masonry. This upper transom often seems to have resulted from carrying such openings to the full height of the story. The transom probably originated from the spaces left between the ends of beams resting on the main girder that spanned the principal opening (see Fig. 81). Somewhat similar balconies are seen in Cibola, both in Zuñi and in the farming villages, but they do not assume so much importance as in Tusayan. An example is shown in Pl. CI, in which the construction of this feature is clearly visible.

In the remains of the ancient pueblos there is no evidence of the use of the half-open terrace rooms described above. If such rooms existed, especially if constructed in the open manner of the Tusayan examples, they must have been among the first to succumb to destruction. The comparative rarity of this feature in Zuñi does not necessarily indicate that it is not of native origin, as owing to the exceptional manner of clustering and to prolonged exposure to foreign influence, this pueblo exhibits a wider departure from the ancient type than do any of the Tusayan villages. It is likely that the ancient builders, trusting to the double protection of the inclosed court and the defensive first terrace, freely adopted this open and convenient arrangement in connection with the upper roofs.

FIG. 79. Rude transoms over Tusayan openings.

The transom-like opening commonly accompanying the large opening is also seen in many of the inclosed doorways of Tusayan, but in some of these cases its origin can not be traced to the roof constructions, as the openings do not approach the ceilings of the rooms. In early days such doorways were closed by means of large slabs of stone set on edge, and these were sometimes supplemented by a suspended blanket. In severe winter weather many of the openings were closed with masonry. At the present time many doorways not provided with paneled doors

are closed in such ways. When a doorway is thus treated its transom
is left open for the admission of light and air. The Indians state that in
early times this transom was provided for the exit of smoke when the

FIG. 80. A large Tusayan doorway with small transom openings.

main doorway was closed, and even now such provision is not wholly
superfluous. Fig. 80 illustrates a large doorway of Tusayan with a
small transom. The opening was being reduced in size by means of
adobe masonry at the time the draw-
ing was made. Fig. 81 shows a
double transom over a lintel composed of two poles; a section of
masonry separating the transom
into two distinct openings rests
upon the lintel of the doorway and
supports a roof-beam; this is shown
in the figure. Other examples of
transoms may be seen in connection
with many of the illustrations of
Tusayan doorways.

FIG. 81. A doorway and double transom in Walpi.

The transom bars over exterior doorways of houses probably bear
some relation to a feature seen in some of the best preserved ruins and
still surviving to some extent in Tusayan practice. This consists of a
straight pole, usually of the same dimensions as the poles of which the
lintel is made, extending across the opening from 2 to 6 inches below
the main lintel, and fixed into the masonry in a position to serve as a
curtain pole. Originally this pole undoubtedly served as a means of
suspension for the blanket or skin rug used in closing the opening, just
as such means are now used in the huts of the Navajo, as well as

occasionally in the houses of Tusayan. The space above this cross stick answered the same purpose as the transoms of the present time.

A most striking feature of doorways is the occasional departure from the quadrangular form, seen in some ruined villages and also in some of the modern houses of Tusayan. Fig. 82 illustrates a specimen of this type found in a small cliff ruin in Canyon de Chelly. Ancient examples of this form of opening are distinguished by a symmetrical disposition of the step in the jamb, while the modern doors are seldom so arranged. A modern example from Mashongnavi is shown in Fig. 83. This opening also illustrates the

FIG. 82. An ancient doorway in Canyon de Chelly cliff ruin.

double or divided transom. The beam ends shown in the figure project beyond the face of the wall and support an overhanging coping or cornice. A door-like window, approximating the symmetrical form described, is seen

FIG. 83. A symmetrically notched doorway in Mashongnavi.

immediately over the passage-way shown in Pl. XXII. This form is evidently the result of the partial closing of a larger rectangular opening.

Fig. 84 shows the usual type of terraced doorway in Tusayan, in which one jamb is stepped at a considerably greater height than the other. In Tusayan large openings occur in which only one jamb is stepped, producing an effect somewhat of that of the large balcony openings with flights of stone steps at one side, previously illustrated. An opening of this form is shown in Fig. 85. Both of the stepped doorways, illustrated above, are provided with transom openings extending from one roof beam to another. In the absence of a movable door the openings were made of the smallest size consistent with convenient use. The stepped form was very likely suggested by the temporary partial blocking up of an opening with loose, flat stones in such a manner as

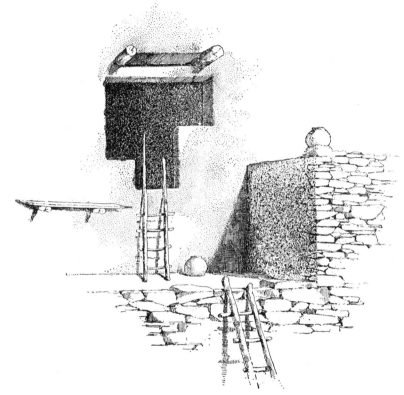

FIG. 84. A Tusayan notched doorway.

to least impair its use. This is still quite commonly done, large openings being often seen in which the lower portion on one or both sides is narrowed by means of adobe bricks or stones loosely piled up. In this connection it may be noted that the secondary lintel pole, previously described as occurring in both ancient and modern doorways, serves the additional purpose of a hand-hold when supplies are brought into the house on the backs of the occupants. The stepping of the doorway, while diminishing its exposed area, does not interfere with its use in bringing in large bundles, etc. Series of steps, picked into the faces of the cliffs, and affording access to cliff dwellings, frequently have a supplementary series of narrow and deep cavities that furnish a secure hold for the hands. The requirements of the precipitous environment of these people have led to the carrying of loads of produce, fuel, etc., on the back by means of a suspending band passed across the forehead;

this left the hands free to aid in the difficult task of climbing. These
conditions seem to have brought about the use, in some cases, of hand-
holds in the marginal frames of interior trapdoors as an aid in climbing the ladder.

FIG. 85. A large Tusayan doorway with one notched jamb.

One more characteristic type of the ancient pueblo doorway remains
to be described. During the autumn of 1883, when the ruined pueblo
of Kin-tiel was surveyed, a number of excavations were made in and
about the pueblo. A small room on the east side, near the brink of
the arroyo that traverses the ruin from east to west, was completely
cleared out, exposing its fireplace, the stone paving of its floor, and
other details of construction. Built into an inner partition of this room
was found a large slab of stone, pierced with a circular hole of sufficient
size for a man to squeeze through. This slab was set on edge and
incorporated into the masonry of the partition, and evidently served as
a means of communication with another room. The position of this
doorway and its relation to the room in which it occurs may be seen
from the illustration in Pl. C, which shows the stone in situ. The
doorway or "stone-close" is shown in Fig. 86 on a sufficient scale to
indicate the degree of technical skill in the architectural treatment of
stone possessed by the builders of this old pueblo. The writer visited
Zuñi in October of the same season, and on describing this find to Mr.
Frank H. Cushing, learned that the Zuñi Indians still preserved traditional knowledge of this device. Mr. Cushing kindly furnished at the

time the following extract from the tale of "The Deer-Slayer and the Wizards," a Zuñi folk-tale of the early occupancy of the valley of Zuñi.

"'How will they enter ?' said the young man to his wife. 'Through the stone-close at the side,' she answered. In the days of the ancients, the doorways were often made of a great slab of stone with a round hole cut through the middle, and a round stone slab to close it, which was called the stone-close, that the enemy might not enter in times of war."

Mr. Cushing had found displaced fragments of such circular stone doorways at ruins some distance northwest from Zuñi, but had been

FIG. 86. An ancient circular doorway or "stone-close" in Kin-tiel.

under the impression that they were used as roof openings. All examples of this device known to the writer as having been found in place occurred in side walls of rooms. Mr. E. W. Nelson, while making collections of pottery from ruins near Springerville, Arizona, found and sent to the Smithsonian Institution, in the autumn of 1884, "a flat stone about 18 inches square with a round hole cut in the middle of it. This stone was taken from the wall of one of the old ruined stone houses near Springerville, in an Indian ruin. The stone was set in the wall between two inner rooms of the ruin, and evidently served as a means of communication or perhaps a ventilator. I send it on mainly as an example of their stone-working craft." The position of this feature in the excavated room of Kin-tiel is indicated on the ground plan, Fig. 60, which also shows the position of other details seen in the general view of the room, Pl. c.

A small fragment of a "stone-close" doorway was found incorporated into the masonry of a flight of outside stone steps at Pescado, indicating its use in some neighboring ruin, thus bringing it well within the Cibola district. Another point at which similar remains have been brought to light is the pueblo of Halona, just across the river from the present Zuñi. Mr. F. Webb Hodge, recently connected with the Hemenway Southwestern Archeological Exposition, under the direction of Mr. F. H. Cushing, describes this form of opening as being of quite common occurrence in the rooms of this long-buried pueblo. Here the doorways are associated with the round slabs used for closing them. The latter were held in place by props within the room. No slabs of this form were seen at Kin-tiel, but quite possibly some of the large slabs of nearly rectangular form, found within this ruin, may have served the same purpose. It would seem more reasonable to use the rectangular slabs for this purpose when the openings were conveniently near the floors. No example of the stone-close has as yet been found in Tusayan.

The annular doorway described above affords the only instance known to the writer where access openings were closed with a rigid device of aboriginal invention; and from the character of its material this device was necessarily restricted to openings of small size. The larger rectangular doorways, when not partly closed by masonry, probably were covered only with blankets or skin rugs suspended from the lintel. In the discussion of sealed windows modern examples resembling the stone-close device will be noted, but these are usually employed in a more permanent manner.

The small size of the ordinary pueblo doorway was perhaps due as much to the fact that there was no convenient means of closing it as it was to defensive reasons. Many primitive habitations, even quite rude ones built with no intention of defense, are characterized by small doors and windows. The planning of dwellings and the distribution of openings in such a manner as to protect and render comfortable the inhabited rooms implies a greater advance in architectural skill than these builders had achieved.

The inconveniently small size of the doorways of the modern pueblos is only a survival of ancient conditions. The use of full-sized doors, admitting a man without stooping, is entirely practicable at the present day, but the conservative builders persist in adhering to the early type. The ancient position of the door, with its sill at a considerable height from the ground, is also retained. From the absence of any convenient means of rigidly closing the doors and windows, in early times external openings were restricted to the smallest practicable dimensions. The convenience of these openings was increased without altering their dimensions by elevating them to a certain height above the ground. In the ruin of Kin-tiel there is marked uniformity in the height of the openings above the ground, and such openings were likely to be quite uniform when used for similar purposes. The most common elevation of the sills of doorways was such that a man could readily step over at one stride. It will be seen that the same economy of space has effected the use of windows in this system of architecture.

WINDOWS.

In the pueblo system of building, doors and windows are not always clearly differentiated. Many of the openings, while used for access to the dwellings, also answer all the purposes of windows, and, both in their form and in their position in the walls, seem more fully to meet the requirements of openings for the admission of light and air than for access. We have seen in the illustrations in Chapters III and IV, openings of considerable size so located in the face of the outer wall as to unfit them for use as doorways, and others whose size is wholly inadequate, but which are still provided with the typical though diminutive single-paneled door. Many of these small openings, occurring most frequently in the back walls of house rows, have the jambs, lintels, etc., characteristic of the typical modern door. However, as the drawings above referred to indicate, there are many openings concerning the use of which there can be no doubt, as they can only provide outlook, light, and air.

In the most common form of window in present use in Tusayan and Cibola the width usually exceeds the height. Although found often in what appear to be the older portions of the present pueblos, this shape probably does not date very far back. The windows of the ancient pueblos were sometimes square, or nearly so, when of small size, but when larger they were never distinguishable from doorways in either size or finish, and the height exceeded the width. This restriction of the width of openings was due to the exceptionally small size of the building stone made use of. Although larger stones were available, the builders had not sufficient constructive skill to successfully utilize them. The failure to utilize this material indicates a degree of ignorance of mechanical aids that at first thought seems scarcely in keeping with the massiveness of form and the high degree of finish characterizing many of the remains; but as already seen in the discussion of masonry, the latter results were attained by the patient industry of many hands, although laboring with but little of the spirit of cooperation. The narrowness of the largest doors and windows in the ancient pueblos suggests timidity on the part of the ancient builders. The apparently bolder construction of the present day, shown in the prevailing use of horizontal openings, is not due to greater constructive skill, but rather to the markedly greater carelessness of modern construction.

The same contrast between modern and ancient practice is seen in the disposition of openings in walls. In the modern pueblos there does not seem to be any regularity or system in their introduction, while in some of the older pueblos, such as Pueblo Bonito on the Chaco, and others of the same group, the arrangement of the outer openings exhibits a certain degree of symmetry. The accompanying diagram, Fig. 87, illustrates a portion of the northern outer wall of Pueblo Bonito,

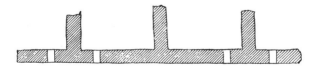

FIG. 87. Diagram illustrating symmetrical arrangement of small openings in Pueblo Bonito.

in which the small windows of successive rooms, besides being uniform in size, are grouped in pairs. The degree of technical skill shown in the execution of the masonry about these openings is in keeping with the precision with which the openings themselves are placed. Pl. CV, gives a view of a portion of the wall containing these openings.

In marked contrast to the above examples is the slovenly practice of the modern pueblos. There are rarely two openings of the same size, even in a single room, nor are these usually placed at a uniform height from the floor. The placing appears to be purely a matter of individual taste, and no trace of system or uniformity is to be found. Windows occur sometimes at considerable height, near or even at the ceiling in some cases, while others are placed almost at the base of the wall; examples may be found occupying all intermediate heights between these extremes. Many of the illustrations show this characteristic irregularity, but Pls. LXXIX and LXXXII of Zuñi perhaps represent it most clearly.

The framing of these openings differs but little from that of the ancient examples. The modern opening is distinguished principally by the more careless method of combining the materials, and by the introduction in many instances of a rude sash. A number of small poles or sticks, usually of cedar, with the bark peeled off, are laid side by side in contact, across the opening, to form a support for the stones and earth of the superposed masonry. Frequently a particularly large tablet of stone is placed immediately upon the sticks, but this stone is never long enough or thick enough to answer the purpose of a lintel for larger openings. The number of small sticks used is sufficient to reach from the face to the back of the wall, and in the simplest openings the surrounding masonry forms jambs and sill. American or Spanish influence occasionally shows itself in the employment of sawed boards for lintels, sills, and jambs. The wooden features of the windows exhibit a curiously light and flimsy construction.

A large percentage of the windows, in both Tusayan and Cibola, are furnished with glass at the present time. Occasionally a primitive sash of several lights is found, but frequently the glass is used singly; in some instances it is set directly into the adobe without any intervening sash or frame. In several cases in Zuñi the primitive sash or frame has been rudely decorated with incised lines and notches. An example of this is shown in Fig. 88. The frame or sash is usually built solidly into the wall. Hinged sashes do not seem to have been adopted as yet. Often the introduction of lights shows a curious and awkward compromise between aboriginal methods and foreign ideas.

Characteristic of Zuñi windows, and also of those of the neighboring pueblo of Acoma,

FIG. 88. Incised decoration on a rude window sash in Zuñi.

is the use of semitranslucent slabs of selenite, about 1 inch in thickness and of irregular form. Pieces are occasionally met with about 18 inches long and 8 or 10 inches wide, but usually they are much smaller and very irregular in outline. For windows pieces are selected that approximately fit against each other, and thin, flat strips of wood are fixed in a vertical position in the openings to serve as supports for the irregular fragments of selenite, which could not be retained in place without some such provision. The use of window openings at the bases of walls probably suggested this use of vertical sticks as a support to slabs of selenite, as in this position they would be particularly useful, the windows being generally arranged on a slope, as shown in Fig. 89. Similar glazing is also employed in the related, obliquely pierced openings of Zuñi, to be described later.

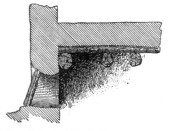

FIG. 89. Sloping selenite window at base of Zuñi wall on upper terrace.

Selenite, in all probability, was not used in pre-Spanish times. No examples have as yet been met with among ruins in the region where this material is found and now used. Throughout the south and east portion of the ancient pueblo region, explored by Mr. A. F. Bandelier, where many of the remains were in a very good state of preservation, no cases of the use of this substance were seen. Fig. 90 illustrates a typical selenite window.

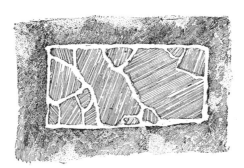

FIG. 90. A Zuñi window glazed with selenite.

In Zuñi some of the kivas are provided with small external windows framed with slabs of stone. It is likely that the kivas would for a long time perpetuate methods and practices that had been superseded in the construction of dwellings. The use of stone jambs, however, would necessarily be limited to openings of small size, as such use for large openings was beyond the mechanical skill of the pueblo builders.

Fig. 91 illustrates the manner of making small openings in external exposed walls in Zuñi. Stone frames occur only occasionally in what seem to be the older and least modified portions of the village. At Tusayan, however, this method of framing windows is much more notice-able, as the exceptional crowding that has exercised such an influence on Zuñi construction has not occurred there. The Tusayan houses are arranged more in rows, often with a suggestion of large inclosures resembling the courts of the ancient pueblos. The inclosures have not been encroached upon, the streets are wider, and altogether the earlier methods seem to have been retained in greater purity than in Zuñi. The unbroken outer wall, of two or three stories in height, like the same feature of the old villages, is pierced at various heights with small open-ings that do not seriously impair its efficiency for defense. Tusayan examples of these loop-hole-like openings may be seen in Pls. XXII, XXIII, and XXXIX.

FIG. 91. Small openings in the back wall of a Zuñi house-cluster.

In some of the ancient pueblos such openings were arranged on a dis-tinctly defensive plan, and were constructed with great care. Openings of this type, not more than 4 inches square, pierced the second story outer wall of the pueblo of Wejegi in the Chaco Canyon. In the pueblo of Kin-tiel (Pl. LXIII) similar loop-hole-like openings were very skill-fully constructed in the outer wall at the rounded northeastern corner of the pueblo. The openings pierced the wall at an oblique angle, as shown on the plan. Two of these channel-like loopholes may be seen in Pl. LXV. This figure also shows the carefully executed jamb corners and faces of three large openings of the second story, which, though greatly undermined by the falling away of the lower masonry, are still held in position by the bond of thin flat stones of which the wall is built.

It is often the practice in the modern pueblos to seal up the windows of a house with masonry, and sometimes the doors also during the tem-porary absence of the occupant, which absence often takes place at the seasons of planting and harvesting. At such times many Zuñi families occupy outlying farming pueblos, such as Nutria and Pescado, and the

Tusayans, in a like manner, live in rude summer shelters close to their fields. Such absence from the home pueblo often lasts for a month or more at a time. The work of closing the opening is done sometimes in the roughest manner, but examples are seen in which carefully laid masonry has been used. The latter is sometimes plastered. Occasionally the sealing is done with a thin slab of sandstone, somewhat larger than the opening, held in place with mud plastering, or propped from the inside after the manner of the "stone close" previously described. Fig. 92 illustrates specimens of sealed openings in the village of Hano of

FIG. 92. Sealed openings in Tusayan.

the Tusayan group. The upper window is closed with a single large slab and a few small chinking stones at one side. The masonry used in closing the lower opening is scarcely distinguishable from that of the adjoining walls. Pl. CVI illustrates a similar treatment of an opening in a detached house of Nutria, whose occupants had returned to the home pueblo of Zuñi at the close of the harvesting season. The door-way in this case is only partly closed, leaving a window-like aperture at

UPRIGHT BLOCKS OF SANDSTONE BUILT INTO AN ANCIENT PUEBLO WALL.

ANCIENT WALL OF UPRIGHT BLOCKS IN SOUTHWESTERN COLORADO.

ANCIENT FLOOR BEAMS AT KIN-TIEL.

ADOBE WALLS IN ZUÑI.

WALL COPING AND OVEN AT ZUÑI.

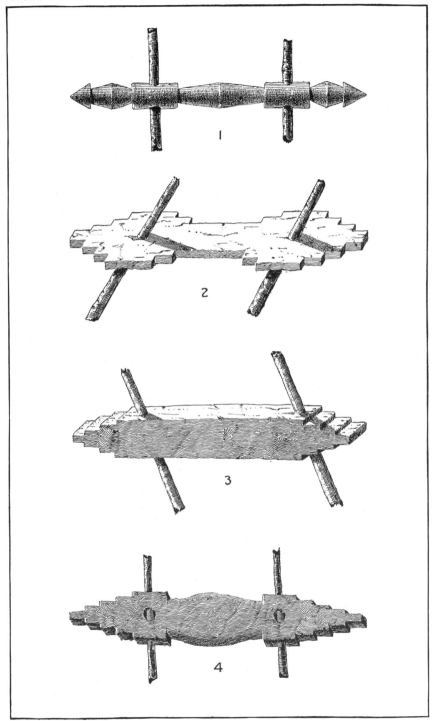

CROSS PIECES ON ZUÑI LADDERS.

H.Hobart Nichols.

OUTSIDE STEPS AT PESCADO.

AN EXCAVATED ROOM AT KIN-TIEL.

MASONRY CHIMNEYS OF ZUÑI.

REMAINS OF A GATEWAY IN AWATUBI.

ANCIENT GATEWAY, KIN-TIEL.

A COVERED PASSAGEWAY IN MASHONGNAVI.

SMALL SQUARE OPENINGS IN PUEBLO BONITO.

SEALED OPENINGS IN A DETACHED HOUSE OF NUTRIA.

PARTIAL FILLING-IN OF A LARGE OPENING IN ORAIBI, CONVERTING IT INTO A DOORWAY.

LARGE OPENINGS REDUCED TO SMALL WINDOWS, ORAIBI.

STONE CORRALS AND KIVA OF MASHONGNAVI.

PORTION OF A CORRAL IN PESCADO.

its top, and the stones used for the purpose are simply piled up without the use of adobe mortar.

Windows and doors closed with masonry are often met with in the remains of ancient pueblos, suggesting, perhaps, that some of the occupants were absent at the time of the destruction of the village. When large door-like openings in upper external walls were built up and plastered over in this way, as in some ruins, the purpose was to economize heat during the winter, as blankets or rugs made of skins would be inadequate.

Besides the closing and reopening of doors and windows just described, the modern pueblo builders frequently make permanent changes in such openings. Doors are often converted into windows, and windows are reduced in size or enlarged, or new ones are broken through the walls, apparently, with the greatest freedom, so that they do not, from their finish or method of construction, furnish any clue to the antiquity of the mud-covered wall in which they are found. Occasionally surface weathering of the walls, particularly in Zuñi, exposes a bit of horizontal pole embedded in the masonry, the lintel of a window long since sealed up and obliterated by successive coats of mud finish. It is probable that many openings are so covered up as to leave no trace of their existence on the external wall. In Zuñi particularly, where the original arrangement for entering and lighting many of the rooms must have been wholly lost in the dense clustering of later times, such changes are very numerous. It often happens that the addition of a new room will shut off one or more old windows, and in such cases the latter are often converted into interior niches which serve as open cupboards. Such niches were sometimes of considerable size in the older pueblos. Changes in the character of openings are quite common in all of the pueblos. Usually the evidences of such changes are much clearer in the rougher and more exposed work of Tusayan than in the adobe-finished houses of Zuñi. Pl. CVII illustrates a large balcony-like opening in Oraibi that has been reduced to the size of an ordinary door by filling in with rough masonry. A small window has been left immediately over the lintel of the newer door. Pl. CVIII illustrates two large openings in this village that have been treated in a somewhat similar manner, but the filling has been carried farther. Both of these openings have been used as doorways at one stage of their reduction, the one on the right having been provided with a small transom; the combined opening was arranged wholly within the large one and under its transom. In the further conversion of this doorway into a small window, the secondary transom was blocked up with stone slabs, set on edge, and a small loophole window in the upper lefthand corner of the large opening was also closed. The masonry filling of the large opening on the left in this illustration shows no trace of a transom over the smaller doorway. A small loophole in the corner of this large opening is still left open. It will be noted that the original transoms of the large openings have in all these cases been entirely filled up with masonry.

The clearness with which all the steps of the gradual reduction of these openings can be traced in the exposed stone work is in marked contrast with the obscurity of such features in Zuñi. In the latter group, however, examples are occasionally seen where a doorway has been partly closed with masonry, leaving enough space at the top for a window. Often in such cases the filled-in masonry is thinner than that of the adjoining wall, and consequently the form of the original doorway is easily traced. Fig. 93, from an adobe wall in Zuñi, gives an illustration of this. The entrance doorway of the detached Zuñi house illustrated in Pl. LXXXIII, has been similarly reduced in size, leaving traces of the orignal form in a slight offset. In modern times, both in Tusayan and Cibola, changes in the form and disposition of openings seem to have been made with the greatest freedom, but in the ancient pueblos altered doors or windows have rarely been found. The original placing of these

FIG. 93. A Zuñi doorway converted into a window.

features was more carefully considered, and the buildings were rarely subjected to unforeseen and irregular crowding.

In both ancient and modern pueblo work, windows, used only as such, seem to have been universally quadrilateral, offsets and steps being confined exclusively to doorways.

ROOF OPENINGS.

The line of separation between roof openings and doors and windows is, with few exceptions, sharply drawn. The origin of these roof-holes, whose use at the present time is widespread, was undoubtedly in the simple trap door which gave access to the rooms of the first terrace. Pl. XXXVIII, illustrating a court of Oraibi, shows in the foreground a kiva hatchway of the usual form seen in Tusayan. Here there is but little difference between the entrance traps of the ceremonial chambers and those that give access to the rooms of the first terrace; the former are in most cases somewhat larger to admit of ingress of costumed dan-

cers, and the kiva traps are usually on a somewhat sharper slope, conforming to the pitch of the small dome-roof of the kivas, while those of
the house terraces have the scarcely perceptible fall of the house roofs
in which they are placed. In Zuñi, however, where the development
and use of openings has been carried further, the kiva hatchways are
distinguished by a specialized form that will be described later. An
examination of the plans of the modern villages in Chapter II and III
will show the general distribution of roof openings. Those used as hatchways are distinguishable by their greater dimensions, and in many cases
by the presence of the ladders that give access to the rooms below. The
smaller roof openings in their simplest form are constructed in essentially the same manner as the trap doors, and the width is usually regulated by the distance between two adjacent roof beams. The second

Fig. 94. Zuñi roof-openings.

series of small roof poles is interrupted at the sides of the opening, which
sides are finished by means of carefully laid small stones in the same
manner as are projecting copings. This finish is often carried several
inches above the roof and crowned with narrow stone slabs, one on each
of the four sides, forming a sort of frame which protects the mud plastered sides of the opening from the action of the rains. Examples of
this simple type may be seen in many of the figures illustrating Chapters II and III, and in Pl. XCVII. Fig. 94 also illustrates common types
of roof openings seen in Zuñi. Two of the examples in this figure are

of openings that give access to lower rooms. Occasional instances are seen in this pueblo in which an exaggerated height is given to the coping, the result slightly approaching a square chimney in effect. Fig. 95 illustrates an example of this form.

FIG. 95. A Zuñi roof opening, with raised coping.

In Zuñi, where many minor variations in the forms of roof openings occur, certain of these variations appear to be related to roof drainage. These have three sides crowned in the usual manner with coping stones

FIG. 96. Zuñi roof-openings, with one elevated end.

laid flat, but the fourth side is formed by setting a thin slab on edge, as illustrated in Fig. 96.

Fig. 94 also embodies two specimens of this form.

The special object of this arrangement is in some cases difficult to determine; the raised end in all the examples on any one roof always takes the same direction, and in many cases its position relative to drainage suggests that it is a provision against flooding by rain on the slightly sloping roof; but this relation to drainage is by no means constant. Roof holes on the west side of the village in such positions as to be directly exposed to the violent sand storms that prevail here during certain months of the year seem in some cases to have in view protection against the flying sand. We do not meet with evidence of any fixed system to guide the disposition of this feature. In many cases these trap holes are provided with a thin slab of sandstone large enough to cover the whole opening, and used in times of rain. During fair weather these are laid on the roof, near the hole they are designed to cover, or lie tilted against the higher edge of the trap, as shown in Fig. 97.

Fig. 97. A Zuñi roof hole with cover.

When the cover is placed on one of these holes, with a high slab at one end, it has a steep pitch, to shed water, and at the same time light and air are to some extent admitted, but it is very doubtful if this is the result of direct intention on the part of the builder. The possible development of this roof trap of unusual elevation into a rudimentary chimney has already been mentioned in the discussion of chimneys. A development in this direction would possibly be suggested by the desirability of separating the access by ladder from the inconvenient smoke hole. This must have been brought very forcibly to the attention of the Indian when, at the time a fire was burning in the fireplace, they were compelled to descend the ladder amidst the smoke and heat.

The survival to the present time of such an inconvenient arrangement
in the kivas can be explained only on the ground of the intense conservatism of these people in all that pertains to religion.   In the small
roof holes methods of construction are seen which would not be so practicable on the larger scale of the ladder holes after which they have
been modeled.   In these latter the sides are built up of masonry or
adobe, but the framing around them is more like the usual coping
over walls.   The stone that, set on edge in the small openings built for
the admission of light, forms a raised end never occurs in these.   The
ladder for access rests against the coping.

When occurring in connection with kivas, ladder holes have certain
peculiarities in which they differ from the ordinary form used in dwellings.   The opening in such cases is made of large size to admit dancers
in costume with full paraphernalia.   These, the largest roof openings to
be found in Zuñi, are framed with pieces of wood.   The methods of

FIG. 98. Kiva trapdoor in Zuñi.

holding the pieces in place vary somewhat in minor detail.   It is quite
likely that recent examples, while still preserving the form and general
appearance of the earlier ones, would bear evidence that the builders
had used their knowledge of improved methods of joining and finishing.

As may readily be seen from the illustration, Fig. 98, this framing, by
the addition of a cross piece, divides the opening unequally.   The
smaller aperture is situated immediately above the fireplace (which
conforms to the ancient type without chimney and located in the open
floor of the room) and is very evidently designed to furnish an outlet to
the smoke.   In a chamber having no side doors or windows, or at most

very small square windows, and consequently no drafts, the column of smoke and flame can often on still nights be seen rising vertically from the roof. The other portion of the opening containing the ladder is used for ingress and egress. This singular combination strongly suggests that at no very remote period one opening was used to answer both purposes, as it still does in the Tusayan kivas. It also suggests the direction in which differentiation of functions began to take place, which in the kiva was delayed and held back by the conservative religious feeling, when in the civil architecture it may have been the initial point of a development that culminated in the chimney, a development that was assisted in its later steps by suggestions from foreign sources. In the more primitively constructed examples the cross pieces seem to be simply laid on without any cutting in. The central piece is held in place by a peg set into each side piece, the weight and thrust of the ladder helping to hold it. The primitive arrangement here seen has been somewhat improved upon in some other cases, but it was not ascertained whether these were of later date or not.

In the best made frames for kiva entrances the timbers are "halved" in the manner of our carpenters, the joint being additionally secured by a pin as shown in Fig. 99.

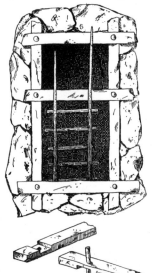

FIG. 99. Halved and pinned trapdoor frame of a Zuñi kiva.

The use of a frame of wood in these trapdoors dates back to a comparatively high antiquity, and is not at all a modern innovation, as one would at first be inclined to believe. Their use in so highly developed a form in the ceremonial chamber is an argument in favor of antiquity. Only two examples were discovered by Mr. L. H. Morgan in a ruined pueblo on the Animas. "One of these measured 16 by 17 inches and the other was 16 inches square. Each was formed in the floor by pieces of wood put together. The work was neatly done."[1]

Unfortunately, Mr. Morgan does not describe in detail the manner in which the joining was effected, or whether the pieces were halved or cut to fit. It seems hardly likely, considering the rude facilities possessed by the ancients, that the enormous labor of reducing large pieces of wood to such interfitting shapes would have been undertaken. A certain neatness of finish would undoubtedly be attained by arranging the principal roof beams and the small poles that cross them at right angles, in the usual careful manner of the ancient builders. The kiva roof opening, with the hole serving for access and smoke exit, is paralleled in the excavated lodges of the San Francisco Mountains, where a single opening served this double purpose. A slight recess or excavation in the side of the entrance shaft evidently served for the exit of smoke.

At the village of Acoma the kiva trapdoors differ somewhat from the Zuñi form. The survey of this village was somewhat hasty, and no opportunity was afforded of ascertaining from the Indians the special purpose of the mode of construction adopted. The roof hole is divided, as in Zuñi, but the portion against which the ladder leans, instead of being made into a smoke vent, is provided with a small roof. These roof holes to the ceremonial chamber are entered directly from the open air, while in the dwelling rooms it seems customary (much more customary than at Zuñi) to enter the lower stories through trapdoors within upper rooms. In many instances second-story rooms have no exterior rooms but are entered from rooms above, contrary to the usual arrangement in both Tusayan and Cibola. All six of the kivas in this village are provided with this peculiarly constructed opening.

In Zuñi close crowding of the cells has led to an exceptionally frequent use of roof-lights and trapdoors. The ingenuity of the builders was greatly taxed to admit sufficient light to the inner rooms. The roof hole, which was originally used only to furnish the means of access and light for the first terrace, as is still the case in Tusayan, is here used in all stories indiscriminately, and principally for light and air. In large clusters there are necessarily many dark rooms, which has led to the employment of great numbers of roof holes, more or less directly modeled after the ordinary trapdoor. Their occurrence is particularly frequent in the larger clusters of the village, as in house No. 1. The exceptional size of this pile, and of the adjoining house No. 4, with the consequent large proportion of dark rooms, have taxed the ingenuity of the Zuñi to the utmost, and as a result we see roof openings here assuming a degree of importance not found elsewhere.

In addition to roof openings of the type described, the dense clustering of the Zuñi houses has led to the invention of a curious device for lighting inner rooms not reached by ordinary external openings. This consists of an opening, usually of oval or subrectangular form in elevation, placed at the junction of the roof with a vertical wall. This opening is carried down obliquely between the roofing beams, as shown in the sections, Fig. 100, so that the light is admitted within the room just at the junction of the ceiling and the inner face of the wall. With the meager facilities and rude methods of the Zuñi, this peculiar arrangement often involved weak construction, and the openings, placed so low in the wall, were in danger of admitting water from the roof. The difficulty of obtaining the desired light by this device was much lessened where the outer roof was somewhat lower than the ceiling within.

These oblique openings occur not only in the larger clusters of houses Nos. 1 and 4, but also in the more openly planned portions of the village, though they do not occur either at Acoma or in the Tusayan villages. They afford an interesting example of the transfer and continuance in use of a constructional device developed in one place by unusual conditions to a new field in which it was uncalled for, being less efficient and more difficult of introduction than the devices in ordinary use.

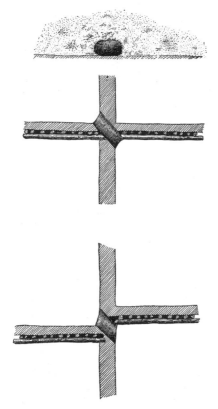

FIG. 100. Typical sections of Zuñi oblique openings.

### FURNITURE.

The pueblo Indian has little household furniture, in the sense in which the term is commonly employed, but his home contains certain features which are more or less closely embodied in the house construction and which answers the purpose. The suspended pole that serves as a clothes rack for ordinary wearing apparel, extra blankets, robes, etc., has already been described in treating of interiors. Religious costumes and ceremonial paraphernalia are more carefully provided for, and are stored away in some hidden corner of the dark storerooms.

The small wall niches, which are formed by closing a window with a thin filling-in wall, and which answer the purpose of cupboards or receptacles for many of the smaller household articles, have also been described and illustrated in connection with the Zuñi interior (Pl. LXXXVI).

In many houses, both in Tusayan and in Cibola, shelves are constructed for the more convenient storage of food, etc. These are often constructed in a very primitive manner, particularly in the former province. An unusually frail example may be seen in Fig. 67, in connection with a fireplace. Fig. 101, showing a series of mealing stones in a Tusayan house, also illustrates a rude shelf in the corner of the room, supported at one

FIG. 101. Arrangement of mealing stones in a Tusayan house.

end by an upright stone slab and at the other by a projecting wooden peg. Shelves made of sawed boards are occasionally seen, but as a rule such boards are considered too valuable to be used in this manner. A more common arrangement, particularly in Tusayan, is a combination of three or four slender poles placed side by side, 2 or 3 inches apart, forming a rude shelf, upon which trays of food are kept.

Another device for the storage of food, occasionally seen in the pueblo house, is a pocket or bin built into the corner of a room. Fig. 101 illustrating the plan of a Tusayan house, indicates the position of one of these cupboard-like inclosures. A sketch of this specimen is shown in

8 ETH——14

Fig. 102. This bin, used for the storage of beans, grain, and the like, is formed by cutting off a corner of the room by setting two stone slabs

into the floor, and it is covered with the mud plastering which extends over the neighboring walls.

A curious modification of this device was seen in one of the inner rooms in Zuñi, in the house of José Pié. A large earthen jar, apparently an ordinary water vessel, was built into a projecting masonry bench near the corner of the room in such a manner that its rim projected less than half an inch above its surface. This jar was used for the same purpose as the Tusayan corner bin.

FIG. 102. A Tusayan grain bin.

Some of the Indians of the present time have chests or boxes in which their ceremonial blankets and paraphernalia are kept. These of course have been introduced since the days of American boards and boxes. In

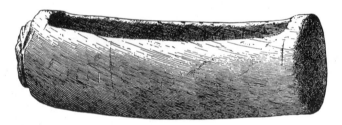

FIG. 103. A Zuñi plume box.

Zuñi, however, the Indians still use a small wooden receptacle for the precious ceremonial articles, such as feathers and beads. This is an oblong box, provided with a countersunk lid, and usually carved from a single single piece of wood. Typical specimens are illustrated in Figs. 103 and

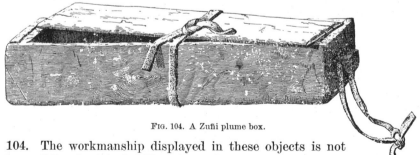

FIG. 104. A Zuñi plume box.

104. The workmanship displayed in these objects is not beyond the aboriginal skill of the native workman, and their use is undoubtedly ancient.

Perhaps the most important article of furniture in the home of the pueblo Indian is the mealing trough, containing the household milling apparatus. This trough usually contains a series of three metates of varying degrees of coarseness firmly fixed in a slanting position most convenient for the workers. It consists of thin slabs of sandstone set into the floor on edge, similar slabs forming the separating partitions between the compartments. This arrangement is shown in Fig. 105, illustrating a Tusayan mealing trough. Those of Zuñi are of the same form, as may be seen in the illustration of a Zuñi interior, Fig. 105.

FIG. 105. A Tusayan mealing trough.

Occasionally in recently constructed specimens the thin inclosing walls of the trough are made of planks. In the example illustrated one end of the series is bounded by a board, all the other walls and divisions being made of the usual stone slabs. The metates themselves are not usually more than 3 inches in thickness. They are so adjusted in their setting of stones and mortar as to slope away from the operator at the

FIG. 106. An ancient pueblo form of metate.

proper angle. This arrangement of the mealing stones is characteristic of the more densely clustered communal houses of late date. In the more primitive house the mealing stone was usually a single large piece of cellular basalt, or similar rock, in which a broad, sloping depression was carved, and which could be transported from place to place. Fig. 106 illustrates an example of this type from the vicinity of Globe, in southern Arizona. The stationary mealing trough of the present day is undoubtedly the successor of the earlier moveable form, yet it was in use among the pueblos at the time of the first Spanish expedition, as the following extract from Castañeda's account[1] of Cibola will show. He says a special room is designed to grind the grain: "This last is apart, and contains a furnace and three stones made fast in masonry.

---

[1] Given by W. W. H. Davis in El Gringo, p. 119.

Three women sit down before these stones; the first crushes the grain, the second brays it, and the third reduces it entirely to powder." It will be seen how exactly this description fits both the arrangement and the use of this mill at the present time. The perfection of mechanical devices and the refinement of methods here exhibited would seem to be in advance of the achievement of this people in other directions.

The grinding stones of the mealing apparatus are of correspondingly varying degrees of roughness; those of basalt or lava are used for the first crushing of the corn, and sandstone is used for the final grinding on the last metate of the series. By means of these primitive appliances the corn meal is as finely ground as our wheaten flour. The grinding stones now used are always flat, as shown in Fig. 105, and differ from those that were used with the early massive type of metate in being of cylindrical form.

One end of the series of milling troughs is usually built against the wall near the corner of the room. In some cases, where the room is quite narrow, the series extends across from wall to wall. Series comprising four mealing stones, sometimes seen in Zuñi, are very generally arranged in this manner. In all cases sufficient floor space is left behind the mills to accommodate the women who kneel at their work. Pl. LXXXVI illustrates an unusual arrangement, in which the fourth mealing stone is set at right angles to the other stones of the series.

Mortars are in general use in Zuñi and Tusayan households. As a rule they are of considerable size, and made of the same material as the rougher mealing stones. They are employed for crushing and grinding the chile or red pepper that enters so largely into the food of the Zuñi, and whose use has extended to the Mexicans of the same region. These mortars have the ordinary circular depressions and are used with a round pestle or crusher, often of somewhat long, cylindrical form for convenience in handling.

Parts of the apparatus for indoor blanket weaving seen in some of the pueblo houses may be included under the heading of furniture. These consist of devices for the attachment of the movable parts of the loom, which need not be described in this connection. In some of the Tusayan houses may be seen examples of posts sunk in the floor provided with holes for the insertion of cords for attaching and tightening the warp, similar to those built into the kiva floors, illustrated in Fig. 31. No device of this kind was seen in Zuñi. A more primitive appliance for such work is seen in both groups of pueblos in an occasional stump of a beam or short pole projecting from the wall at varying heights. Ceiling beams are also used for stretching the warp both in blanket and belt weaving.

The furnishings of a pueblo house do not include tables and chairs. The meals are eaten directly from the stone-paved floor, the participants rarely having any other seat than the blanket that they wear, rolled up or folded into convenient form. Small stools are sometimes seen, but the need of such appliances does not seem to be keenly felt by these Indians, who can, for hours, sit in a peculiar squatting position on their haunches, without any apparent discomfort. Though moveable chairs or stools are rare, nearly all of the dwellings are provided with the low ledge or bench around the rooms, which in earlier times seems to have been confined to the kivas. A slight advance on this fixed form of seat was the stone block used in the Tusayan kivas, described on p. 132, which at the same time served a useful purpose in the adjustment of the warp threads for blanket weaving.

The few wooden stools observed show very primitive workmanship, and are usually made of a single piece of wood. Fig. 107 illustrates two forms of wooden stool from Zuñi. The small three-legged stool on

FIG. 107. Zuñi stools.

the left has been cut from the trunk of a piñon tree in such a manner as to utilize as legs the three branches into which the main stem separated. The other stool illustrated is also cut from a single piece of tree trunk, which has been reduced in weight by cutting out one side, leaving the two ends for support.

A curiously worked chair of modern form seen in Zuñi is illustrated in Fig. 108. It was difficult to determine the antiquity of this specimen, as its rickety condition may have been due to the clumsy workmanship quite as much as to the effects of age. Rude as is the workmanship, however, it was far beyond the unaided skill of the native craftsman to join and mortise the various pieces that go to make up this chair. Some decorative effect has been sought here, the ornamentation, made up of notches and sunken grooves,

FIG. 108. A Zuñi chair.

closely resembling that on the window sash illustrated in Fig. 88, and somewhat similiar in effect to the carving on the Spanish beams seen in the Tusayan kivas. The whole construction strongly suggests Spanish influence.

Even the influence of Americans has as yet failed to bring about the use of tables or bedsteads among the pueblo Indians. The floor answers all the purposes of both these useful articles of furniture. The food dishes are placed directly upon it at meal times, and at night the blankets, rugs, and sheep skins that form the bed are spread directly upon it. These latter, during the day, are suspended upon the clothes pole previously described and illustrated.

CORRALS AND GARDENS.

The introduction of domestic sheep among the pueblos has added a new and important element to their mode of living, but they seem never to have reached a clear understanding as to how these animals should be cared for. No forethought is exercised to separate the rams so that the lambs will be born at a favorable season. The flocks consist of sheep and goats which are allowed to run together at all times. Black sheep and some with a grayish color of wool are often seen among them. No attempt is made to eliminate these dark-fleeced members of the flock, since the black and gray wool is utilized in its natural color in producing many of the designs and patterns of the blankets woven by these people. The flocks are usually driven up into the corrals or inclosures every evening, and are taken out again in the morning, frequently at quite a late hour. This, together with the time consumed in driving them to and from pasture, gives them much less chance to thrive than those of the nomadic Navajo. In Tusayan the corrals are usually of small size and inclosed by thin walls of rude stone work. This may be seen in the foreground of Pl. XXI. Pl. CIX illustrates several corrals just outside the village of Mashongnavi similarly constructed, but of somewhat larger size. Some of the corrals of Oraibi are of still larger size, approaching in this respect the corrals of Cibola. The Oraibi pens are rudely rectangular in form, with more or less rounded angles, and are also built of rude masonry.

In the less important villages of Cibola stone is occasionally used for inclosing the corrals, as in Tusayan, as may be seen in Pl. LXX, illustrating an inclosure of this character in the court of the farming pueblo of Pescado. Pl. CX illustrates in detail the manner in which stone work is combined with the use of rude stakes in the construction of this inclosure. On the rugged sites of the Tusayan villages corrals are placed wherever favorable nooks happen to be found in the rocks, but at Zuñi, built in the comparatively open plain, they form a nearly continuous belt around the pueblo. Here they are made of stakes and brush held in place by horizontal poles tied on with strips of rawhide. The rudely contrived gateways are supported in natural forks at the top and sides of posts. Often one or two small inclosures used for burros or horses occur near these sheep corrals. The construction is identical with those above described and is very rude. It is illustrated in Fig. 109, which shows the manner in which the stakes are arranged, and also

the method of attaching the horizontal tie-pieces. The construction of
these inclosures is frail, and the danger of pushing the stakes over by
pressure from within is guarded against by employing forked braces
that abut against horizontal pieces tied on 4 or 5 feet from the ground.
Reference to Pl. LXXIV will illustrate this construction.

FIG. 109. Construction of a Zuñi corral.

Within the village of Zuñi inclosures resembling miniature corrals
are sometimes seen built against the houses; these are used as cages
for eagles. A number of these birds are kept in Zuñi for the sake of
their plumage, which is highly valued for ceremonial purposes. Pl. CXI
illustrates one of these coops, constructed partly with a thin adobe wall
and partly with stakes arranged like those of the corrals.

In both of the pueblo groups under discussion small gardens contiguous to the villages are frequent. Those of Tusayan are walled in with
stone.

Within the pueblo of Zuñi a small group of garden patches is inclosed
by stake fences, but the majority of the gardens in the vicinity of the

principal villages are provided with low walls of mud masonry. The small terraced gardens here are near the river bank on the southwest and southeast sides of the village. The inclosed spaces, averaging in size about 10 feet square, are used for the cultivation of red peppers, beans, etc., which, during the dry season, are watered by hand. These inclosures, situated close to the dwellings, suggest a probable explanation for similar inclosures found in many of the ruins in the southern and eastern portions of the ancient pueblo region. Mr. Bandelier was informed by the Pimas[1] that these inclosures were ancient gardens. He

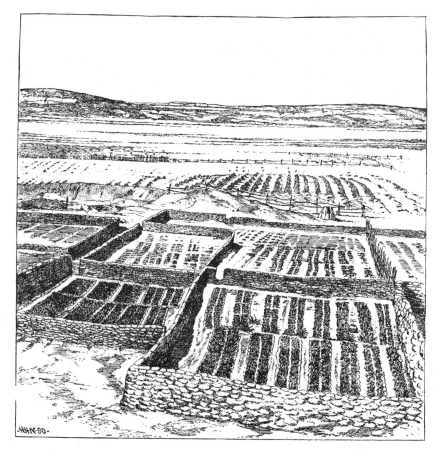

Fig. 110. Gardens of Zuñi.

concluded that since acequias were frequent in the immediate vicinity these gardens must have been used as reserves in case of war, when the larger fields were not available, but the manner of their occurrence in Zuñi suggests rather that they were intended for cultivation of special crops, such as pepper, beans, cotton, and perhaps also of a variety of

---

[1] Fifth Ann. Rept. Arch. Inst. Am., p. 92.

tobacco—corn, melons, squashes, etc., being cultivated elsewhere in larger tracts. There is a large group of gardens on the bank of the stream at the southeastern corner of Zuñi, and here there are slight indications of terracing. A second group on the steeper slope at the southwestern corner is distinctly terraced. Small walled gardens of the same type as these Zuñi examples occur in the vicinity of some of the Tusayan villages on the middle mesa. They are located near the springs or water pockets, apparently to facilitate watering by hand. Some of them contain a few small peach trees in addition to the vegetable crops ordinarily met with. The clusters here are, as a rule, smaller than those of Zuñi, as there is much less space available in the vicinity of the springs. At one point on the west side of the first mesa, a few miles above Walpi, a copious spring serves to irrigate quite an extensive series of small garden patches distributed over lower slopes.

At several points around Zuñi, usually at a greater distance than the terrace gardens, are fields of much larger area inclosed in a similar manner. Their inclosure was simply to secure them against the depredations of stray burros, so numerous about the village. When the crops are gathered in the autumn, several breaches are made in the low wall and the burros are allowed to luxuriate on the remains. Pl. LIX indicates the position of the large cluster of garden patches on the southeastern side of Zuñi. Fig. 110, taken from photographs made in 1873, shows several of these small gardens with their growing crops and a large field of corn beyond. The workmanship of the garden walls as contrasted with that of the house masonry has been already described and is illustrated in Pl. XC.

## "KISI" CONSTRUCTION.

Lightly constructed shelters for the use of those in charge of fields were probably a constant accompaniment of pueblo horticulture. Such shelters were built of stone or of brush, according to which material was most available.

In very precipitous localities, as the Canyon de Chelly, these outlooks naturally became the so-called cliff-dwellings or isolated shelters. In Cibola single stone houses are in common use, not to the exclusion, however, of the lighter structures of brush, while in Tusayan these lighter forms, of which there are a number of well defined varieties, are almost exclusively used. A detailed study of the methods of construction employed in these rude shelters would be of great interest as affording a comparison both with the building methods of the ruder neighboring tribes and with those adopted in constructing some of the details of the terraced house; the writer, however, did not have an opportunity of making an examination of all the field shelters used in these pueblos. Two of the simpler types are the "tuwahlki," or watch house, and the "kishoni," or uncovered sl de. The former is constructed by first planting a short forked stick in the ground, which supports one end of a pole, the other end resting on the ground.   The interval between this ridge pole and the ground is roughly filled in with slanting sticks and brush, the inclosed space being not more than 3 feet in height, with a maximum width of four or five feet.   These shelters are for the accommodation of the children who watch the melon patches until the fruit is harvested.

The kishoni, or uncovered shade, illustrated in Fig. 111, is perhaps

Fig. 111. Kishoni, or uncovered shade, of Tusayan.

the simplest form of shelter employed.   Ten or a dozen cottonwood saplings are set firmly into the ground, so as to form a slightly curved inclosure with convex side toward the south.   Cottonwood and willow boughs in foliage, grease-wood, sage brush, and rabbit brush are laid with stems upward in even rows against these saplings to a height of 6 or 7 feet.   This light material is held in place by bands of small cottonwood branches laid in continuous horizontal lines around the outside of the shelter and these are attached to the upright saplings with cottonwood and willow twigs.

Figs. 112 and 113 illustrate a much more elaborate field shelter in Tusayan. As may readily be seen from the figures this shelter covers a

FIG. 112. A Tusayan field shelter, from southwest.

considerable area; it will be seen too that the upright branches that inclose two of its sides are of sufficient height to considerably shade the level roof of poles and brush, converting it into a comfortable retreat.

FIG. 113. A Tusayan field shelter, from northeast.

The following nomenclature, collected by Mr. Stephen, comprises the terms commonly used in designating the constructional details of Tusayan houses and kivas:

| | |
|---|---|
| Kiko′li | The ground floor rooms forming the first terrace. |
| Tupu′bi | The roofed recess at the end of the first terrace. |
| Ah′pabi<br>Ih′pobi | A terrace roof. |
| Tupat′ca ih′pobi | The third terrace, used in common as a loitering place. |
| Tumtco′kobi | "The place of the flat stone;" small rooms in which "piki," or paper-bread, is baked. "Tuma," the piki stone, and "tcok" describing its flat position. |
| Tupa′tca | "Where you sit overhead;" the third story. |
| O′mi Ah′pabi | The second story; a doorway always opens from it upon the roof of the "kiko′li." |
| Kitcobi | "The highest place;" the fourth story. |
| Tuhkwa | A wall. |
| Puce | An outer corner. |
| Apaphucua | An inside corner. |
| Lestabi | The main roof timbers. |
| Wina′kwapi | Smaller cross poles. "Winahoya," a small pole, and "Kwapi," in place. |
| Kaha′b kwapi | The willow covering. |
| Süibi kwapi | The brush covering. |
| Si′hü kwapi | The grass covering. |
| Kiam′ balawi | The mud plaster of roof covering. "Balatle′lewini," to spread. |
| Tcukat′cvewata | Dry earth covering the roof. "Tcuka," earth, "katuto," to sit, and "at′cvewata," one laid above another. |
| Kiami | An entire roof. |
| Kwo′pku | The fireplace. |
| Kwi′tcki | "Smoke-house," an inside chimney-hood. |
| Sibvu′tütük′mula | A series of bottomless jars piled above each other, and luted together as a chimney-top. |
| Sibvu′ | A bottomless earthen vessel serving as a chimney pot. |
| Bok′ci | Any small hole in a wall, or roof, smaller than a doorway. |
| Hi′tci | An opening, such as a doorway. This term is also applied to a gap in a cliff. |
| Hi′tci Kalau′wata | A door frame. |
| Tûñañ′iata | A lintel; literally, "that holds the sides in place." |
| Wuwûk′pi | "The place step;" the door sill. |
| Niñuh′pi | A hand hold; the small pole in a doorway below the lintel. |
| Pana′ptca ütc′pi bok′ci | A window; literally, "glass covered opening." |
| Ut′cpi | A cover. |
| Ahpa′bütc′pi<br>Wina′ütc′pi | A door. "Apab," inside; wina, a pole. |
| O′wa ütc′ppi | "Stone cover," a stone slab. |

Tüi′ka ............................A projection in the wall of a room suggesting a partition, such as shown in Pl. LXXXV. The same term is applied to a projecting cliff in a mesa.

Kiam′i ..........................An entire roof. The main beams, cross poles, and roof layers have the same names as in the kiva, given later.

Wĭna′kü′i......................Projecting poles; rafters extending beyond the walls.

Bal′kakini ....................."Spread out;" the floor.

O′tcokpü′h....................."Leveled with stones;" a raised level for the foundation.

Ba′lkakini tü′wi..............."Floor ledge;" the floor of one room raised above that of an adjoining one.

Hako′la ........................"Lower place;" the floor of a lower room. Sand dunes in a valley are called "Hakolpi."

Ko′ltci .........................A shelf.

Owako′ltci .....................A stone shelf.

Ta′pü kü′ita...................A support for a shelf.

Wina′ koltci...................A hewn plank shelf.

Kokiüni........................A wooden peg in a wall.

Tületa ........................A shelf hanging from the ceiling.

Tület′haipi ...................The cords for suspending a shelf.

Tükûlci .......................A niche in the wall.

Tükûli ........................A stone mortar.

Ma′ta ........................The complete mealing apparatus for grinding corn.

Owa′mata......................The trough or outer frame of stone slabs.

Mata′ki ......................The metate or grinding slab.

Kakom′ta mata′ki.............The coarsest grinding slab.

Tala′kĭ mata′ki...............The next finer slab; from "talaki" to parch crushed corn in a vessel at the fire.

Piñ′nyümta mata′ki ...........The slab of finest texture; from "pin," fine.

Ma′ta ü′tci ...................The upright partition stones separating the metates. The rubbing stones have the same names as the metates.

Hawi′wita .....................A stone stairway.

Tütü′beñ hawi′wita ...........A stairway pecked into a cliff face.

Sa′ka .........................A ladder.

Wina′ hawi′pi .................Steps of wood.

Ki′cka ........................The covered way.

Hitcu′yi′wa ...................."Opening to pass through;" a narrow passage between houses.

Ki′sombi ......................"Place closed with houses;" courts and spaces between house groups.

Bavwa′kwapi .................A gutter pipe inserted in the roof coping.

In kiva nomenclature the various parts of the roof have the same names as the corresponding features of the dwellings. These are described on pp. 148–151.

Le′stabi.......................The main roof timbers.

Wina′kwapi....................The smaller cross poles.

Kaha′b kwapi .................The willow covering.

Süibi kwapi ...................The brush covering.

Si′hü kwapi ...................The grass covering.

Tcuka′tcve wata ..............The dry earth layer of the roof.

Kiam′ba′lawi .................The layer of mud plaster on the roof.

Kiami........................An entire roof.

The following terms are used to specially designate various features of the kivas:

| | | |
|---|---|---|
| Tüpat'caiata, lestabi | | Both of these terms are used to designate the kiva hatchway beams upon which the hatchway walls rest. |
| Lesta'bkwapi, | | |

Süna'cabi le'stabi ............The main beams in the roof, nearest to the hatchway.

Ép'eoka le'stabi ......⸴..........The main beams next to the central ones.

Püep'eoka le'stabi.............The main beams next in order, and all the beams intervening between the "epeoka" and the end beams are so designated.

Kala'beoka lestabi .............The beams at the ends of a kiva.

Mata'owa ......................"Stone placed with hands."

Hüzrüowa .................... "Hard stone."
Both of these latter terms are applied to corner foundation stones.

Kwa'kü üt'cpi.................Moveable mat of reeds or sticks for covering hatchway opening, Fig. 29. "Kwaku," wild hay; "utcpi," a stopper.

Tüpat'caiata ...................The raised hatchway; "the sitting place," Fig. 95.

Tüpat'caiata tü'kwa............The walls of the hatchway.

Kipat'ctjua'ta.................The kiva doorway; the opening into the hatchway, Fig. 28.

Apa'pho'ya ...................Small niches in the wall. "Apap," from "apabi," inside, and "hoya," small.

Si'papüh.......................An archaic term. The etymology of this word is not known.

Kwŏp'kota ....................The fireplace. "Kwuhi," coals or embers; "küaiti," head.

Kŏı'tci ........................Pegs for drying fuel, fixed under the hatchway. "Ko-hu," wood; Fig. 28.

Kokü'ina.......................Pegs in the walls.

Sa'ka .........................A ladder. This term is applied to any ladder. Figs. 45–47.

Sa'kaleta......................Ladder rungs; "Leta," from "lestabi;" see above.

Tüvwibi ......................The platform elevation or upper level of the floor. "Tu-vwi," a ledge; Fig. 24.

Tüvwi ........................Stone ledges around the sides, for seats. The same term is used to designate any ledge, as that of a mesa, etc.

Katcin' Kihü...................."Katcina," house. The niche in a ledge at the end of the kiva.

Kwi'sa........................The planks set into the floor, to which the lower beam of a blanket loom is fastened.

| | |
|---|---|
| Kaintup'ha ................... | Terms applied to the main floor; they both mean "the large space." |
| Kiva' kani ................... | |

Tapü'wü'tci...................Hewn planks a foot wide and 6 to 8 feet long, set into the floor.

Wina'wü'tci...................A plank.

Owa' pühü'imiata.............."Stone spread out;" the flagged floor; also designates the slabs covering the hatchway.

Yau'wiopi.....................Stones with holes pecked in the ends for holding
the loom beam while the warp is being adjusted;
also used as seats; see p. 132.

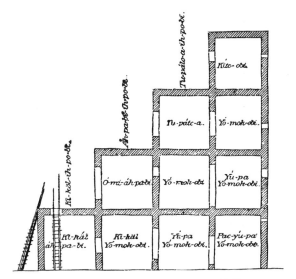

FIG. 114. Diagram showing ideal section of terraces, with Tusayan names.

The accompanying diagram is an ideal section of a Tusayan four-story
house, and gives the native names for the various rooms and terraces.

### CONCLUDING REMARKS.

The modern villages of Tusayan and Cibola differ more widely in
arrangement and in the relation they bear to the surrounding topography
than did their predecessors even of historic times.

Many of the older pueblos of both groups appear to have belonged
to the valley types—villages of considerable size, located in open plains
or on the slopes of low-lying foothills. A comparison of the plans in
Chapters II and III will illustrate these differences. In Tusayan the
necessity of defense has driven the builders to inaccessible sites, so that
now all the occupied villages of the province are found on mesa summits. The inhabitants of the valley pueblos of Cibola, although compelled at one time to build their houses upon the almost inaccessible
summit of Tâaiyalana mesa, occupied this site only temporarily, and
soon established a large valley pueblo, the size and large population of which afforded that defensive efficiency which the Tusayan
obtained only by building on mesa promontories. This has resulted in
some adherence on the part of the Tusayan to the village plans of their
ancestors, while at Zuñi the great house clusters, forming the largest
pueblo occupied in modern times, show a wide departure from the primitive types. In both provinces the architecture is distinguished from
that of other portions of the pueblo region by greater irregularity of

plan and by less skillfully executed constructional details; each group, however, happens to contain a notable exception to this general carelessness.

In Cibola the pueblo of Kin-tiel, built with a continuous defensive outer wall, occupies architecturally a somewhat anomalous position, notwithstanding its traditional connection with the group, and the Fire House occupies much the same relation in reference to Tusayan. The latter, however, does not break in upon the unity of the group, since the Tusayan, to a much greater extent than the Zuñi, are made up of remnants of various bands of builders. In Cibola, however, some of the Indians state that their ancestors, before reaching Zuñi, built a number of pueblos, whose ruins are distinguished from those illustrated in the present paper by the presence of circular kivas, this form of ceremonial room being, apparently, wholly absent from the Cibolan pueblos here discussed.

The people of Cibola and of Tusayan belong to distinct linguistic stocks, but their arts are very closely related, the differences being no greater than would result from the slightly different conditions that have operated within the last few generations. Zuñi, perhaps, came more directly under early Spanish influence than Tusayan.

Churches were established, as has been seen, in both provinces, but it is doubtful whether their presence produced any lasting impression on the people. In Tusayan the sway of the Spaniards was very brief. At some of the pueblos the churches seem to have been built outside of the village proper where ample space was available within the pueblo; but such an encroachment on the original inclosed courts seems never to have been attempted. Zuñi is an apparent exception; but all the house clusters east of the church have probably been built later than the church itself, the church court of the present village being a much larger area than would be reserved for the usual pueblo court. These early churches were, as a rule, built of adobe, even when occurring in stone pueblos. The only exception noticed is at Ketchipauan, where it was built of the characteristic Indian smoothly chinked masonry. The Spaniards usually intruded their own construction, even to the composition of the bricks, which are nearly always made of straw adobe.

At Tusayan there is no evidence that a church or mission house ever formed part of the villages on the mesa summits. Their plans are complete in themselves, and probably represent closely the first pueblos built on these sites. These summits have been extensively occupied only in comparatively recent times, although one or more small clusters may have been built here at an early date as outlooks over the fields in the valleys below.

It is to be noted that some of the ruins connected traditionally and historically with Tusayan and Cibola differ in no particular from stone pueblos widely scattered over the southwestern plateaus which have been from time to time invested with a halo of romantic antiquity, and regarded as remarkable achievements in civilization by a vanished but once powerful race. These deserted stone houses, occurring in the midst of desert solitudes, appealed strongly to the imaginations of early explorers, and their stimulated fancy connected the remains with "Aztecs" and other mysterious peoples. That this early implanted bias has caused the invention of many ingenious theories concerning the origin and disappearance of the builders of the ancient pueblos, is amply attested in the conclusions reached by many of the writers on this subject.

In connection with the architectural examination of some of these remains many traditions have been obtained from the present tribes, clearly indicating that some of the village ruins, and even cliff dwellings, have been built and occupied by ancestors of the present Pueblo Indians, sometimes at a date well within the historic period.

The migrations of the Tusayan clans, as described in the legends collected by Mr. Stephen, were slow and tedious. While they pursued their wanderings and awaited the favorable omens of the gods they halted many times and planted. They speak traditionally of stopping at certain places on their routes during a certain number of "plantings," always building the characteristic stone pueblos and then again taking up the march.

When these Indians are questioned as to whence they came, their replies are various and conflicting; but this is due to the fact that the members of one clan came, after a long series of wanderings, from the north, for instance, while those of other gentes may have come last from the east. The tribe to-day seems to be made up of a collection or a confederacy of many enfeebled remnants of independent phratries and groups once more numerous and powerful. Some clans traditionally referred to as having been important are now represented by few survivors, and bid fair soon to become extinct. So the members of each phratry have their own store of traditions, relating to the wanderings of their own ancestors, which differ from those of other clans, and refer to villages successively built and occupied by them. In the case of others of the pueblos, the occupation of cliff dwellings and cave lodges is known to have occurred within historic times.

Both architectural and traditional evidence are in accord in establishing a continuity of descent from the ancient Pueblos to those of the present day. Many of the communities are now made up of the more or less scattered but interrelated remnants of gentes which in former times occupied villages, the remains of which are to-day looked upon as the early homes of "Aztec colonies," etc.

The adaptation of this architecture to the peculiar environment indicates that it has long been practiced under the same conditions that now prevail. Nearly all of the ancient pueblos were built of the sandstone found in natural quarries at the bases of hundreds of cliffs throughout these table-lands. This stone readily breaks into small pieces of regular form, suitable for use in the simple masonry of the pueblos without receiving any artificial treatment. The walls themselves give an exaggerated idea of finish, owing to the care and neatness with which the component stones are placed. Some of the illustrations in the last chapter, from photographs, show clearly that the material of the walls was much ruder than the appearance of the finished masonry would suggest, and that this finish depended on the careful selection and arrangement of the fragments. This is even more noticeable in the Chaco ruins, in which the walls were wrought to a high degrees of surface finish. The core of the wall was laid up with the larger and more irregular stones, and was afterwards brought to a smooth face by carefully filling in and chinking the joints with smaller stones and fragments, sometimes not more than a quarter of an inch thick; this method is still roughly followed by both Tusayan and Cibolan builders.

Although many details of construction and arrangement display remarkable adaptation to the physical character of the country, yet the influence of such environment would not alone suffice to produce this architectural type. In order to develop the results found, another element was necessary. This element was the necessity for defense. The pueblo population was probably subjected to the more or less continuous influence of this defensive motive throughout the period of their occupation of this territory. A strong independent race of people, who had to fear no invasion by stronger foes, would necessarily have been influenced more by the physical environment and would have progressed further in the art of building, but the motive for building rectangular rooms—the initial point of departure in the development of pueblo architecture—would not have been brought into action. The crowding of many habitations upon a small cliff ledge or other restricted site, resulting in the rectangular form of rooms, was most likely due to the conditions imposed by this necessity for defense.

The general outlines of the development of this architecture wherein the ancient builders were stimulated to the best use of the exceptional materials about them, both by the difficult conditions of their semi-desert environment and by constant necessity for protection against their neighbors, can be traced in its various stages of growth from the primitive conical lodge to its culmination in the large communal village of many-storied terraced buildings which we find to have been in use at the time of the Spanish discovery, and which still survives in Zuñi, perhaps its most striking modern example. Yet the various steps have resulted from a simple and direct use of the material immediately at hand, while methods gradually improved as frequent experiments taught the builders more fully to utilize local facilities. In all cases the material was derived from the nearest available source, and often variations in the quality of the finished work are due to variations in the quality of the stone near by. The results accomplished attest the patient and persistent industry of the ancient builders, but the work does not display great skill in construction or in preparation of material.

The same desert environment that furnished such an abundance of material for the ancient builders, also, from its difficult and inhospitable character and the constant variations in the water supply, compelled the frequent employment of this material. This was an important factor in bringing about the attained degree of advancement in the building art. At the present day constant local changes occur in the water sources of these arid table-lands, while the general character of the climate remains unaltered.

The distinguishing characteristics of Pueblo architecture may be regarded as the product of a defensive motive and of an arid environment that furnished an abundance of suitable building material, and at the same time the climatic conditions that compelled its frequent employment.

The decline of the defensive motive within the last few years has greatly affected the more recent architecture. Even after the long practice of the system has rendered it somewhat fixed, comparative security from attack has caused many of the Pueblo Indians to recognize the inconvenience of dwellings grouped in large clusters on sites difficult of access, while the sources of their subsistence are necessarily sparsely scattered over large areas. This is noticeable in the building of small, detached houses at a distance from the main villages, the greater convenience to crops, flocks and water outweighing the defensive motive. In Cibola particularly, a marked tendency in this direction has shown itself within a score of years; Ojo Caliente, the newest of the farming pueblos, is perhaps the most striking example within the two provinces. The greater security of the pueblos as the country comes more fully into the hands of Americans, has also resulted in the more careless construction in modern examples as compared with the ancient.

There is no doubt that, as time shall go on, the system of building many-storied clusters of rectangular rooms will gradually be abandoned by these people. In the absence of the defensive motive a more convenient system, employing scattered small houses, located near springs and fields, will gradually take its place, thus returning to a mode of building that probably prevailed in the evolution of the pueblo prior to the clustering of many rooms into large defensive villages. Pl. LXXXIII illustrates a building of the type described located on the outskirts of Zuñi, across the river from the main pueblo.

The cultural distinctions between the Pueblo Indians and neighboring tribes gradually become less clearly defined as investigation progresses. Mr. Cushing's study of the Zuñi social, political, and religious systems has clearly established their essential identity in grade of culture with those of other tribes. In many of the arts, too, such as weaving, ceramics, etc., these people in no degree surpass many tribes who build ruder dwellings.

In architecture, though, they have progressed far beyond their neighbors; many of the devices employed attest the essentially primitive character of the art, and demonstrate that the apparent distinction in grade of culture is mainly due to the exceptional condition of the environment.

ZUÑI EAGLE CAGE.

Harbert Nichols 1889.

# LOCALIZATION OF TUSAYAN CLANS

BY

COSMOS MINDELEFF

# ILLUSTRATIONS

PLAN OF SUMMER SETTLEMENT

# LOCALIZATION OF TUSAYAN CLANS

By Cosmos Mindeleff

Of the many problems which perplex the student of the cliff ruins and other house remains of pueblo origin in the Southwest, two are of the first importance and overshadow all the others. These are (1) the enormous number of ruins scattered over the country and (2) the peculiarities of ground-plan and their meaning. The two phenomena are so intimately connected that one can not be understood or even studied without the other.

The ancient pueblo region extends from Great Salt lake to beyond the southern boundary of the United States and from the Grand canyon of the Colorado to the vegas or plains east of the Rio Grande and the Pecos. Within this area of about 150,000 square miles ruins can be numbered almost by thousands. Such maps as have been prepared to show the distribution of remains exhibit a decided clustering or grouping of ruins in certain localities. Much of this is doubtless due to the state of our knowledge rather than to the phenomena themselves; that is to say, we know more about certain regions than about others. Yet from the data now in hand it is a fair inference that ruins are generally clustered or grouped in certain localities. There were apparently a number of such centers, each the source of many subordinate settlements more or less scantily distributed over the regions between them.

This distribution of ruins lends color to a hypothesis advanced by the writer some years ago, which affords an at least plausible explanation of the immense number of ruins found in the Southwest. The key to this problem is the extended use of outlying farming settlements. All lines of evidence—history, tradition, mythology, arts, industries, habits and customs, and above all the ruins themselves—agree in establishing the wide prevalence, if not the universal use, of such settlements, as much in the olden days as in modern times, and as much now as ever.

The ruins are of many kinds and varieties; no two are quite alike, but there are external resemblances which have led to several attempts

639

at classification. The results, however, are not satisfactory, and it is apparent that we must look further into the subject before we can devise a good classificatory scheme. It seems to the writer that all the plans of classification hitherto published have put too much stress on the external appearance of ruins and not enough on the character of the sites which they occupy or on the social and tribal conditions indicated by such sites.

Pueblo architecture is essentially a product of the plateau country, and its bounds are, in fact, practically coincident with those of that peculiar region popularly known as the mesa country. Peculiar geological conditions have produced a peculiar topography, which in turn has acted on the human inhabitants of the country and produced that characteristic and distinctive phase of culture which we call pueblo art. The region is in itself not favorable to development; in three essentials, cultivable land, water, and vegetation, it is anything but an ideal country, although blessed with an ideal climate which has done much to counteract the unfavorable features. But through a great abundance of excellent building material, the product of the mesas, and through peculiar social conditions, the product of the peculiar environment, whereby a frequent use of such materials was compelled, pueblo architecture developed.

It seems probable that in the early stages of the art of house building among these people they lived in small settlements located in or near the fields which they cultivated, for the pueblo tribes have always been an agricultural people, living principally by the products of the soil. In the olden days, before the introduction of sheep and cattle, they were even more agricultural than they are now, although at that time they had a food resource in their hunting grounds which is now lost to them. It seems probable that for several centuries the people pursued the even, placid course of existence which comes from the undisturbed cultivation of the ground, with perhaps now and then some internecine war or bloody foray to keep alive their stronger passions.

In the course of time, however, other tribes drifted into the region, and, being wild and accustomed to the hardy life of warriors, they soon found that they were more than a match for the sedentary tribes which had preceded them. The latter were industrious, and, being more or less attached to certain localities, were enabled to lay by stores against a possible failure of crops. At the present day in some of the pueblos the corn is thus stored, and sometimes great rooms full of it can be seen, containing the full crops of one or two years. Undoubtedly the same custom of storing food prevailed in ancient times, and the wilder tribes found in the sedentary villages and in the fields tributary to them convenient storehouses from which to draw their own supplies. If the traditions are at all to be trusted, there was no open war nor were there determined sieges, but foray after foray was made by the wilder spirits of the nomadic tribes; fields were raided when ripe for the harvest, and the fruit of a season's labor was often swept away in a night. It soon became unsafe to leave the village unguarded, as a descent might be made upon it at any time when the men were away, and the stores accumulated for the winter might be carried off. But the detail of a number of men to guard the home was in itself a great hardship when men were few and subsistence difficult to obtain. Such were the conditions according to the ancient traditions.

Under the pressure described the little villages or individual houses, located primarily with reference to the fields under cultivation, were gradually forced to aggregate into larger villages, and, as the forays of their wild neighbors continued and even increased, these villages were moved to sites which afforded better facilities for defense. But through it all the main requirement of the pueblo builder—convenience to and command of agricultural land—was not lost sight of, and the villages were always located so as to meet these requirements. Generally they were placed on outlying spurs or foothills overlooking little valleys, and it should be noted that at the time of the Spanish discovery and conquest, three centuries and a half ago, a considerable number of the villages were so located.

There seems to be little doubt that the first troubles of the pueblo builders, aside from those arising among themselves, which were not sufficiently important to influence their arts or architecture, were caused by the advent of some tribe or tribes of Athapascan stock. Afterward, and perhaps as late as the beginning of the eighteenth century, the Comanche extended their range into the pueblo country, and still later the Ute found profit in occasional raids over the northern border. It is quite probable, however, that in the beginning, when pueblo architecture was still in an early stage of development, none of the tribes mentioned were known in that country.

Eventually the housebuilders found it necessary to remove their homes to still more inaccessible and still more easily defended sites, and it was at this period that many of the mesas were occupied for the first time. The country is practically composed of mesas, and it was an easy matter to find a projecting tongue or promontory where a village could be built that would be accessible from one side only, or perhaps would be surrounded by cliffs and steep slopes that could be scaled only after a long and arduous climb over a tortuous and difficult trail. Building material was everywhere abundant and could generally be found within a stone's throw of almost any site selected.

Few of the villages at the time of the Spanish conquest were located on mesa sites, but numbers of them were on the foothills of mesas and sometimes commanded by higher ground. At that time Acoma occupied its present location on the mesa summit, one of the best if not the best and most easily defended in New Mexico, as the

Spaniards found to their cost after an unsuccessful assault.    But this
location was at that time unusual, and was doubtless due to the fact
that the people of Acoma were, like the wilder tribes, predatory in
their instincts and habits, and lived upon their neighbors.

When the little settlements of the first stage of development were
compelled to cluster into villages for better protection, a new element
came into pueblo architecture.    The country is an arid one, and but a
small percentage of the ground can be cultivated.    Except in the valleys of the so-called rivers, arable land is found only in small patches
here and there—little sheltered nooks in the mesas, or bits of bottom
land formed of rich alluvium in the canyons.    Easily defended sites
for villages could be found everywhere throughout the country, but
to find such a site which at the same time commanded an extensive
area of good land was a difficult matter.    It must be borne in mind
that the pueblo tribes in ancient times, as now, were first and fore-
most agriculturists, or rather horticulturists, for they were not farmers but gardeners.    Depending as they did upon the products of the
soil, their first care was necessarily to secure arable lands.    This was
always the dominating requirement, and as it came in conflict with
the clustering of houses into villages, some means had to be devised to
bring the two requirements into accord.    This was accomplished by
the use of farming shelters, temporary establishments occupied only
during the farming season and abandoned on the approach of winter,
but located directly on or overlooking the fields under cultivation.

The ultimate development of pueblo architecture finds expression
in the great clustered houses which remind one of a huge beehive.
As the wilder tribes continued their depredations among the inoffensive
villagers, and, with the passing of time, grew more numerous and more
and more bold in their attacks and forays, the pueblo tribes were
forced to combine more and more for protection.    Groups of related
villages, each offering a point of attack for savage foes and rich plunder when looted, were compelled to combine into a single larger
pueblo, and as reliance was now placed on the size of the village and
the number of its inhabitants, these large villages were located in wide
valleys or on fertile bottom lands, the people again returning to their
original desire to live upon the lands they worked.

Under modern conditions, when the depredations of the wild tribes
have been terminated by the interference of a higher and stronger
civilization, the houses are reverting to the primitive type from which
the great pueblos developed.    But so late as ten or twelve years ago the
Hopi or Tusayan villages were under the old conditions and were subjected to periodical forays from their immediate neighbors, the Navaho.
Young warriors of the latter tribe ravaged the fields of the Hopi, more
perhaps for the pleasure it afforded them and on account of the old
traditions than from any real necessity for food as they destroyed more

than they took away. If they found anyone in the fields, they would beat him, or perhaps kill him, merely for the amusement it seemed to afford. It was the Navaho method of "sowing wild oats." There is little doubt that the pressure which bore on the Pueblos for at least some centuries was of this nature, annoying rather than actually dangerous. No doubt there were also occasional invasions of the country of more than usual magnitude, when from various causes the nomadic tribes had either an abundance or a scarcity of food, and, knowing the character of the villages as storehouses of corn and other products, or impelled by old grudges growing out of former forays, a whole tribe might take part in the incursion, and perhaps try themselves by an assault on some village of considerable size. But such expeditions were rare; the pueblo tribes were annoyed rather than menaced. Eventually, however, they found it necessary to provide against the ever-present contingency of an invasion of their country, and the great valley pueblos were developed.

As aggregation of the little settlements into villages and of villages into great valley pueblos continued, the use of farming shelters grew apace. No matter what the conditions might be, the crops must be grown and harvested, for the failure of the crops meant the utter annihilation of the people. They had no other resource. They were compelled to combine into large pueblos containing often a thousand or fifteen hundred souls, a condition which was at variance with their requirements and manner of life; but they were also compelled to till the soil or starve. The lands about the home villages were never sufficient for the needs of the people, and in consequence a considerable portion of the population was compelled to work fields more or less distant from them. Thus, in the ultimate stage of pueblo development the use of farming shelters was as much or more in evidence, and as much a necessity to the people, as in the prior stages.

This sketch of the development of pueblo architecture exhibits a sequence; but it is a cultural, not a chronologic, one. The data in hand will not permit the determination of the latter now, but within a given group sequence in culture and sequence in time are practically synonymous. The time relations of the various groups, one to another, must be determined from other evidence.

The use of farming shelters has been a most important factor in producing the thousands of ruins which dot the mesas and canyons of the Southwest, while another factor, the localization of clans, has worked with it and directed it, as it were, in certain channels. All the evidence which investigation has revealed, from traditions to the intrinsic evidence of the ruins themselves, concur in establishing the fact that the pueblo tribes were in slow but essentially constant movement; that movement has continued down to the present time and is even now in progress. Viewed across long periods of time it might be regarded as a migration, but the term has not the same meaning here that it has when applied to the movements of great masses of humanity which have taken place in Europe and Asia. In the pueblo country migration was almost an individual movement; it was hardly a tribal, certainly not a national, exodus. Outlying farming settlements were established in connection with each important village. In the course of time it might come about that some of the people who used these establishments at first only during the summer, retiring to the home village during the winter, would find it more convenient to remain there throughout the year. At the present day some of the summer villages are fifteen miles and more from the home pueblo, and it must have been at best inconvenient to live in two places so far apart.

The home villages can be distinguished from the summer places by the presence or absence of the kivas, or sacred ceremonial chambers. For as practically all the rites and dances take place after the harvest is gathered and before planting time in the spring—that is, at the season when the men have some leisure—they are performed in the home pueblos, and only such villages have kivas.

When, from prolonged peace or for other reasons, some families allowed the inconvenience of moving back and forth to dominate over counter motives, and remained throughout the year at the summer place, they might build a kiva or two, and gradually, as others also decided to remain, the summer place would become a home village. As the population grew by increment from outside and by natural increase this village would put out farming shelters of its own, which in the course of time might supplant their parent in the same way. The process is a continuous one and is in progress to-day. The summer village of Ojo Caliente, 15 miles from Zuñi, and attached to that pueblo, has within the last decade become a home village, occupied throughout the year by several families, and during the farming season by many others. Eventually kivas will be built there, if this has not already been done, and Ojo Caliente will become a real home village and put out farming shelters of its own. Such is also the case with the pueblo of Laguna, which is gradually being abandoned by its inhabitants, who are making their permanent homes at what were formerly only summer villages.

It will thus be seen that a comparatively small band might in the course of a few centuries leave behind them the remains of many villages. In the neighborhood of the Hopi towns there are at least 50 ruins, all, or practically all, of which were left by the people who found their present resting places on the summits of the rocky mesas of Tusayan. And with it all it is not necessary to assume great periods of time; it is doubtful whether any of the ruins of Tusayan are much more than four hundred years old, and some of them were partly inhabited so late as fifty years ago.  Including the present location, three sites of Walpi, one of the Hopi towns, are visible from the summit of the mesa.  According to the native traditions the last movement of this village, only completed in the present century, was commenced when the Spaniards were in control, over two centuries ago.  It is said that the movement was brought about by the women of the village, who took their children and household goods up on the summit of the mesa, where a few outlooks had been built, and left the men to follow them or remain where they were.  The men followed.

Among the inhabited villages the home pueblo can be distinguished from the summer establishments by the presence of the kivas, and often the same distinction can be drawn in the case of ruins.  In many of the latter the kivas are circular and are easily found even when much broken down.  Aside from this the plans of the two classes of villages can often be distinguished from each other through their general character, the result of the localization of clans previously alluded to.

The migratory movements of a band of village builders often consumed many years or many decades.  During this time subordinate settlements were put out all along the line as occasion or necessity demanded, and were eventually abandoned as the majority of the people moved onward.  Hopi traditions tell of such movements and rests, when the people remained for many plantings in one place and then continued on.  As a rule there was no definite plan to such a movement and no intention of going to any place or in any direction; the people simply drifted across the country much as cattle drift before a storm.  They did not go back because they knew what was back of them, but they went forward in any direction without thought of where they were going, or even that they were going at all.  It was a little trickling stream of humanity, or rather many such streams, like little rivulets after a rain storm, moving here and there as the occurrence of areas of cultivable land dictated, sometimes combining, then separating, but finally collecting to form the pueblo groups as we now know them.

There is no doubt that in addition to this unconscious drifting migration there were also more important movements, when whole villages changed their location at one time.  Such changes are mentioned in the traditions and evidenced in the ruins.  There is a multiplicity of causes which bring about such movements, many of them very trivial, to our way of thinking.  While the climate of the pueblo country is remarkably equable and the water supply, although scanty, is practically constant over the whole region, local changes often occur; springs fail at one place and burst out at another; some seasons are marked by comparatively abundant rains, others by severe droughts.  The failure of some particularly venerated spring would be deemed good cause for the abandonment of a village situated near it, or the occurrence of several years of drought in succession would be construed as a mark of disfavor of the gods, and would be followed by a movement of the people from the village. Even a series of bad dreams which might be inflicted on some prominent medicine-man by overindulgence in certain articles of food would be regarded as omens indicating a necessity for a change of location. Such instances are not unknown. Toothache also is dreaded for mythic reasons, and is construed as a sign of disfavor of the gods; so that many a village has been abandoned simply because some prominent medicine-man was in need of the services of a dentist. Many other reasons might be stated, but these will suffice to show upon what slight and often trivial grounds great villages of stone houses, the result of much labor and the picture of permanence, are sometimes abandoned in a day.

But while such movements en masse are not unknown, they have been comparatively rare. The main movement of the people, which was a constant one, was accomplished through the custom of using out-lying farming settlements. Such settlements were commonly single houses, but where the conditions permitted and the area of cultivable land justified it, the houses were grouped into villages. These were always located on or immediately adjacent to the land which was worked, and in some instances attained considerable size, but as a rule they were small. The practice was universal throughout the length and breadth of the pueblo country, and the farming shelters took various forms as the immediate topographic environment dictated. Even the cliff ruins are believed to be farm shelters of a type due to peculiar physical con-ditions, but as this idea has been exploited elsewhere[1] by the writer it need not be developed here.

The occupancy of farm shelters, whether individual rooms or small villages, was necessarily more or less temporary in character, and as the population moved onward the places would be finally and completely abandoned. It would often be difficult to obtain from the study of the ground-plan of a ruin, generally all that is left of it, any idea of the people who inhabited it and of the conditions under which they lived; but there is another element by the aid of which the length of time during which the village was inhabited and of the conditions under which such occupancy continued may often be approximated. This is the localization of clans, to which allusion has been made.

The constant movement of the tribe, due to the use of outlying farm-ing settlements, which has been sketched above, has its analogue within each village, where there is an equally constant movement from house to house and from row to row. The clans which inhabit a village are combined into larger units or groups known as phratries; locally such

---

[1] The Cliff Ruins of Canyon de Chelly, in the Sixteenth Annual Report of the Bureau of American Ethnology.

clans are said to "belong together." In the olden days each phratry occupied its own quarters in the village, its own cluster or row, as the case might be, and while the custom is now much broken down, just how far it has ceased to exercise its influence is yet to be determined.

In the pueblo social system descent and inheritance are in the female line. This custom is widely distributed among the tribes of mankind all over the world and has an obvious basis. Among the Pueblos it works in a peculiar manner. Under the old rule, when a man marries, not having any house of his own, he goes to his wife's home and is adopted into her clan. The children also belong to the mother and are members of her clan. In many of the villages at the present day a man may marry any woman who will marry him, but in former times marriage within the clan, and sometimes within the phratry, was rigidly prohibited. Thus it happened that a clan in which there were many girls would grow and increase in importance, while one in which the children were all boys would become extinct.

There was thus a constant ebb and flow of population within each clan and consequently in the home or houses of each clan. The clans themselves were not fixed units; new ones were born and old ones died, as children of one sex or the other predominated. The creation of clans was a continuous process. Thus, in the Corn clan of Tusayan, under favorable conditions there grew up subclans claiming connection with the root, stem, leaves, blossom, pollen, etc. In time the relations of clans and subclans became extremely complex; hence the aggregation into larger units or phratries. The clan is a great artificial family, and when it comprises many girls it must necessarily grow. Such is also the case with the individual family, for as the men who are adopted into it by marriage take up their quarters in the family home and children are born to them more space is required. But additional rooms, which are still the family property, must be built in the family quarter, and by a long-established rule they must be built adjoining and connected with those already occupied. Therefore in each village there are constant changes in the plan; new rooms are added here, old rooms abandoned there. It is in miniature a duplication of the process previously sketched as due to the use of outlying shelters. It is not unusual to find in an inhabited village a number of rooms under construction, while within a few steps or perhaps in the same row there are rooms vacant and going to decay. Many visitors to Tusayan, noticing such vacant and abandoned rooms, have stated that the population was diminishing, but the inference was not sound.

On the other hand, the addition of rooms does not necessarily mean growth in population. New rooms might be added year after year when the population was actually diminishing; such has been the case in a number of the villages. But the way in which rooms are added may suggest something of the conditions of life at the time of building.

The addition of rooms on the ground floor, and the consequent extension of the ground plan of a house cluster, indicates different conditions from those which must have prevailed when the village, without extending its bounds, grew more and more compact by the addition of small rooms in the upper stories.

The traditions collected from the Hopi by the late A. M. Stephen, part of which have been published,[1] present a vivid picture of the conditions under which the people lived. The ancestors of the present inhabitants of the villages reached Tusayan in little bands at various times and from various directions. Their migrations occupied very many years, although there were a few movements in which the people came all together from some distant point. Related clans commonly built together, the newcomers seeking and usually obtaining permission to build with their kindred; thus clusters of rooms were formed, each inhabited by a clan or a phratry. As occupancy continued over long periods, these clusters became more or less joined together, and the lines of division on the ground became more or less obliterated in cases, but the actual division of the people remained the same and the quarters were just as much separated and divided to those who knew where the lines fell. But as a rule the separation of the clusters is apparent to everyone; it can nearly always be traced in the ground plans of ruins, and even in the great valley pueblos, which were probably inhabited continuously for several centuries, the principal divisions may still be made out. In the simpler plans the clusters are usually well separated, and the irregularities of the plan indicate with a fair degree of clearness the approximate length of time during which the site was occupied.

A plan of this character is reproduced in figure 3, showing a ruin near Moenkapi, a farming settlement of the people of Oraibi situated about 45 miles from that village. There were altogether 21 rooms, disposed in three rows so as to partially inclose three sides of an open space or court. The rows are divided into four distinct clusters, with a single room outside, forming a total of five locations in a village which housed at most twenty-five or thirty persons. The continuity of the wall lines and comparative regularity of the rooms within each cluster, the uniformity in height of the rooms, which, if the débris upon the ground may be accepted as a criterion, was one story, and the general uniformity in the character of the masonry, all suggest that the site was occupied a short time only. This suggestion is aided by the almost complete absence of pottery fragments. It is a safe inference that persons of at least five different clans occupied this site.

A plan of interest in connection with the last is that shown in plate XXI, which illustrates the modern village of Moenkapi, occupied only during the summer. Here we have two main clusters and two

---

[1] A Study of Pueblo Architecture, in the Eighth Annual Report of the Bureau of Ethnology.

detached houses, but the clusters are not nearly so regular as in the plan above, nor are the wall lines continuous to the same extent. This place is spoken of by the people of Oraibi as of recent establishment, but it has certainly been occupied for a much longer period than was the ruin near it. It is apparent from an inspection of the plan that the clusters were formed by the addition of room after room as year by year more people used the place in summer. It will be noticed that the rooms constituting the upper right-hand corner of the larger cluster on the map, while distinct from the other rooms, are still attached to them, while two other rooms in the immediate vicinity

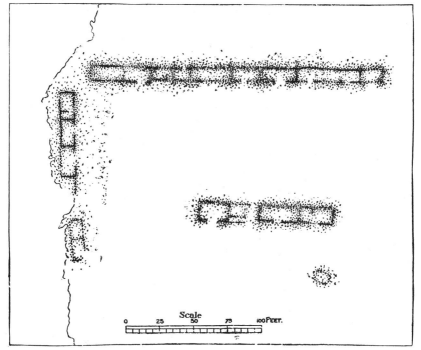

Fig. 3—Plan of ruin showing brief occupancy.

are wholly detached. This indicates that the cluster was occupied by one clan or by related families, while the detached houses were the homes of other families not related to them. Thus we have in this village, comprising about the same number of rooms as the ruin first described, at least four distinct clans.

Detached rooms, such as those shown on these plans, always indicate a family or person not connected directly with the rest of the inhabitants, perhaps the representative of some other clan or people. A stranger coming into a village and wishing to build would be required to erect his house on such a separate site. In the village of Sichumovi (shown in plan in plate xxiv) there are two such detached houses directly in front of the main row. One had been built and was inhabited at the time when the map was made by a white man who made his home there, while the other, which had been abandoned and was falling into ruin, was built some years before by a Navaho who wished to live in the village. The former was subsequently surrendered by the white man and occupied by some of the natives. The localization of clans worked both ways. Not only was a member of a clan required to build with his own people, but outsiders were required to build outside of the cluster.

The same requirement is illustrated in plate XXII, which shows the plan of Hawikû, one of the ancient "Seven Cities of Cibola," near the present Zuñi. The standing walls which occupy the southeastern corner of the ruin are the remains of an adobe church, while the buildings which stood near and to the north of it, now marked only by lines of débris, were the mission buildings and offices connected with the church. They are pointed out as such by the natives of Zuñi to-day. All these buildings were set apart and were distinct from the village proper, which occupied the crest of the hill, while the buildings mentioned were on the flat below.

This was the first discovered city of Cibola,[1] the first pueblo village seen by the friar Niza in 1539, and the first village stormed by Coronado and his men in 1540. It was abandoned about 1670 (?) on account of the depredations of the Apache. The plan shows that the site was inhabited for a long time, and that the village grew up by the addition of room after room as space was needed by the people. Notwithstanding the fact that no standing walls remain, and that the place was abandoned over two centuries ago, six or seven house-clusters can still be made out in addition to the buildings erected by or for the monks in the flat below. Dense clustering, such as this, indicates prolonged occupancy by a considerable number of people, and probably two centuries at least would be required to produce such a plan. The long and comparatively narrow row to the left of the main cluster suggests an addition of much later date than the main portion of the village.

The maps of the villages Walpi, Sichumovi, Hano, Mishongnovi, Shipaulovi, and Oraibi, which are presented herewith, show the distribution of the clans at the time the surveys were made (about 1883). At first glance the clans appear to be located with the utmost irregularity and apparently without system, but a closer study shows that notwithstanding the centuries which have elapsed since the period covered by the old traditions of the arrival of clans[2] the latter are in a measure corroborated by the maps. It is also apparent that notwithstanding the breakdown of the old system, whereby related peoples were required to build together, traces of it can still be seen. It is a matter of regret

---

[1] See Hodge, First Discovered City of Cibola, in American Anthropologist, VIII, April, 1895.
[2] These traditions are given in detail in the preceding paper.—ED.

that the data are incomplete. The accompanying table shows the distribution of the families within the villages at the time of the surveys, but some of the clans represented, which do not appear in the traditions collected, are necessarily given as standing alone or belonging to unknown phratries, as their phratral relations were not determined. The clustering of houses was a requirement of the phratry rather than of the clan.

*Distribution of families*

| | Walpi | Sichumovi | Hano | Mishonginovi | Shipaulovi | Oraibi | Total families |
|---|---|---|---|---|---|---|---|
| Bear families................ | | | 6 | 9 | 6 | 5 | 26 |
| Rope families ............... | | | | 5 | | | 5 |
| Spider families ............. | 1 | | | | | 2 | 3 |
| Snake families ............. | 5 | | | | | 1 | 6 |
| Cactus families ............ | 1 | | | | | | 1 |
| Horn families .............. | 5 | | | | | | 5 |
| Flute families ............... | 2 | | | | | | 2 |
| Firewood families.......... | | | | 3 | | | 3 |
| Eagle families.............. | 1 | | 8 | 8 | | 6 | 23 |
| Sun families................ | 1 | 1 | 2 | 1 | 15 | 9 | 29 |
| Hawk families.............. | | | | 2 | | 1 | 3 |
| Katcina families ........... | 2 | | | 2 | | 1 | 5 |
| Paroquet families ......... | | | | 1 | | 10 | 11 |
| Cottonwood families ....... | | | 3 | | | | 3 |
| Asa families ................ | 3 | 9 | 1 | | | | 13 |
| Badger families ............ | | 3 | | 8 | | 13 | 24 |
| Water (Corn) families...... | 1 | | 4 | 5 | | 9 | 19 |
| Water (Cloud) families..... | 8 | 3 | 6 | 4 | 1 | | 22 |
| Reed families ............... | 6 | | | | | 25 | 31 |
| Lizard families ............. | 1 | 4 | 1 | | | 14 | 20 |
| Rabbit families............. | 3 | 1 | | | | 11 | 15 |
| Sand families.............. | | | | 1 | | 8 | 9 |
| Tobacco families .......... | 1 | 1 | 2 | | | | 4 |
| Sivwap (Shrub) families.... | 2 | | | | | | 2 |
| Coyote families............. | 2 | | 2 | 1 | | 17 | 22 |
| Owl families................ | 2 | | | | | 9 | 11 |
| Red Ant families........... | 7 | | | | | | 7 |
| Bow families ............... | | | | | | 4 | 4 |
| Squash families........... | | | | 3 | | 1 | 4 |
| Snow families .............. | 3 | | | | | | 3 |
| Batkin families............ | | 1 | | | | | 1 |
| Moth families ............. | | 1 | | | | 1 | 2 |
| Crane families............. | | | | | | 1 | 1 |
| Mescal-cake families ...... | | | | | | 1 | 1 |
| | 57 | 24 | 35 | 53 | 22 | 149 | 340 |

The determination of the clans shown on the maps was made by the late A. M. Stephen, whose qualifications for the work were exceptional. Doubtless there are some errors in it, for it is a difficult matter to determine the relationships of nearly 400 families, and the work was brought to an end before it was entirely finished. But the maps illustrate a phase of life of the village builders which has not heretofore attracted attention, and which has had a very important effect on the architecture of the people.

Through the operation of the old custom of localizing clans, although it is now not rigidly adhered to as formerly, the plans of all the villages have been modified. The maps here presented show them as they were in 1883, but in a few cases known to the writer the changes up to 1888 are shown by dotted lines. If now or in the future new surveys of the villages be made and the clans be relocated, a mass of data will be obtained which will throw much light on some of the conditions of pueblo life, and especially on the social conditions which have exercised an important influence on pueblo architecture.

The table showing the distribution of families in the villages presents also the number of families. The most numerous were the Water people, comprising in various clans no fewer than 121 families, or over a third of the total number. These were among the last people to arrive in Tusayan and they are well distributed throughout the villages. It will be noticed, also, that while a scattering of clans throughout the villages was the rule, some of them, generally the older ones, were confined to one village or were concentrated in one village with perhaps one or two families in others. The Snow people were found only in Walpi, but these may be properly Water people and of recent origin. The Snake people were represented by 5 families in Walpi and 1 in Oraibi, although they were among the first to arrive in Tusayan, and for a long time exercised proprietary rights over the entire region and dictated to each incoming clan where it should locate. The largest clan of all, the Reed clan, was represented by 6 families in Walpi and 25 in Oraibi, a total of 31 families, or, by applying the general average of persons to a family, by 155 persons. In Oraibi, the largest village, there were 21 distinct clans, although 7 of them were represented by only 1 family each. In Shipaulovi, the smallest village, there were 20 families of 2 clans, and three-fourths of the inhabitants belonged to one of them. In addition there is one family of the Water people, and in fact in each of the villages one or more clans is represented by one family only. It will be noticed that in Shipaulovi the two clans were still well separated and occupied distinct quarters, although the houses of the village were continuous.

The scattered appearance of the clans on the maps is more apparent than real. It is unfortunate that the phratral relations of the clans could not be completely determined, and it is probable that were this done the clans would be found to be well grouped even now. Even the insufficient data that we have appear to show a tendency on the part of the clans to form into groups at the present day, notwithstanding the partial disintegration of the old system. At the present time the house of the priestess of the clan is considered the home of that clan, and she has much to say about proposed marriages and other social functions. There is no doubt that in ancient times the localization of clans was rigidly enforced, as much by circumstances as by rule, and the ground plans of all the ruins were formed by it. As has been before suggested, a resurvey of the villages of Tusayan and a relocation of the clans, after an interval of some years, would probably develop data of the greatest value to the student of pueblo architecture, when compared with the plans here presented.

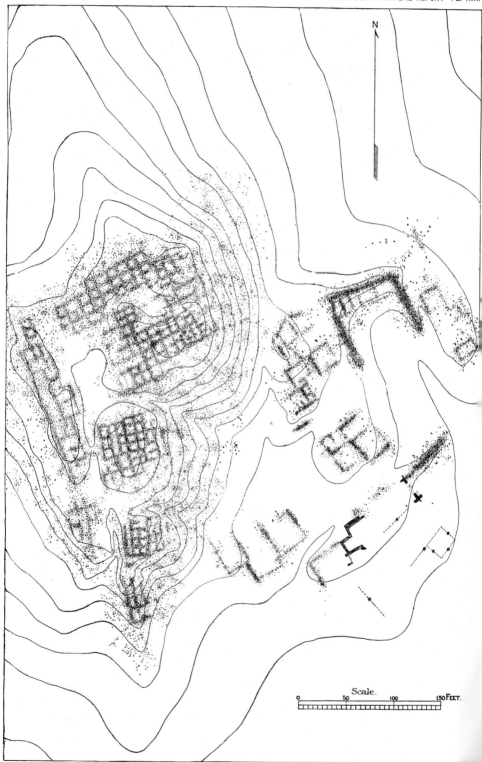

PLAN OF RUIN SHOWING LONG OCCUPANCY

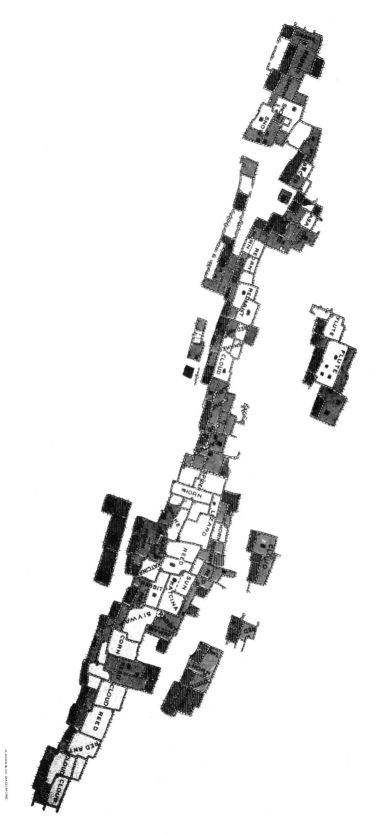

PLAN OF WALPI SHOWING DISTRIBUTION OF CLANS

A. HOEN & CO. BALTIMORE.

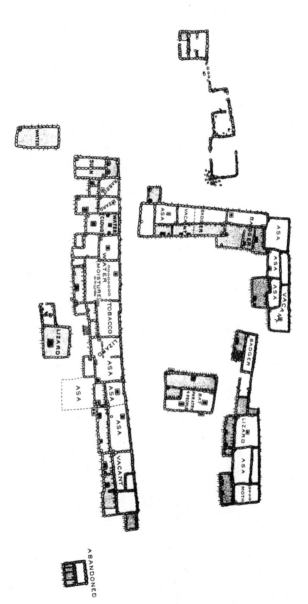

PLAN OF SICHUMOVI SHOWING DISTRIBUTION OF CLANS

NINETEENTH ANNUAL REPORT PL. XXV

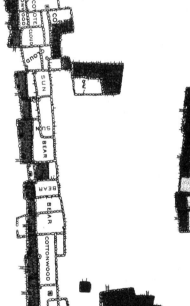

PLAN OF HANO SHOWING DISTRIBUTION OF CLANS

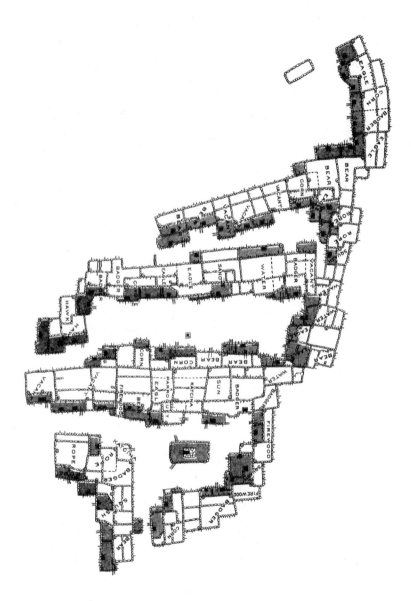

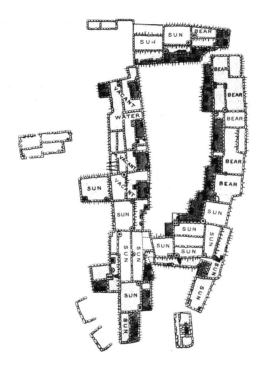

PLAN OF SHIPAULOVI SHOWING DISTRIBUTION OF CLANS

PLAN OF ORAIBI SHOWING DISTRIBUTION OF CLANS

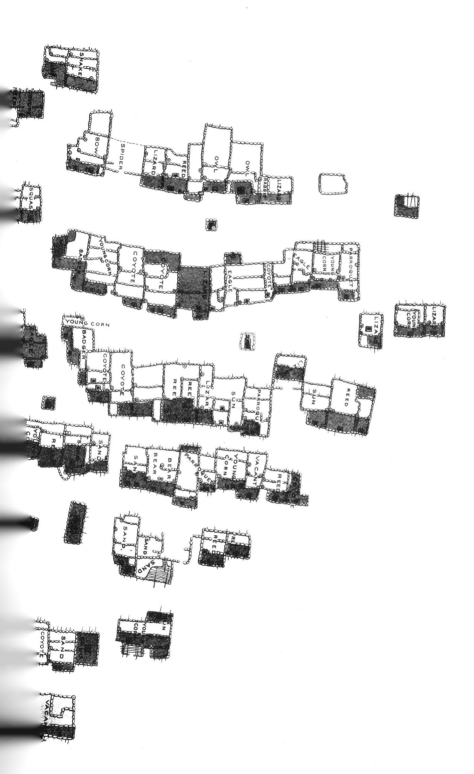